Timber Wars

Judi Bari

Common Courage Press   Monroe, Maine

Library of Congress Cataloging-in-Publication Data
Bari, Judi.
Timber Wars / Judi Bari
p.   cm.
Includes index.
ISBN 1-56751-027-2 (cloth),
ISBN 1-56751-026-4 (pbk.)
1. Old growth forests—California, Northern.
2. Forest conservation—California, Northern—Citizen par-
ticipation.
3. Earth First! (Organization).
4. Timber—California, Northern.
I. Title.
SD387.043B37 1994
333.75'137'09794—dc20   94-12124
CIP

Common Courage Press
P.O. Box 702
Monroe, ME 04951
207-525-0900 fax: 207-525-0934

First Printing

Contents

Introduction

I know, I know. I need to write a book about all this. Fighting to save the redwoods, building alliances with the loggers, getting car-bombed and finding out that we're up against not just the timber industry but also the FBI. Then coming back home and ending up back on the front lines again. I fully intend to write about it eventually, but it's hard to write about something when you're still in the middle of it.

In the meantime, though, I am publishing this compilation of articles I have written over the past few years. It won't tell the whole story, but it will begin to give an idea of what's been going on here on the front lines of Ecotopia.

This collection of articles is very spotty, mainly because I hardly wrote anything before the bombing. I mean, I put out leaflets and stuff, but mostly I was too busy doing the actions to write about them. Then, for a while after the bombing I was too disabled to write. So I have included a few interviews from that time period, to document what was certainly a poignant time for me, and I think an important point in the movement.

Most of the articles in this collection, though, were written since the bombing. Now that I can no longer hike through the woods or throw my body in front of bulldozers, I've become a much more prolific writer. Those who can, do. Those who can't, write.

Because this collection was written over a period of time, and because the articles were written in the heat of the moment in a changing and developing movement, the ideas expressed in them should not be considered Eternal Truths, or even Eternal Truths as I see them. In fact, some of my ideas and analysis change substantially from the beginning of the book to the end.

Most of these articles were first printed in the *Anderson Valley Advertiser*, a radical weekly newspaper that fans the flames of discontent in our area, and to which I am a regular contributor. For subscription info, see below.

Anderson Valley Advertiser
P.O. Box 459
Boonville, CA 95415
$30.00 per year (52 issues)
$16.00 for 6 months
Senior citizens deduct $5.00
for one-year subscription

"You fucking commie hippies, I'll kill you all!" Logger Dave Lancasster, with loaded shotgun, faces off with EF!ers at a demo in whitethorne, August 1989. He later punched 50-year-old EF!er Mem Hill, breaking her nose and knocking her unconscious. Mendo County sheriffs refused to arrest him, and District Attorney Susan Massini refused to prosecute despite all our efforts. (photo Greg King)

Timber Wars

Industrial Worker,
October, 1989

"You fucking commie hippies, I'll kill you all!" A shotgun blast went off, and the Earth First!ers scattered. What started as a peaceful logging road blockade had turned violent when a logger sped his truck through our picket line and swerved it towards the demonstrators. The loggers also grabbed and smashed an Earth First!er's camera and, for no apparent reason, punched a 50-year-old protester in the face, knocking her cold and breaking her nose.

The environmental battle in the Pacific Northwest has reached such a level of intensity that even the press now refers to it as the Timber Wars. At stake is the survival of one of the nation's last great forest ecosystems. Our adversaries are giant corporations—Louisiana-Pacific, Georgia Pacific, and Maxxam in Northern California, where I live.

These companies are dropping trees at a furious pace, clogging our roads no less than 18 hours a day, with a virtual swarm of logging trucks. Even old timers are shocked at the pace and scope of today's strip-logging, ranging from 1000-year-old redwoods, one tree trunk filling an entire logging truck, to six-inch diameter baby trees that are chipped up for the pulp mills and particle-board plants.

One-hundred-forty years ago the county I live in was primeval redwood forest. At the current rate of logging, there will *no* marketable trees left here in 22 years. Louisiana-Pacific President Harry Merlo put it this way in a recent newspaper interview:("It always annoys me to leave anything on the ground when we log our own land. We don't log to a 10-inch top, we don't log to an 8-inch top or a 6-inch top. We log to infinity. It's out there, it's ours, and we want it all. Now.")

So the battle lines are drawn. On one side are the environmentalists, ranging from the big-money groups like The Wilderness Society and Sierra Club to the radical Earth First!ers and local mountain people fighting the front-line battles in the woods. Tactics being used include tree-sitting, logging road blockading, and bulldozer dismantling, as well as the more traditional lawsuits and lobbying.

On the other side are the big corporations and the local kulaks who do their bidding. Tactics used by them have included falling trees into demonstrators, suing protesters for punitive damages (and winning), buying politicians, and even attempting to ban the teaching at a local elementary school of a Dr. Seuss book, "The Lorax," which the timber companies say portrays logging in a bad light.

Position of the Workers

But what about the timber workers? Where do they fit into this scenario? Their true interest lies with the environmentalists, because, of course, when the trees are gone, the jobs will be gone too. Logging is listed by the US Labor Department as the most dangerous job in the US, yet the current speed-up has some loggers and millworkers working 10 or more hours a day, six days a week.

Clearcutting is the most environmentally devastating logging method, and also the least labor-intensive. In the long run, the only way to save timber jobs in our area is to change over to sustained yield logging, where logs can only be taken in a manner and at a rate that doesn't destroy the forest. This is exactly what the environmentalists are asking for.

Yet in spite of all this, those timber workers who are organized at all have been organized by the companies *against* the environmentalists. There are a few noteworthy exceptions, which I'll discuss later, but by and large timber workers around here are either doing the companies' dirty work or keeping their mouths shut.

A good example of this is the spotted owl campaign. Scientists and environmentalists have been trying to get the owl listed as an endangered species, as 90–95% of its habitat, the old growth forest, has already been annihilated. The timber companies have responded with a vicious campaign promoting the extinction of the owl so that it would no longer stand in the way of them destroying the last of the old growth. Loggers are the pawns of this game, wearing T-shirts that read: "Save A Logger, Eat An Owl" and "Spotted Owl Tastes Like Chicken." Recently a hearing on the owl's status was held in Redding, CA. The timber companies closed the mills and logging operations for the day and bused 5,000 workers to the hearing, carrying anti-owl banners and cheering as speakers denounced environmentalists.

Then there's the Nazi-like Yellow Ribbon campaign, where workers, their families, and local businesses are asked to fly yellow ribbons to show solidarity with management against the environmentalist "threat." It is dangerous not to fly these ribbons in some timber-dependent small towns. And, of course, there's always the few crazies who harass us face to face, like the logger who came to one of our demos last June, revved a live chainsaw in a peaceful crowd, then sucker-punched and floored an Earth First! organizer.

Why have the companies been so successful at misdirecting the workers' anger? One obvious reason is fear—timber workers can see the end of the forest (and their jobs) in northern California as well as we can. Many of these families have lived and worked in small one-job towns for generations. The environmentalists are often relative newcomers, culturally different and easy to vilify.

But there's another reason not often discussed. That is the utter lack of class consciousness by virtually all of the environmental groups. I have even had an international Earth First! spokesman tell me that there is no difference between the loggers and the logging companies!

I have heard various environmentalists say that working in the woods and mills is not an "honorable" profession, as if the workers have any more control over the corporations' policies (or are gaining any more from them) than we do. As long as people on our side hold these views, it will be easy pickins for the bosses to turn their employees against us.

Potential For Organizing

Into this battleground, our local Earth First! group has tried to bring some class consciousness of the variety prescribed by the Industrial Workers of the World. The first step is to stop blaming the loggers and millworkers for the destruction of the planet. (The timber companies treat them the same way they treat the forest—as objects to exploit for maximum profit.)We can't form an alliance by saying, "Hey, worker, come help save the trees." We have to recognize that their working conditions are not separate from or subordinate to the rape of the forest. They are part and parcel of the same thing.

With this in mind, it has been surprisingly easy to make contact with timber workers who don't buy the companies' line. The fact that Earth First! is number one on the companies' hit list doesn't seem to faze anyone, and we have managed to meet good, intelligent, and politically astute people working for all three of the big corporations in our area. They have leaked us inside information which has helped us pull off tree-sits, blockades, etc. without getting caught.

But far more important, we have found that conditions among the workers in the woods and mills could mean the opening of a whole new front in the Timber Wars.

Georgia Pacific (G-P) is a good example. Three years ago they cut wages by 25%, saying they needed the money to "modernize" the mill, and would restore the pay scale in the next contract. G-P is the only unionized outfit around here, but its union (International Woodworkers of America, AFL-CIO) went right along with the pay cut, just like they go along with everything else the company does. So G-P "modernized," eliminating jobs, and raked in record profits with the new low wages. Comes the new contract this year end and, lo and behold, instead of 25% the company offers a 3% wage increase. The millworkers were furious and voted by an 88% margin to strike. But the union, assisted by a federal "mediator," squashed the strike vote by telling the workers they would all just get fired if they went out. They then eliminated the radicals from the vote counting committee, took a re-vote, and passed the contract.

Earlier this year, a G-P millworker was poisoned when a PCB-filled capacitor broke and spilled on his head. The company refused to give the man adequate medical care or close off the area, saying it was just mineral oil. The union, as usual, stuck up for the company. At least 11 more people were contaminated before the workers themselves managed to get OSHA to shut down the plant for three days and fine the company $114,000.

Pacific Lumber is another of the "big three" timber companies in the area. Until recently, it was a locally based, family-run operation paying good wages and amazing benefits. Pacific Lumber also treated the forest better than most and, because of its conservative logging and avoidance of clearcutting, has ended up owning most of the privately owned old-growth redwood that's left in the world.

But in 1986, Pacific Lumber was taken over in a leveraged buyout by Maxxam Corp., a high-finance holding company owned by Texas sleazebag Charles Hurwitz. Hurwitz financed the takeover with junk bonds, and is now liquidating the assets of the company to pay off the debt. But in this case, the assets of the company are the last of the ancient redwoods. Hurwitz has tripled the cut, instituting clearcutting, gutted the pension plan, and started working people overtime.

Employees reacted by attempting to organize an ESOP, or Employee Stock Ownership Plan, so that they could buy the company back and protect their jobs and community. As many as 300 people came to an ESOP meeting at its height. But Hurwitz, of course, refused to sell, and the ESOP plan died. Maxxam expected everyone to just shut up and go back to work at that point. Instead, some of the workers started publishing an underground paper called Timberlyin' (as opposed to the company's paper, Timberline), which lampoons management and, while rejecting the misleadership of both the ESOP and the AFL unions, calls on the workers to organize for self-protection.

The other big timber company around here is Louisiana "We Log To Infinity" Pacific (L-P). This is absolutely the most crass company in the county. They busted the union in 1986, and the workforce is still scattered and disorganized, but they left a vast pool of resentment. Recently, L-P closed down a sawmill which had employed 136 people. They then opened a chipmill nearby which employs 15. Earth First! songwriter Darryl Cherney wrote a song, about the mill closing, called Potter Valley Mill, which includes two references to sabotage. The song became the most requested song on the local country music station as the millworkers called in for it and sold tapes of it in Potter Valley. Shortly after the mill closed, three men (who were definitely NOT Earth First!ers) tried—unsuccessfully—to torch the new chip mill with a molotov cocktail.

Role of the IWW

So, while the environmental struggle is raging, and while the public is watching loggers bashing owls, the flames of discontent are slowly igniting among the workers. What's needed is some direction, and it's certainly not coming from the AFL unions. Earth First! is still leading the battle in the woods, but Earth First! can only do so much because it is not a workers' organization.

Historically, it was the IWW who broke the stranglehold of the timber barons on the loggers and millworkers in the nineteen teens. The ruling class fought back with brutality, and eventually crushed the IWW, settling instead for the more cooperative business unions. Now the companies are back in total control, only this time they're taking down not only the workers but the Earth as well. This, to me, is what the IWW-Earth First! link is really about. And if the IWW would like to be more than a historical society, it seems that the time is right to organize again in timber.

Greg "Tarzan" King traverses two Redwood giants at 150' as part of his seven-day aerial occupation in 1987 with Jane Cope to bring attention to the destruction. (photo by CEMPA)

Waferboard:
The Final Solution

June 16, 1989

(Speech given at an Earth First! demonstration in front of Louisiana-Pacific's new chipping mill near Ukiah.)

We are at the site of the new Calpella chipping mill for Louisiana-Pacific. Starting this logging season, L-P has instituted a new logging practice that they call "logging to infinity." The log deck over there is stacked up with all kinds of little treetops and hardwoods. All kinds of stuff that's got no business on a log deck. It ought to be in the forest.

I want to point out that we are not here to protest against either the loggers or the millworkers or anyone who is an employee of Louisiana-Pacific. They don't have any more control over these logging practices than we do. At the beginning of this logging season, Louisiana-Pacific called a meeting in Willits of the people that are going to be logging for them to explain their new logging practices. And I want you to know that their own employees, their own contract loggers, many of them are just as disgusted with this as we are. That's how we found out about a lot of this stuff. One comment from an old-timer was, "When they start telling us to take the tops of the trees, we know it's the end."

So the person we're here to protest is not the logger, not the millworker. It's the president of

Waferboard: The Final Solution

Louisiana-Pacific: a man named Harry Merlo. Harry Merlo is the ultimate tree Nazi. He wants to cut every last tree and implement The Final Solution of waferboard in our county. Now you've all heard this quote, but I'm going to read it again 'cause you can't say anything about Harry Merlo as bad as what Harry Merlo says about himself. We can thank Mike Geniella of the *Press Democrat* for coming up with this quote. In an interview with Harry Merlo about his logging practices, Harry had this to say: "You know it always annoys me to leave anything on the ground when we log our own land. There shouldn't be anything left on the ground. We need everything that's out there. We don't log to a 10-inch top or an 8-inch top or even a 6-inch top. We log to infinity. Because it's out there, it's ours and we need it all, now."

This maniac is actually in charge of most of the forestland in Mendocino County. Here are some astounding photos of what logging to infinity means. These were taken on L-P cuts in the Mendocino National Forest, but it looks the same all over. Clearcuts, mudslides, devastation where the forest used to grow. So what we are dealing with here is a man who not only does not believe in obeying the laws of humans—as far as forestry practices—this man does not even believe in the laws of nature. Any farmer knows that you can't keep taking out of the soil without putting back into the soil, but Harry Merlo has not yet discovered this basic principle of nature.

(Fifty percent of the organic matter on the ground in a natural forest is decaying wood.) Yet Harry Merlo wants to remove all this wood. His plan, he says, is to strip everything off the ground, leaving it completely bare and replant tree farms with 20-year rotations.

TIMBER WARS

According to Chris Maser, the forestry expert, there has never been a tree farm that survived beyond three generations. Without putting something into the soil, the soil gets poorer and poorer and the trees just don't grow back. So what Harry Merlo is talking about if he implements his plan is desertification in 60 years. That's why we're here. That's why this is so serious.

Now Merlo says don't worry if we got hardwoods and we got slash out on that deck. It's okay. We are going to replant it with conifers, we're going to replant it with Douglas fir, which are much better sawlogs, much better trees. What he's talking about is monoculture. He's talking about eliminating biodiversity. Right now, one of the things that is happening is that they are exporting the logs to Japan, where they are paying a much higher price. The reason they are willing to pay more for this wood is because they have already destroyed their own forest. They took the advice of the United States Forestry Service and replanted their forest with monoculture pine. And several years later, much to their dismay, they were attacked by an infestation of pine beetles destroying this monoculture forest. In a natural forest there is enough diversity that something like a pine beetle won't destroy the whole ecosystem. In a tree farm, that diversity doesn't exist. The people in Japan saw it as an infestation of pine beetles, nature saw it as an infestation of pine trees.

The other thing that Harry Merlo is not considering when he says he owns this land and can do what he wants with it, is the climate. We all know about the greenhouse effect. We all know what this is doing to our climate. I saw something really dismaying in the *Press Democrat* just a few days ago. It was an advertisement for a new product called a solar prism. It says "protects your garden against 120-degree heat." Now here where I live is called Redwood Valley, and there's hardly a redwood left in it. Last year it hit 115 degrees on the clearcut where I live, and I know it didn't hit any 115 degrees when there were redwood trees there. So what we are seeing here is a changing of the climate, a drying up of the land. And we are seeing the greenhouse effect kicking in.

Now some of those counter-demonstrators across the street are wearing "No Earth First!" shirts. And one of the things they like to holler about is jobs. I'd like to see these people defend waferboard, because not only is waferboard eliminating the forest, it is also eliminating the forest jobs. L-P just closed down the Potter Valley sawmill in the next valley over from here. That sawmill employed 136 people. Subsequently they opened up this chip plant here and it employs 15. And that's what we are looking at. It doesn't take a logger to harvest a tree farm. It's done with machinery. We are talking about farmworkers, not loggers. We are talking about less jobs in the mills. We are talking about more toxic jobs. Just to show you how sensitive Harry Merlo is to the jobs situation, here's his comment on the Potter Valley mill: "I feel sorry for Potter Valley and all the people that are there. But when you look at the total picture, our future is so bright, even though some product lines are at their end." Well, I don't know who's future he thinks is so bright. Certainly not the Potter Valley millworkers. When he says product lines are at their end, he's not talking about product lines, he's talking about trees and forests that are at their end.

TIMBER WARS

There's no benefit from waferboard, no benefit at all. Here's an example of it over here. As a carpenter, I can tell you that this is totally inferior product. Wood chips floating in a gel of toxic glue. Do you want your house built out of this stuff? I know I don't and I bet Harry Merlo's house isn't built out of it either.

Some Earth First!ers say they don't want any logging at all, and I'm not really sure if human beings can log and still have the forest there or not. I do feel that we have to base our society on what the Earth can sustain. Not trying to strip everything we can off the Earth without worrying about the future. If this is the future, I don't want to be here for it. There's no benefit to this strip logging except to the greedy millionaire, Harry Merlo. (Harry is practicing the economics of extinction. Well we have a surprise for him in Mendocino County. He's about to run into the politics of resistance.)

We don't recognize Harry Merlo's claim to ownership of beings that are 2,000 years old. Beings in whose life Harry Merlo is just a blip in their history. We don't recognize his right to strip our forest and leave nothing. Or to strip our children's future. The forest doesn't belong to Harry Merlo, the forest belongs to the ages. The logs on that log deck don't belong to Harry Merlo, they belong to the future. They belong to the forest creatures who need them for habitat. We are not going to let Harry Merlo chip up our county to satiate his greed. This is not the last demonstration Harry, this is the first. The next one will be at your office, and the next one will be at your house. Harry Merlo Last! Earth First!

"Some People Just Don't Get It"

A Conversation with
Bruce Anderson, Editor of the
Anderson Valley Advertiser (AVA)

June 13, 1990

Interview with Judi Bari in Highland Hospital two weeks after she was car-bombed and nearly killed in Oakland while organizing for Redwood Summer.

Bari: Since we aren't going to be so loud, keep the door open a little bit. I hate these fucking windows that don't open. I want to get a glass cutter and cut a little square in it. How do they expect people to get well in a room painted all white with windows that don't open, with no air, and food prepared by a chef they hired from the airlines?

AVA: *You're not permitted to talk about the bombing itself at all—or the ramifications?*

Bari: No.

AVA: *But you can talk about when it went boom, or whatever it did?*

Bari: Well, it did go boom. I will agree that it went boom. That's about all.

AVA: *You left Ukiah on a Tuesday night?*

Remember, you said you were going to call me?

Bari: I'm going to have a hard time remembering dates... There was a meeting on Tuesday night with the gyppos, and I think we spent the night in Redwood Valley—me, Dakota Sid, Utah Phillips, and Joanna Robinson...

AVA: *Joanna Robinson is Mrs. Utah Phillips?*

Bari: No, she's Joanna Robinson.

AVA: *Is she married to him?*

Bari: Yes. He is Mr. Joanna Robinson. (laughs)

AVA: *Okay, all right.*

Bari: You never learn. It doesn't matter; I can purge your papers, I can burn them—I can do anything, and you never learn. (laughs)

AVA: *Judi's my harshest critic. So you went to Seeds of Peace...*

Bari: Yeah. There was a meeting at Seeds of Peace, and we left Wednesday afternoon to get there for an evening meeting, and that night I slept at somebody's house in Berkeley. Then the next morning Darryl came over and we started to rehearse music, because I never get a chance to play anymore and I'm losing my ability to perform—so we rehearsed about two songs, and we decided to go back to the Seeds house and rehearse with George, too. So we got in the car to drive back to the Seeds of Peace house, and it was on the way to the Seeds of Peace house that...

AVA: *And from the Seeds of Peace you were going to Santa Cruz...*

Bari: We were going to Santa Cruz that evening where the gig was. We were on our way to rehearse for the gig.

"Some People Just Don't Get It"

AVA: *People up north are saying that there's no way they could have stuck the bomb in your car up there at the gyppo (contract logger) meeting, because your vehicle was clearly visible from inside the room.*

Bari: No comment.

AVA: *So the bomb went off, and the next thing you knew you were in the hospital...*

Bari: The next thing I knew it was Sister Morphine—from shot to shot.

AVA: *Actually, I think there's an old song...*

Bari: Yeah that's what I was referring to, "Come on, Sister Morphine." I will talk about that. I didn't want to live. I wanted to die. I begged them to let me die.

AVA: *It was that painful?*

Bari: It was real bad. It's still pretty bad. Right now I'm okay. I wasn't very okay this morning. I'm not just here for fun. It's not just a show, I'm really sick. That's why I'm not doing press interviews, except for the AVA, which is a sick newspaper anyway, so it doesn't matter. (laughs) It hurt so bad, that I just begged them to put me out, and they told me they were going to operate and cut out my colon and give me a bag that my shit would come out of, and I told them to let me die instead. And they went in there (surgery) and apparently they didn't have to do it. And they told me I wouldn't walk and I wouldn't be able to control my body functions, but to their great surprise and my great relief—I was wondering who was going to change my diapers for the next 50 years—but it turns out that was an incorrect diagnosis and I'm already regaining control. I don't know if I'm going to walk, but I'm definitely going to be able to control my body functions.

AVA: *Was it your right leg that was damaged?*

Bari: Yeah. My left leg still works, though my pelvis is broken in ten different places and my coccyx looks like oatmeal on the x-rays.

AVA: *So the last time you saw a doctor, what did they say?*

Bari: They say I will probably have to have a brace on my leg and I'll probably be able to walk. I'll have to be in traction, flat on my back in the most uncomfortable bed I've ever been in my life for six more weeks. I have to be flat on my back for eight weeks—I cannot leave this bed, I cannot sit up, I cannot turn over. It's real uncomfortable. I want to say, though, that this huge outpouring from people I know and people I don't know has really been what has sustained me, and when I wanted to give up, people wouldn't let me give up, and I don't know how I can express my appreciation for that. There's somebody with me 24-hours a day. If I wake up crying, there's somebody to hold my hand, and I don't even always know the person, but there's always someone here, and I really appreciate it. I'm not strong enough to respond to cards and letters, but I'm reading them and I really appreciate them, and I hope they don't get tired of writing them, because they're the only thing that keeps my spirits high.

AVA: *You know, of course, that the story has been in all the media across the country...*

Bari: Some people will do anything to be famous...(laughs)

AVA: *I know Darryl wanted to get on TV... (laughter)...that may account for the placement of the device...*

Bari: No, Darryl, first of all, has some of the least mechanical skills of anyone I've ever known. I once tried to hire him to hang sheet rock and found him to be unemployable, because he didn't know how to hammer. And, secondly, whatever else I know about Darryl—Darryl and I have been broken up as a romantic couple for several months now—but I love Darryl and Darryl loves me, and there is no question in my mind that Darryl would never, ever do such a thing.

AVA: *Yeah, I think we can eliminate Darryl as a suspect.*

Bari: But I did appreciate Rob's article about the [imaginary] argument that we had: "Oh, Darryl, you're such a wimp, you put the bomb under my seat instead of yours..." (laughter) I thought that was great!

AVA: *So, no suspicious persons...you can't speculate on any of that?*

Bari: No comment. You will not trick me into commenting.

AVA: *See, that's the problem when the lawyers move into a case, you know.*

Bari: The problem for me, Bruce, is that I know that perfectly innocent people have gone to jail for 10 years, 20 years—for their lives—and I know that I'm perfectly innocent, and I don't want to go to jail.

AVA: *That's what's astounding about this case, because, at this late date, you two are still the only suspects.*

Bari: I know. They've never even considered anybody else.

AVA: *You would think that at this point in our history, there would be some sophistication in these police agencies, but now they've dredged up the old*

29

"Patty Hearst" photo of you ["Judi Bari—AVA Poster Gal of the Week," AVA, April 4, 1989]—the Patty Hearst take-off—which, if they had any sort of historical reference, they would know immediately, at a glance, that's what it was...

Bari: They're totally lacking in a sense of humor. They cannot understand why someone who doesn't know which end of an Uzi to fire would pose with one. The actual purpose of that pose, how we came to take that picture, was we were trying to think of the most outrageous cover we could for Darryl's album, "They Sure Don't Make Hippies Like They Used To." That was an out-take, one that was not used. It was a joke. I've never fired an Uzi. I don't know how to fire an Uzi. I don't own an Uzi. I don't own any fire arms. I don't know how to use fire arms. I've never killed anything bigger than a potato bug.

AVA: *So there's no truth to the rumor that you've been on maneuvers with the "camo buddies" in Comptche? The "Camo buddies," I love that phrase. That really describes them—retarded 50-year olds in paramilitary drills, getting ready for the summer. What can you say? Tactically, it looks very promising for the first demo in Samoa [where timber is exported]. At the grass roots level, I don't know what the tactics are going to be—massive civil disobedience, or what?*

Bari: It was supposed to be, but I've been out of it and things have changed. Back when I was involved in the organizing of this, the idea was that we would do massive civil disobedience as close as we could get. I think there's a public beach across from the dock—I don't know what recon has been done or what's on. But I was dismayed to hear some people in Arcata say, "Let's not do civil disobedience." When people were killed in Mississippi, the organizers didn't say, "Well, gee, let's not register black people. Let's just interview them instead." You can't back down to terrorism. You can't back down to this kind of thing. We're all in shock. Our community is in shock. We were all naive little kids, never thinking this could happen to us. When we talked about non-violence training, we were worried about getting punched. It never occurred to us that someone would use something as unspeakable as a bomb that would do the type of damage they've done to me. It never crossed my mind that that would happen. It really didn't.

AVA: *It hadn't crossed mine. I was thinking it was more likely that we would occasionally be way-laid by groups of camo buddies...*

Bari: Right. And that's all I was worried about. I felt very safe in the city. I didn't feel there was any danger, and I think I was real naive, because we know that we're going against the biggest corporations, the biggest greed-mongers...

AVA: *In many ways they're not only the biggest, but some of the worst, some of the most vicious, some of the most relentless concentrations of money in the world.*

Bari: Right. And we know what their tactics have been against black people, against Indians, etc. And because we've grown up with this white, middle-class privilege, it never crossed our minds that they would use the same unspeakable tactics on us. But we have to grow up and to realize that's no reason to stop, because the alternative is to let not just the forests go, but to let the entire life support of the Earth go. If that's the alternative, there is no alternative. We can't back down no matter what they do.)

AVA: *How do you account for the fact that there's only been one equivocating denunciation from Supervisor de Vall about what happened to you. He said something like, "Gee, I don't think they'd be crazy enough to carry a bomb." Which, of course, leaves open the possibility that you were. But nothing from Bowsker [Congressman Bosco, State Senator Keene, Assemblyman Hauser], nothing from the County Supervisors—even from Liz Henry. And, of course, absolutely nothing from District Attorney Massini and those thugs in the D.A.'s office or local law enforcement. I mean, not even the usual pro forma thing, about how we're opposed to violence on all sides.*

Bari: Pacific-Lumber did, though. P-L sent a very nice get-well message. And Bill Bailey and Art Harwood.... I was touched by that. But I really do think some of those locals are as shocked by this as we are. I think Bill Bailey was sincere. I've heard him denounced as an opportunist, but I don't agree with that. Those who fail to condemn it—it puts them right in the camp with the murderers. I think it's despicable.

AVA: *It's certainly a green light for the murderers.*

Bari: They had no hesitation to condemn us. They had no hesitation to call us violent when we called for non-violent civil disobedience. We called for mass, non-violent civil disobedience. The loggers responded, at that famous supervisors' meeting, ("If you do that, we'll beat you up; therefore, you're violent.") And the supervisors condemned us. They have spent much of their energy condemning us, and I think their failure to condemn the other side

32

really shows which side they're on. I don't think they're neutral. I don't think they have any morality, and I don't know how they can look at themselves in the mirror in the morning.

AVA: *Will you be here for the next six weeks?*

Bari: This room, this bed. I cannot move from this bed. I cannot go out in the goddamn hall. There's one danger: If they do arrest me, I'm supposed to go up to the jail ward, and that's real dangerous for me, because there's only one nurse on the jail ward, and I'm real sick, and one nurse for the whole ward is not enough to take care of me.

AVA: *That's upstairs in this hospital, on the eighth floor?*

Bari: They actually took me there out of the critical care unit, and when the doctors came looking for me, I was gone and they were outraged. I was up there only a half hour, just long enough to make friends with my roommate.

AVA: *You're out of protective custody?*

Bari: The hospital's been very cooperative. Though I'm out of protective custody, they've allowed me to have a 24-hour guard—that Movement has been astounding. There's not been one second that the shift has not been covered.

AVA: *[To the on-shift guard] And your name is...?*

Guard: Grace Nichols.

AVA: *You're doing this shift, Grace?*

Bari: Some of them have been Earth First!ers. Some of them are college kids here for Redwood Summer, Sacramento Earth First! was my guard last night—you know, the new group that did the dock action in Sacramento. Some of them I know, and some of them I don't know. In addition to the security of having people guarding me and having people there for me when I get too depressed, I'm getting to meet the movement. I'm finding out who these people are. It's fascinating. They're such a diverse group.

AVA: *You don't see any diminishing spirit for this summer's activity?*

Bari: No, I see it greatly increasing in spirit. I think [the bombing] had the exact opposite effect than intended. They don't understand us. They're looking for a leader, and they can't find a leader. They tried to knock off Dave Foreman, and it didn't work. I get my juice from these demonstrations, and it's going to be real hard to not be there. But I think it's going to be good for the movement to have it happen without me this summer, because we've had a problem of people being too dependent on me, that if I don't organize something, it doesn't happen. I'm really glad to see—I've known this all along—the community discovering that they don't need me. No movement is dependent on one person, and if it is, it's not a movement. The fact that it's going to go on stronger and better without me—I think that's good. Everyone contributes, but no one is essential.

AVA: *I heard Supervisor Nelson Redding the other day on National Public Radio, of all places, and he said that everything that was happening in Mendocino County—Earth First!, Judi Bari, Darryl Cherney—was worse than the People's Temple. [laughter]*

Bari: That sounds like a Tim Stoen quote to me. Worse than People's Temple? What exactly is he referring to that's so horrible? I guess to him murdering black kids isn't so horrible.

AVA: *It's going to be interesting to see how people like Redding and Butcher handle the national media this summer.*

Bari: I think they're going to be totally out of their league.

AVA: *They're already out of their league.*

Bari: The whole reason we called this—and that's one of the reasons we drew the analogy to Mississippi—just like they could get away with beating up black kids when no one but the locals were looking, they can get away with their bizarre behavior in Mendocino County when no one but Mendocino County is watching. But the rest of the world sees them for what they are—which is a bunch of small-town, small-minded, petty powermongers. There are very few people who think the right of a few people to make $7.00 an hour for a few more years is worth the extinction of a 10,000 year-old eco-system. I'm one of the strongest advocates for the loggers and the millworkers. I'm certainly a stronger advocate for them than their own unions are, and I'm certainly a stronger advocate for them than their employers are. I think they're victims. I love Grace's song she just sang for me. It goes, "Come on now millworkers. It's time to organize. What they're doing to the old growth, they're doing to our lives."

AVA: *About the camo buddies...*

Bari: I do think the camo buddies are the equivalent of the white racists in Mississippi. They don't really have much to be gained from the system. They're being used by the system. But they are people who are not real bright who have bought into it and they're getting their kicks and playing their games.

AVA: *Historically they're sort of like Pinkertons. They've always used goons against the labor movement.*

Bari: Right. I think the threat of violence does come from people like that. We used to have a chant at the Concord Naval Weapons Station that we should say to the camo buddies: "You are not boys, those are not toys, this is not a game." That's why they are dangerous, because they are playing games. It's a game to them, but it's real life to us.

AVA: *In Mendocino County, Jerry Philbrick can make a threat to take out 150 people, and there's no official concern, there's no official denunciation.*

Bari: Well, Mendocino County, as we all know, is known as the largest out-patient ward in America and we who live there are completely used to this stuff. I really think that things are going to change. Everybody out of the County I've told the story to, for example, about selling the County Courthouse to the Japanese is absolutely astounded, and yet nobody blinks an eye in Mendocino County. These things happen every day up there. I think we're going to bring a little reason to the area by having people come in from outside, who are not used to complete loonies running the government, the police, the schools, the hospitals, and the newspapers.

AVA: *Watch it lady, when you talk about newspapers. But the Mississippi parallel was a stroke of genius, because Mendocino County is very similar to Mississippi in the early sixties. Local authority uses this violent fringe to do their dirty work.*

Bari: That's a real difference that we need to

emphasize between this non-violent action and the Nevada Test Site, Diablo Canyon, and even Concord Naval Weapons Station: The only adversary there was the government or their agents, but here we have this lunatic fringe. That's why the comparison was made to Mississippi, because we have a whole different level we have to deal with. I have a lot of respect for most of the loggers and the workers and most of them know what's going on, but there's a certain element among them who are busy cutting themselves right out of the jobs and will defend to the death their right to do it. When it's all over and it's all gone, I don't know if they'll ever wake up. Maybe they think they're going to go to Oregon, but it's already happened in Oregon.

AVA: *The wildest talk seems to be coming from gyppos themselves, and they're essentially small businessmen, younger men, who've inherited business and equipment. They've never really been out in the world.*

Bari: There's too much inbreeding, too. It's a rural area. The genetic pool is not large, and some of these families have lived here for five generations.

AVA: *That's right. Incest has not been a happy experience in Mendocino County...European royalty...Mendocino gyppos...So the tactics this summer: large public demos, like a loading dock, maybe a CDF office...*

Bari: There will be several large demos that will be publicized in advance, but there will be continuous smaller demos that are happening everywhere. There are so many possibilities for things that could be done without disrupting operations, without causing a lot of danger, so we could leave the actual slowing down, the actual standing in front of the cutting to the hardcore.

AVA: *People should be clear on that, because the camo buddies are the authority up there—including Bosco, Keene, Hauser, the utterly contemptible Don Nelson, the alleged union man—God, he's disgraceful...*

Bari: He really is. And his son is going to be teaching seminars on how to talk to loggers at our base camp. He does a good workshop on that.

AVA: *He's a good guy. But what they're saying is—especially their intellectual leadership, like Tom Loop...*

Bari: [laughter]

AVA: *That's what we're talking about, Judi. They say it's an all-out physical attack on loggers and their equipment.*

Bari: And, of course, it is not at all. We all know that these people are cutting themselves out of jobs. And they all know it, too. But I want to explain the attacks on the equipment, too. Louisiana-Pacific, for example, sets the price per thousand (board feet), and as the woods become more depleted, it takes more and more labor to get the thousand out. And, since they have no collective bargaining—these wonderful, rugged individualists don't believe in such things—they have no say in what the price is that they're offered. So the price per thousand has become so low the gyppos can not make enough off the cut to maintain their own equipment. What's happening is that wages have gone to a disgracefully low level—people are starting at $9.00 an hour in the woods. That is an embarrassment. This is the most dangerous job in the United States, according to the Labor Department. I've heard that undocumented Mexicans start even lower...

AVA: *Yeah, Mexicans start at $5.00.*

Bari: I've never seen that proven, but I have seen the $9.00 proven. I know that for sure. As the gyppos get squeezed by these corporations, getting the last few years out of it before they ditch them entirely, before these "loyal" idiots get ditched by their corporate masters...

AVA: *They were already ditched once when L-P and G-P got rid of their woods crews.*

Bari: Sure, but I'm talking about the gyppos now. I'm talking about who is threatening the gyppo jobs and equipment, and I'm saying that the corporations are threatening their jobs and equipment. They're doing it by paying them so little per thousand that they can't pay their employees a living wage, and they can't afford to maintain their own equipment. That's where the danger is coming from. It's not coming from Earth First!

AVA: *And the gyppos are going to be left competing with each other for private tracts.*

Bari: This has been happening, and what is happening is that the smaller gyppos are being squeezed out, as the laws of capitalism play themselves out. The smaller companies have been increasingly squeezed out, and only the larger, more crass gyppos have survived.

AVA: *Even they subdivide and are into real estate and all kinds of other ventures, so this business that they're trying to preserve a noble history.... This old-timer in Navarro—he's in his eighties now— he started out when they were cutting trees by hand. He remembers the first chainsaws after World War II. They didn't even have chainsaws until then. I don't*

39

think a lot of people know that.

Bari: Philbrick is so proud of his grandfather cutting down trees "with no technology."

AVA: *Why doesn't he do it that way, then? This old guy says, these guys with their pickup trucks and their big ugly dogs wouldn't have lasted three minutes under the old conditions in the old days.*

Bari: But the timber industry has a real brutal history, one of the most brutal of any industry. And the way that they busted the loggers' attempts at self-organization—what you have to realize is that what you see now is the result of the military suppression of the loggers' attempts to organize themselves against these really violent companies. These are the same companies we're dealing with today, and we shouldn't forget that today.

AVA: *Philbrick alluded to a possible environmentalist-gyppo coalition to oppose certain corporate practices. Do you foresee anything like that?*

Bari: I see more hope of coalitions with the workers than with the gyppos. I think there's a difference between a gyppo employee and a gyppo owner. I would be willing to work in coalition with anybody against the corporations. Even Philbrick or any of them who sincerely wanted to form a coalition to oppose corporate practices. I would do that. But I wouldn't compromise my principles to do so; I wouldn't say that I will form this coalition instead of Redwood Summer. I would certainly do it in addition to Redwood Summer.

AVA: *If they haven't opposed corporate practices by now, there's little indication that they will anytime soon.*

Bari: It's a little late. I was upset when I read—I

was basically unconscious for two weeks and afterwards Karen Pickett gave me a press packet of all the clippings—and I didn't read anything about the forest. I read about myself a lot, and I read about bombs and about loggers and this and that, but I didn't read about the forest. And people who are willing to make compromises we shouldn't be making, people are ready to back down, they should remember why we called this in the first place. They should to take a walk on Big River, or go to Navarro, or to Albion, Whale Gulch, Pudding Creek, and Sherwood Road. And if they don't remember after that why we're having Redwood Summer, we don't need 'em.

AVA: *You're aware that the base camps have already been set up, and Seeds of Peace are already up there.*

Bari: Seeds of Peace are wonderful and give me hope for the future, because I've been a political activist for 20 years and for 20 years I've been the youngest generation, and it's so nice to have a bunch of kids coming in who are so wise. I mean, they are 19-year old kids with this wisdom, this ability, and this spirit to fight back. It really gives me hope for the future of the movement that I wasn't sure I had before. The other thing that's so exciting about Redwood Summer is the passing of the torch to the next generation, just like the 40-year olds set us in motion 20 years ago when I was in the anti-war movement.

AVA: *I think we should go over the misunderstanding—deliberate, of course, in Mendocino County—that Earth First! is an aggressively violent, terrorist organization.*

Bari: Earth First! is an aggressively prankster

41

organization. Our sense of humor is what distinguishes us from virtually every other group I've ever been in.

AVA: *So the literal-minded are going to have a very difficult time understanding...*

Bari: Something they fail to understand about Earth First! is our style, our spirit, our lack of respect, and our sense of humor. And people with no sense of humor will never understand Earth First! In fact, one of my favorite Earth First! slogans is, "Some People Just Don't Get It."

KPFA Interview

July 5, 1990

Conducted at Highland Hospital by Sami Riest

SR: *How has the bombing affected Redwood Summer? Are things going on as planned?*

Bari: Well, Redwood Summer is going on the way that it was anticipated, and that's pretty amazing because this bomb blast had a lot of effects on us. It knocked out virtually all of our experienced leadership. It didn't just knock me out. Some of the people who have been working on the issues for years who have also been targeted by death threats as well as I have, have been intimidated from being right up there on the front lines. And then of course there's a lot of support going on for me down here, so people who we had expected to be up there working on Redwood Summer are down here working on support for me, and that even includes our legal team. So what happened is in the absence of our experienced leadership, instead of falling apart, a whole group of people have risen to the occasion. There must be 20 people who have come up and just risen to it and assumed leadership positions and are holding it together.

One thing to me that's very impressive is that most of these people are women. This is the feminization of Earth First! Redwood Summer is an almost entirely women-led action. There are women holding the base camp together, there are women holding the actions together, even the attorney team is women.

43

SR: *It must be fairly frustrating for you to be outside of the main action, when you were one of the main planners in the beginning.*

Bari: Yeah, it really is. It's very hard. It's not the way I had planned to spend my summer. I unfortunately recognize the fact that this bombing has galvanized people and increased support for Redwood Summer. People who were thinking about it casually and maybe would and maybe wouldn't, have showed up and were so outraged by the bombing that they vowed to do it. But it sure wasn't any price I had intended to pay, and it's not fun, that's for sure.

SR: *So how are you doing, health-wise? Are you feeling like you're recovering well?*

Bari: Yeah, actually apparently I'm recovering way ahead of schedule. They just took me out of traction two weeks early. The problem is I'm really in constant pain and it's a long, hard road. Even though I'm out of traction now, not only can I not walk, I can't sit. So it's not like I can just, y'know, jump into a wheelchair and start zipping around. I have a lot of physical therapy to go before I can do anything like that. I can't get a straight answer out of anybody as to how long that's expected to take, or even what exactly is going to be involved. The only thing they'll say is that it's going to be painful, and I think I already know that, 'cause it's been pretty painful so far.

SR: *Have you been, in the last while at least, left fairly much alone by the police and the FBI, or are they still coming by?*

Bari: I've had no contact from the police at all here. However, they've been up where I live. They've

44

been home harassing my family, and they've raided my house twice and the last time that they raided it they took finishing nails out of the window trim. They're really grasping at straws apparently. I don't think I need to say on KPFA, I think the listeners are perfectly aware of my absolute innocence. I have a 20-year history as a non-violent organizer, and I didn't suddenly turn into a bomb thrower. And I'm certainly not stupid enough to put a bomb under my own car seat and blow myself up. I think it's pretty preposterous that I'm being charged with this, that they're saying I'm the only suspect.

This is the second assassination attempt on me in 10 months, and that's pretty scary. The last one was really the most violent thing that had ever happened to me in my life. I got run off the road by a logging truck. Karen Silkwood-style. The guy just sped up and kept going. My car was moving at the time, and he overtook me and rammed me without hitting his brakes. It was a horrible, violent impact and my car sailed through the air and crashed. But the bombing was 20 times worse. I mean there's just no describing how awful it felt, and just the horrificness of being blown up by a bomb is not something I can describe in words. And not only having to go through the physical pain and the psychological terror of having this done, but then on top if this, to have somebody trying to frame me and blame me for it and making no effort whatsoever to find out who these assassins are really makes it a lot worse. It really adds a whole other dimension to it, and it's real difficult to go through this.

SR: *Do you still fear that someone might try to get you while you're in the hospital here?*

Bari: I feel fairly secure here in the hospital. The hospital recognizes my security needs and allows me to have somebody here 24 hours a day. I'm too scared to go home. I feel like I need to, because this is really going to be quite an ordeal to recover from this on many levels. And I need to be where my support system is, and that's home. I also have two small children that need their Mom. So I feel a very strong need to go home, and I'm scared to death to go home. The police in Mendocino County, over the last year or so have been encouraging violence against Earth First!ers by refusing to arrest or prosecute people who punch us, shoot at us, and now even bomb us. The message that they've given very clearly in Mendocino County is that it's open season on Earth First!ers, and it's OK to attack Earth First!ers in general and me in particular, and that you won't be apprehended.

I think we were incredibly naive. When I look back over the events leading up to this, it's really surprising to me that I wasn't more careful, and that I didn't realize that something awful was about to happen. I guess this is still white, middle-class privilege. They don't do this to white people. They do this to Black Panthers, they do this to the American Indian Movement, but the idea of using a car bomb on an environmental organizer is fairly unprecedented, and I had never anticipated this level of violence. People in other places certainly live under much greater threats than this. I mean, look at the Salvadorans who continue to fight in spite of the death threats and the death squads. If they can do it, we can do it. But we're going to have to face the way it is now in this movement.

SR: *It's interesting. As I look around the room, I can see you're obviously getting a tremendous outburst of support.*

Bari: It's been really phenomenal, and I have to say it's kept me going. Last year when I got run off the road by the logging truck, I reached deep-down inside myself and found the courage to go on. It wasn't easy. It took me about a month to make the decision that I would go on. And then this year, immediately preceding this bomb blast, I was subjected to a very frightening death threat campaign, and I had to do the same thing. I had to reach down inside myself and find the resources to go on. This time when I reached down inside myself, there wasn't anything there. I wasn't able to go on by myself. I spent a couple of weeks without much of a will to live and acting very passive about the whole thing, and it was the outpouring from the movement that gave me that will to go on.

SR: *Are there any other things that you feel you would like to say?*

Bari: I guess I'd like to talk a little about what I've learned being here in this hospital bed, because it's a real different experience for me. I've never even sprained an ankle before. I know that they've been reading an old interview with me from New Settler Magazine over KPFA, and in that interview one of the things that I talk about is my opinion of men, and that I basically don't have much hope for them based on my experience. I said no matter how far you go with men, eventually you're going to get down to a point where their misogyny is going to show. That had been my personal experience in relationships. One of the things that I've learned in this hospital room is that there is such a thing as nurturing men. There's been some incredible men who've come in here, and I have met enough people now that I have really changed my opinion and I no longer think that there's no hope for men. I think that there is a new kind of man that is coming out in the movement that we can build a new society based on different kinds of relationships with men and women. So my opinion that there's no hope for relationships with men and women has changed based on some of the incredibly nurturing men who have come into my hospital room and helped me and held my hand when I cried and just offered themselves in a way that I thought only women would do. So that's one of the lessons I've learned here.

SR: *What about the future, what are your plans? Do you look that far forward or are you just going day to day right now?*

Bari: It's really hard. I feel like I'm a public person this summer, whether I want to be or not. So I think it would be futile for me to say I'm going to retreat this summer because especially with the FBI trying to frame me in this case, and my involvement in Redwood Summer, I think it's foolish for me to try to be a private person right now. But I do feel eventually I'm going to have to take a break away from public life and take some time with my children and take some time to heal my body and my spirit from what's been done to me, because in addition to the fact that my body has been broken, if I recover fully at all it will be a very long time I have to live with this constant reminder of this. It's a real change for me having always been strong and all of a sudden to find myself very limited, and at best they say I'm going to be able to eventually walk with a brace in my shoe. To which I reply, you mean I have to wear shoes? But, I don't really know the extent of my recovery with Western medicine.

That's another thing I've learned in this hospital is that Western medicine knows how to cut you up and sew you back together, but they don't know a thing about healing. The alternative healing communities have been just as incredible to me as the nurturing men. I mean the things that I've learned from them is that there are other ways to heal ourselves. The other thing they've taught me is that they consider themselves and their alternative healing methods to be part of the same movement that we're in with our ecological and social justice issues.

So I don't know what the extent of my recovery is, but I know that it's going to be long and difficult, and I think that I'm going to have to take some private time probably in the fall, just to go back and—because in addition to these physical injuries I've been really terrorized to the depths of my soul. It's hard to describe that, but I know it's going to take a long time to get back the confidence that I used to have and it's a really frightening thing to have people try to kill you and it's an even more frightening thing to have them nearly succeed. They actually did nearly succeed. I came really close to dying, and it's going to be a long, hard road back. So I think after the summer you probably won't hear much from me for awhile while I recover. Hopefully after that recovery, I'll be able to come back strong again and be in the movement again.

SR: *Well I know most of the people out there listening are really hoping that too.*

Bari: Being here and being subjected to this terrorism, I've had to do a lot of soul-searching. It took me a while even to face it. I was unable to sleep for a long time, because I was afraid to sleep. I was afraid to face what my subconscious had in it. So I've had to do a lot of thinking about violence and no-nviolence and terrorism and things like that. I met Brian Willson one week before this happened, and at the time I had a discussion with him and I told him that I considered nonviolence to be the only appropriate tactic in our country at this time, but that I considered it only a tactic. I wasn't a Gandhian who considered non-violence to be the only way ever. I would never tell a Salvadoran to use non-violence only. And Brian gave me an answer that has played out in my mind a thousand times since then. He said, "Your belief in non-violence as a tactic only will not be enough to sustain you through the hatred you're going to experience this summer." So that one has really gone through me a lot of times. I realize that the person who ran me off the road with the logging truck last summer, I wouldn't have used this word, but I guess that I could say I forgave him in that I saw that he was a victim who took his anger out on the wrong person. I could see that about him. They hauled him out of his truck and made him confront me, and I could see that he was horrified at what he had done. When he saw that my children were in the car too, he kept saying, "The children, the children, I didn't see the children." But the person who bombed me was a monster. I've been unable to understand him. I've been unable to understand somebody who would deliberately and coldly, premeditatedly place something like that in my car with the intent to kill me. Knowing who I was and knowing that I have small children and that I'm their sole support, and certainly their emotional support as well as physical support. And what I realized about myself, I never really thought of myself as a Gandhian, I still don't actually because I'm just not that pious. But what I realized is that if you gave me the same bomb, and you gave me the person's car who did this to me, I don't have it in me to do that back to him. What I have discovered is that there's a level of violence, there's a level of terrorism that's really unacceptable to me, and I think that's one of the things that we really need to change in the world. The existence of this kind of violence in the world and this kind of terrorism, this is part of the problem. The same mentality that would level a redwood forest and destroy it's ability to regenerate, this is the same mentality that would place this bomb in my car and would do this kind of violence to me. I think that the problem isn't just the economic system, isn't just the social relations, I think that part of the problem is the violence in the society. Violence against humans and violence against the Earth. That's the lesson that this has really taught me.

For F.B.I., Back to Political Sabotage?

New York Times Op-Ed,
August 23, 1990

On May 24 a car bomb exploded under my seat as I drove through Oakland, Calif. The attack followed a series of death threats against me and occurred as I was traveling to organize nonviolent protests with Earth First! against overcutting of the redwood forest in northern California. My injuries are painful and severe, and will leave me permanently crippled.

But the unspeakable terrorism of this ordeal did not end there. The Federal Bureau of Investigation, working with the Oakland police, immediately concluded that I was responsible for the bombing myself. They attempted to charge me with the assassination attempt that nearly took my life.

Within hours after the bombing, they declared that my passenger, Darryl Cherney, and I were the only suspects. They based this on an F.B.I. agent's statement that since the bomb was on the floor in the back seat of the car, we should have seen it, and therefore we knew we were carrying it. Later they admitted that the bomb was hidden well under the seat and could not have been seen. Nonetheless, Mr. Cherney and I were arrested.

During the next eight weeks, the police and the F.B.I. raided my house twice and even pulled finishing nails from my window trim in a vain attempted to link me to nails found in the bomb. Meanwhile, a local newspaper received a letter claiming credit for the bombing. The letter said that the author wanted to kill me for my political activities and described the bomb in such detail that police had to admit that the writer had personal knowledge of it. But instead of searching for the letter's author, the F.B.I. concluded that the letter writer must be my accomplice, and Mr. Cherney and I remained the only suspects.

While I was in the hospital, too weak to respond, the police and F.B.I. carried on a media campaign against me. Using selected leaks and innuendo, they continued to imply my guilt. Yet the filing of charges against me was delayed twice, then finally dropped on July 18 for lack of evidence. In spite of this, the F.B.I. successfully damaged my reputation and discredited the nonviolent movement I was helping to organize.

Political sabotage of this nature is reminiscent of the activities the F.B.I. engaged in during the 1960s under the name "Cointelpro." This program of covert operations was formally suspended in 1971 after the media revealed that the F.B.I. had deliberately disrupted legitimate movements for social change.

Congressional investigations established that the F.B.I.'s activities included a 10-year secret war against Dr. Martin Luther King, and court documents show that agents acted improperly in the murders of members of the Black Panther Party and the American Indian Movement. The F.B.I. agent in charge of investigating my case is Richard W. Held, who worked with Cointelpro. And although Cointelpro was formally suspended, a former agent, Wesley Swearingen, has said that its activities continued.

The F.B.I. admitted at a news conference that one of its agents, Michael Fain, set up Earth First! activists for arrest in Arizona, and it has been widely reported that the bureau spent more than $2 million to infiltrate and disrupt Earth First! Considering this history, it seems wildly improper for the F.B.I. to be conducting any investigation of the bombing attack on me in Oakland.

The reaction of the F.B.I. to the bombing was so improper that a coalition of 50 environmental and women's groups, including the Sierra Club, the Audubon Society and the National Organization for Women, joined Representative Ron Dellums of California in calling for a Congressional investigation. The House Judiciary subcommittee on civil and constitutional rights, headed by Representative Don Edwards of California, has agreed to question the F.B.I. about its handling of the case.

Earth First! is not a terrorist organization, although the F.B.I. has done its best to present us as one. If it can succeed in framing and discrediting us, then domestic dissent is not safe from government sabotage. The right to advocate social change without fear of harassment is the cornerstone of a free society. We cannot allow ourselves to be manipulated by police agencies that have no respect for our democratic principles.

Breaking Up
Is Hard To Do

AVA, September 1990

I'd rather be sitting around base camp listening to Bob Marley, smoking a hooter, and writing this on the back of a rolling paper. But if Dave Foreman wants a divorce from all the hippie leftist anarchist humanists in Earth First!, I've got a few things to say.

First of all, I'm not out to trash Dave Foreman. I have a lot of respect for him, both for introducing me and many others to the idea of biocentrism, and for the decentralized, non-hierarchical non-organization he helped set up in EF! But this divorce has been a long time coming, and it's based on real political differences.

Dave Foreman calls himself a conservationist, and believes that the focus of EF! should be limited to preserving wilderness in public land set-asides. I absolutely agree that we need to save everything we can, and I support all efforts to preserve or re-establish wilderness. But I don't think preserving wilderness in set-asides is enough. (Our society is so destructive that any wilderness we preserve may be destroyed by acid rain, drought, or greenhouse effect. And, as the Earth continues to deteriorate under the weight of human abuse, social pressure to consume any unspoiled land will become so great that we will lose it eventually.)

The only way to preserve wilderness and the

EF! blockade during Redwood Summer, 1990, shuts down logging in the Sequoia National Forest. (photo by Peter Fisk)

only way to save our planet's life support system from collapse is to find a way to live on the Earth that doesn't destroy the Earth. In other words, Earth First! is not just a conservation movement, it is also a social change movement. (This is why EF! has attracted so many people who live alternative lifestyles. It doesn't make sense to bemoan the destruction of nature while supporting the system that is destroying it.) Yet Dave Foreman proudly calls himself a patriot, and glorifies the dominant culture of our corrupt society. He says he is a no-compromise defender of biodiversity, yet he has made the ultimate compromise of accepting a society that is literally based on the destruction of the Earth.

But in spite of the fact that many of us think putting the Earth first involves profound social change, it is wrong for Dave Foreman to characterize us simply as "leftists" or "a class struggle group." We are not trying to overthrow capitalism for the benefit of the proletariat. In fact, the society we envision is not spoken to in any leftist theory that I've ever heard of. Those theories deal only with how to redistribute the spoils of exploiting the Earth to benefit a different class of humans. We need to build a society that is not based on the exploitation of Earth at all—a society whose goal is to achieve a stable state with nature for the benefit of all species.

Of course we are nowhere near such a society. But having this kind of worldview does not mean we are working on social rather than ecological issues. It just helps shape the strategies used in our Earth First! organizing. For example, Dave Foreman would like to keep the movement small and pure. But profound social changes don't happen without mass movements, and I think we need a whole lot more of us to bring about even the modest reforms we need to save the redwoods. So the strategy for Redwood Summer was to increase our numbers. We had 2,000 people at the Earth First! rally in Fort Bragg, and we have been staging constant actions all summer. We're not watering down the movement—we're spreading our radicalism by sending all those people home with new experience in direct action.

Another change that goes with our worldview is the prominence of women in EF! Ed Abbey's retrogressive view of women as sex objects doesn't make it here, where about three-quarters of the EF! organizers are strong and competent women. And, although male dominance is not the only problem with our society or the sole reason for the destruction of nature, it is definitely a factor. Any change towards a non-exploitive culture would have to include a balance between masculine and feminine, and we had better start with our own movement.

It is particularly ironic that Dave Foreman sees us as having strayed from EF!'s principles, because we are the front line warriors of Earth First!, literally risking our lives out there defending the forest. And that is the most important part of our movement. (We are a direct action group, and our policy is set on the front lines, not on the lecture circuit or in the minds of theoreticians.)

Nobody has all the answers, and one of the strengths of Earth First! has always been our diversity. Rednecks for Wilderness and Hippie Wu-Wu's can co-exist in Earth First!, as long as we are all fighting to save this planet. Our decentralized non-structure leaves room for many strategies to be followed at once. But if Dave Foreman or anyone else starts insisting on conventionality, we will lose our spark.

I don't see Dave's leaving as a split in Earth First!, but rather as an evolution. We are not moving away from his ideas, we are expanding them. The activities he proposes are not in competition with ours, and there is no reason for anyone to have to choose sides. Things are not the same as they were 10 years ago, and Earth First! is changing too. But we will continue, and a year from now we'll still be out there kicking corporate butt.

Earth First! blockade of L-P logging operation in Navarro, CA, August 18 1989. Less than 24 hours later, this same truck and driver rammed my car from behind at full speed.(photo by Judi Bari)

The Revolution Will Not Be Televised

AVA, September 26, 1990

In case anyone still had any delusions about freedom of the press in Mendocino County, the Santa Rosa *Press Democrat* laid them to rest last week when they removed Ukiah Bureau Chief Mike Geniella from covering timber issues. Geniella has been the lead reporter in the timber region, and has broken important stories and won awards for his coverage. Removing him was an outrageous act of censorship, and marked a new low in corporate media kowtowing to big timber.

Geniella's crime was that he gave an interview to the AVA in which he told the truth about Redwood Summer. "Clearly Redwood Summer accomplished a number of things," admitted Geniella. "Earth First! used to attract 30 or 40 people here on the steps of the Court House, so bringing 2000 to a rally in Fort Bragg is quite impressive. The sensational aspect of the bombing [of Judi Bari and Darryl Cherney], I'm convinced, having been to some of the colleges, frightened some of the people away. For Redwood Summer to be able to regroup and do Samoa, which I think was absolutely critical, and to pull it off like they did, and then go do Fort Bragg, well, you have to give them a lot of credit.... There was all this talk about violence and when the test came clearly it was the Redwood Summer people who kept the lid on." Geniella also admitted that The *Press Democrat*'s coverage of the Fort Bragg action "probably was unfair."

That's it. That's the worst of what he said. Of course, the fact that he said it in the big bad AVA didn't help matters. But the real irony of the *Press Democrat*'s actions is that, while still holding naive ideas about his right to free speech off the job, Mike Geniella had already caved in to timber industry pressure on the job. His reporting on timber issues, once among the most fair and hard-hitting around, had been watered down to satisfy his editors' pro-timber bias. The last piece he wrote before being pulled off timber issues was a blatant piece of industry propaganda titled "Foresters Contend Logging In Balance." It cited 53 professional foresters, "all of whom work in the private sector in Mendocino County," claiming that there is no over-cut here. By calling them "private sector" instead of "corporate" foresters he gives the impression that they are independent. He never asks the simple question of who they work for (which in Mendo County is usually L-P or G-P), or why, if there's no overcut, are they logging six-inch pecker poles.

Geniella also sacrificed truth in reporting to brown-nose his editors in his Redwood Summer wrap-up piece. You won't find any of his legitimate praise of EF! organizers in this article. Instead he starts out, "Redwood Summer, the series of logging protests christened by a violent explosion, is set to end this week." The implication, of course, is that EF! was the cause of the explosion, not the victim. No further explanation is given, and when he gets into listing acts of violence associated with Redwood Summer he omits the bombing entirely and bends over backward to make it look like both sides were

Fort Bragg Demonstration, Redwood Summer 1990. (photo by Nicholas Wilson)

violent. His description of the incident with Pacific Lumber President John Campbell was absolutely fraudulent. "Campbell said protesters rocked his car and pounded their fists on rolled up windows as he tried to leave," wrote Geniella. "The timber executive later described the experience as 'very frightening.'" What Geniella didn't write was that Campbell had picked up protester Bob Serena on the hood of his car as Campbell attempted to break through the picket line, and that Campbell then floored it and careened down the road with Serena clinging for his life to the car hood. "That's called balanced reporting," Geniella answered when I complained to him about the inaccuracy.

There are many other examples of Geniella and other reporters engaging in self-censorship this summer by failing to write about attacks on demonstrators and, especially in August, failing to cover our demos at all. But even compromising his integrity in his reporting was not enough for Geniella's editors. They want to shut him up in his private life too. What this really shows is what a hoax any claim of objective reporting is. No reporter has ever been disciplined for being "too close" to Harry Merlo or Charles Hurwitz. Geniella describes a reporter's job as having a front row seat on the parade of life. But when you are dealing with forces as ruthless and powerful as big timber, there are no seats. We are all in the parade. And Geniella's complicity in distorting and suppressing info about the success of our demos and the viciousness of attacks on us helped contribute to the atmosphere in which he could become the next victim of the Timber Wars. First they come for the Earth First!ers, then they come for the reporters.

Geniella has filed a grievance with his union over the *Press Democrat*'s violation of his right to free speech. But the union is encountering its own problems with corporate greed. Wages and working conditions have been deteriorating at the *Press Democrat* ever since it was taken over by *The New York Times* in 1985. As bargaining begins on their new contract, management has put forward their proposal to eliminate wage scales and impose a "merit" system based on management evaluations. Work could also be assigned to anyone, including non-union employees. Severance pay, rehiring rights and union security would be eliminated, and a "management rights" clause would preclude dissent by employees in most areas. Employees would also be subject to drug testing and searches of their belongings and vehicles on company property. These conditions are strikingly similar to the labor practices of Louisiana-Pacific, which might help to explain why the *Press Democrat* is willing to go to such lengths to support their corporate buddies in the timber industry.

Censoring Geniella has had a chilling effect on local reporters of lesser stature, who are rushing to censor themselves so that they won't meet the same fate. An ominous pattern is being established, as shown by the 30 yellow shirts who showed up last week in Mendocino to demand that Kay Rudin's powerful video of the slaughter of Osprey Grove be kept off the air. Despite Geniella's recent weak-kneed reporting, it is important to support him on this issue of censorship. If they can keep him down we are all at risk.

It is a measure of our effectiveness (both EF! and the *AVA*) that the corporados are going to such extremes to suppress us. (When you look as bad as the timber industry, only a complete news blackout can help public opinion.) One thing I learned when that bomb exploded under me last May is that these criminals will go to any lengths to stay in power. It's not surprising that an industry that would use assassination to suppress dissent would also use censorship. We can't depend on the corporate media to publicize our battles with the corporations. That's why papers like the *AVA* are so important. As Gil Scott Heron says: "The revolution will not be televised. The revolution will be live."

1990: A Year in the Life of Earth First!

AVA, January 2, 1991

January

We started out the year by taking over the office of Mendo County District Attorney Susan Massini. About 20 of us forced our way in to protest Massini's refusal to prosecute logger Dave Lancaster for breaking Mem Hill's nose at a protest in Whitethorn. (Note to liberals: Yes, we had already tried talking politely with her, and it didn't work.) Mem said refusal to prosecute would create the impression that violence against EF!ers is okay in Mendo County. Massini said we "suckered" her. Riverhouse Bill said, "The only County service we get in Whitethorn is CAMP [Campaign Against Marijuana Planting]."

Also in January the AFL unions in Humboldt County held a toothless protest against L-P's shipping logs to Mexico. The amazing thing about this rally was that music was supplied by yours truly, IWW-EF! band, Darryl, me and George singing "Where Are We Gonna Work When The Trees Are Gone." Also on the labor front, IWW Local No. 1 successfully intervened in January to stop a sell-out deal between G-P, OSHA, and Don Nelson's union to plea bargain the PCB spill. The case went on to appeal.

Darryl and me at Redwood Summer organizing rally May 1990. Last rally before the bombing.

1990: The Year of Earth First!

February

Boskeenhauser, the three-headed lap-dog, met behind closed doors with their corporate masters Charles Hurwitz and Harry Merlo to work out a "compromise" on the forest. EF! wasted no time denouncing this scam. The very next day, 75 of us stormed all three of their offices in Eureka, instituting our own "open door policy" by taking Hauser's door off its hinges.

The next day we took our protests to the field. To show that the "deal" had not slowed the slaughter of ancient redwoods, we ambushed a logging truck loaded with huge old-growth logs headed for Scotia. When the truck stopped at a stop sign, five EF!ers quickly climbed it and chained themselves to the logs, and 50 more of us jumped out of the bushes and surrounded the truck. This enraged truck owner Don Nolan, who had recently distinguished himself by telling the SF Examiner, "I think I own this land. My ancestors protected it from the Indians and the bears."

March

The first thing we did in March was go to the Oregon Law Conference, where EF!ers were prominent on many panels. My panel was on Labor and the Environment, where Oregon millworker Gene Lawhorn publicly challenged me to make good my statements about labor by renouncing tree-spiking. I did, and to my surprise received overwhelming support from EF!ers there. We met afterward and decided to renounce tree-spiking in Northern California and Southern Oregon.

Meanwhile Pacific Lumber tried to sneak and

put a logging road into Headwaters Forest, where the Timber Harvest Plan (THP) had not been approved. Unfortunately for them, EF! just happened to be trespassing there that day, and caught Maxxam red-handed. Maxxam claimed it was a "trail" for its wildlife biologist. But the Mud Babies Affinity Group videotaped the 30-foot-wide, one-mile-long road. We took it to the press, the Sierra Club took it to court, and Maxxam had to stop.

We also announced Mississippi Summer in the California redwoods around this time. Darryl and I began promoting it at a student environmental rally in Sacramento. We also announced it at an EF! rally in Eureka, when Darryl and George went in to start a 10-day jail term for the heinous crime of tree-sitting. Mike Geniella wrote an article about Mississippi Summer in the *Press Democrat*, and it went national on the wire service. Fortuna's mayor announced that he wants no more EF! demos in his town. Requests for info started coming in from all over, and we realized this thing was bigger than we thought.

We held one last demo in March, at the Redwood Region Logging Show in Ukiah. A bunch of hippie-looking EF!ers created a distraction while two logger-looking EF!ers climbed Okerstrom's prize $700,000 feller-buncher and hung a banner that said "This Things Kills Jobs & Forests." A few weeks later that same feller-buncher burned in the woods near Willits. When asked if we were responsible, I told the press it wasn't me—("I was home in bed with five witnesses.")

April

L-P sent shock waves through Mendo County

by announcing 195 layoffs in Ukiah and Covelo and the closing of the Covelo Mill, while reaping record profits for the quarter. "I know the political timing is lousy," said L-P's silver-tongued spokesman Shep Tucker," but business and politics at this juncture for L-P don't mix."

We reacted by staging the first public display of our worker alliance. EF!, IWW, and L-P employees appeared together at the Board of Supes meeting to demand that Mendo County use the power of Eminent Domain to seize all of L-P's holdings and operate them in the public interest. Darryl brought the house down and made everyone but Marilyn Butcher smile with his legendary song "El Pio."

After that they turned up the heat on us. False press releases claiming to be from EF! began appearing in the mills and logging towns, calling for violence. Death threats against me, Darryl and Greg came thick and heavy, and law enforcement refused to investigate. L-P spent $100,000 to put up a barbed-wire fence in Ukiah to "protect" its employees from us EF! "terrorists." Sheriff Shea introduced the Stupid Sign Ordinance to limit our picket sign sticks to 1/4 inch thick. (In a rare display of sanity, the Board of Supes did not pass it.)

Meanwhile, Earth Day arrived with its message of corporate compromise. But Earth Night saw the dropping of power lines in Santa Cruz, which, although we knew nothing about it, was immediately blamed on us. The next day EF! successfully climbed the Golden Gate Bridge and attempted to unfurl a banner denouncing Earth Day. The ground support crew was arrested along with the climbers, and two EF! cars were illegally seized and towed. Oakland cops mysteriously appeared in Marin to search and confiscate the EF!ers' belongings.

May

May began with the unprecedented denial of Charlie Hiatt's logging plan in Anderson Valley, after local residents made an issue of the cutting of baby trees.

The Board of Supes put Mississippi Summer on their agenda and ordered us to appear. We found the room filled with hostile gyppo owners and L-P security, openly calling for the use of violence against our non-violent protests. When I showed them the death threats, Marilyn Butcher said, "You brought it on yourself, Judi." When I referred to Charlie Stone's right-wing anti-EF! radio show as "radio K-KKK," Butcher and Sheriff Shea stormed out.

We reacted by working with Art Harwood to set up negotiating meetings with the gyppos to try and prevent violence. We held a rally in Ukiah, where 100 people heard Brian Willson call for non-violence. Then, just as it seemed we were making progress, someone put a bomb in my car. It exploded in Oakland, while Darryl and I were traveling to Santa Cruz to recruit students for what was now called Redwood Summer. The bomb nearly killed me. It maimed me for life, and took me out for the entire summer. Darryl and I were arrested, and Darryl was interrogated in jail as the FBI moved in to try and blame us for the bombing. Richard Held, the FBI agent who got famous in COINTELPRO, was in charge of our case. They spent the next few months smearing us in the press with selected leaks and innuendos, before finally admitting that they had no evidence against us. Still, our names have not been cleared by the FBI.

June

With most of the experienced Redwood Summer leaders and legal team taken out by the bombing, and with our community in shock, people started arriving from around the country, and we had to keep going. Many people rose up and took my place, especially women. Karen, Kelpie, Pam, Anna Marie, Mickey, Jennifer, Lisa, Naomi, Debbie, Justine, Betty, Tracy, Roanne, Mary, Karen, Sequoia, Brian, Steve, Mokai, Robert, Zack and many more took on the risks and personal sacrifices needed to keep the movement alive.

New EF!ers in Sacramento staged the first Redwood Summer protest at the export dock. Humboldt EF!ers took to the woods, where they held a "cat and mouse" action to stop logging. The Squirrel Affinity Group also staged a tree-sit in Murrulet Grove and collected biological data on endangered species in the grove before being arrested. "Urban Earth Women" were arrested in costume at Maxxam headquarters in Marin.

The first official Redwood Summer protest took place in Samoa at the L-P export dock. Seven hundred people showed for the rally, and 44 were arrested blocking log and chip trucks. L-P's Shep Tucker called it "a fizzle," but the *Press Democrat* (which was still enamored with us back then) ran its story with the headline, "Practice Makes Perfect Demo."

July

Redwood Summer demonstrators seemed to have trouble finding the woods at first, and several demos were held at mills or holding signs along the highway. The Calpella chip mill demo featured a timber wife counter-demonstrator holding a sign reading, "If you take my husband's job, he takes it out on me." Yellow shirts held a "solidarity" rally in Fort Bragg and started planning for a counter-demo to our upcoming Ft. Bragg rally.

Right before the Fort Bragg rally, neighbors heard L-P falling old growth in Osprey Grove and called in Redwood Summer. Sixty demonstrators blocked the logging and were assaulted by Registered Professional De-Forester Lee Susan and Pardini's logging crew, who threw rocks at the protesters and hit one with an ax-handle. In the perfect Redwood Summer scenario, protesters got arrested and stalled the cut while the Save the Redwoods League offered to buy it. L-P relented, and the old growth was saved.

The climax of the summer, of course, was the Fort Bragg rally. Two thousand of us rallied peacefully in an extremely tense situation, and marched through town chanting "Earth First! Profits Last!" At the other end of town 1,500 yellow shirts rallied to Maribell (the cheerleader from Hell)'s chant of "2-4-6-8, Who do we appreciate? Loggers, loggers, yeah!!" In the middle of town there was a standoff between our people and several hundred angry counter-demonstrators. In a dramatic resolution, Darryl and Pam invited the hecklers to speak on our sound truck. Duane Potter, a logger whom we had never met before, stood up and told the truth—that he used to log in the summer and fish in the winter, and now there are no logs and no fish.)The rally, to everyone's surprise and relief, ended without violence.

At the end of July, Redwood Summer moved to the Sequoia National Forest, where 400 people joined a rendezvous and action that stopped all logging in the area for the day at eight different logging sites.

August

After the Fort Bragg rally, the *Press Democrat* ran an article declaring Redwood Summer over, then proceeded to stop covering it as much as they could get away with. But the protests continued, moving mainly to Humboldt County.

Demonstrators locked themselves to logging equipment with Kryptonite locks in several places. At one protest Pacific Lumber falsely tried to blame us for interfering with firefighting efforts. At the Carlotta log deck 17 people were arrested in a lockdown, and four had their heads shaved in jail by brutal Mississippi-style law enforcement. Five demonstrators outside the jail shaved their own heads in protest, and one was arrested for illegally communicating with prisoners by holding up a sign that said "We Love You."

The Lorax Affinity Group, who had been arrested in June at the Samoa protest, took their case to jury trial and argued that they were blocking trucks to prevent greater crimes by L-P. Legal history was made when they got a hung jury, 7-5 for acquittal.

The most outrageous woods action of the summer took place in Murrelet Grove near Headwaters, where 50 people marched into the active logging site and blocked operations with their bodies. Loggers chased them with bulldozers, and they stood their ground. One protester had his legs run over by a logger's truck. He miraculously escaped serious injury, but when other protesters came to his aid, a grappling match broke out between loggers and protesters. People surrounded an old-growth tree as a logger tried to cut it, and one man place his hand right under the chainsaw, so it could not be turned back on without hurting him.

After Murrelet, 70 protesters assembled outside a timber executives' meeting with HSU professors in Korbel, so they could focus the demo on the execs instead of the loggers. When Pacific Lumber President John Campbell came out, people surrounded his car and tried to place him under citizens arrest. Campbell rammed the picket line and took off, careening down the road, with protester Bob Serena clinging to his car hood. When he stopped a half-mile later, Serena was arrested and Campbell went free. For the next three days, 20 protesters held a 24-hour vigil at Campbell's house. They tried to place him under citizens' arrest for being a Maxxam hood, but the police would not cooperate. Serena is still in jail, serving four months.

Just when it looked like things couldn't get much more outrageous, US Army troops and helicopters, fresh from their "victory" in Panama, landed in the Mattole area of Humboldt County for Operation Greensweep. Their purpose was supposedly to rid the area of the scourge of marijuana on public lands. They flew helicopters low over people's homes and tromped around people's land with assault weapons, scaring and pissing off local residents. Redwood Summer responded by holding Hemp Liberation Day right in front of the place where the troops were stationed. Two hundred and fifty hippies showed up with music and speakers advocating using hemp instead of trees for paper and fiber. They threw marijuana seeds over the line at the soldiers, smoked big hooters right in front of them, and finally ended with a classic drum circle. The troops were withdrawn a few days later because they were "needed in Iraq."

Meanwhile, back in Mendo County, the citizens of Elk took it upon themselves to organize a Redwood Summer-style protest over L-P's cutting near their water supply. Calling themselves "Breakfast First!," they had gourmet chefs serve a champagne breakfast in the middle of a logging road. One arrestee was a longtime logger, and supervisor Norman deVall stood in front of logging equipment as L-P goons ordered it to move on the protesters.

Brave demonstrators in the devastated Sherwood area in Mendo Co. also staged a bicycle ride blockade that ended in wild chase through Willits of a log truck that stole their banner. Several protests were also held at the Maxxam building in Marin, including a Peace Navy Sea Blockade and an arrest action by Central America activists drawing connections between environmental devastation in the redwoods and in Central America. In another outstanding August action the Squirrel Affinity Group closed down Highway 101 for five hours with a single tree climber suspended over the road with a banner saying, "Save Headwaters." Also in August I made my first and only public appearance, still in a wheelchair, at a women's rally at the FBI building in San Francisco. Two hundred women, including United Farmworkers' Dolores Huerta, sang "Burning Times" at that bastion of male power.

The finale of Redwood Summer was supposed to be a mass action at Maxxam. For whatever reasons (it would take another article to discuss it), organizing for this action was taken out of the area and planning was done in the Bay Area, mostly out of control of the locals. The result was what looked like a recipe for disaster—a two-day concert called Redwoodstock held in a hostile area after a court order was obtained to allow the assembly, followed by a march through the legendary Stomper town of Fortuna. In spite of this set-up, the Redwood Summer demonstrators again proved their commitment to non-violent protest. Seven hundred of them marched through Fortuna through a hail of jeers, eggs and bottles. At the end of the march the police seemed unable to hold back the attacking vigilantes. But just as they broke through, the marchers sat down and started singing "We Shall Overcome," once again preventing violence by using non-violence.

This is by no means a complete list of Redwood Summer demos. At least 3,000 people participated, as opposed to about 150 who joined redwood protests the year before. Arrest total was over 250.

September

After the Redwood Summer hordes went home, L-P moved in for the kill in Osprey Grove. Without even notifying Save the Redwoods League, which was still trying to buy it, they brutally slaughtered the old growth while a few EF! demonstrators who heard about it in time desperately tried to stop them. Loggers felled trees feet away from Anna Marie and Zack, and hurled insults at them as they did it. A court order was finally obtained to stop the cutting, but by that time only 12 trees were left. There was so much public outrage over this that L-P made the unprecedented move of apologizing for its "perceived arrogance." Anna Marie called the apology ("as empty as Osprey Grove.")

A few days later, EF! held a protest rally in Ukiah calling for "L-P Out of Mendo County." We also announced the beginning of our next campaign—Corporate Fall. The plan was to bring the demos to the homes and offices of the corporate execs, to show who is really responsible for the destruction of the Earth.

Darryl Cherney traveled to Houston for the first Corporate Fall demo, and led 125 new EF!ers to Maxxam's lair. Charles Hurwitz personally tried to intervene to stop the demo.

Meanwhile the *Press Democrat* struck the final blow in its increasingly hostile and scanty coverage by removing award-winning journalist Mike Geniella from the timber beat. Mike's crime was to give an interview to the Anderson Valley Advertiser in which he admitted that we were non-violent and effective in Redwood Summer. Mike is still gathering dust in his Ukiah office, where he's not allowed to write about anything much that happens here, and we are all still suffering from the press censorship that results.

October

The best demo of Corporate Fall (in fact, probably the best demo of the year, in a year with tight competition) was held at Harry Merlo's secret Shangri-La in Cloverdale. EF!ers hung banners telling Harry to repent for his corporate crimes, dumped chips in his driveway, and blasted him with Earth First! music from the world's biggest bullhorn. Then they walked onto his property, took off their clothes and jumped into his hot-tub. The cops finally arrived and arrested the "leaders," who spent a cold wet 12 hours in jail, but said it was worth it.

On October 29, to commemorate Black Friday and the stock exchange crash, a Corporate Fall demo was held at the Pacific Stock Exchange in San Francisco. It was a coalition demo with Earth Action Network, and included 300 demonstrators blocking the streets while crazed yuppies tried to get to work. The demo ended with 25 random arrests after a smoke bomb mysteriously went off in the corporate office of Chas Schwab.

November

Okerstrom's new feller-buncher was still chugging away in the already moonscaped Noyo area. So IWW-EF! Eco-Trans came to the rescue, blocking the logging road Caltrans-style, with little orange vests and hard hats. They dumped a load of gravel in the road and shoveled it from pothole to pothole, taking long coffee breaks and leaning on their shovels.

Eco-Trans was called into action a second time on election day. As Propositions 130, 128 and 138 all went down to defeat, the real Caltrans was out on Highway 20 cutting old growth to make the world safer for automobiles. EF!-Eco-Trans warriors responded like the volunteer fire department, jumping into their vests and rushing to the scene. They threw their bodies in front of logging equipment, climbed trees and hugged trees. With some timely help from Supervisors Norm deVall and Liz Henry, the cut was stopped, and all but two trees were saved.

December

There was still time for one more Corporate Fall demo. EF! Corporate Fallers went carolling at Pacific Lumber President John Campbell's house. Children delivered gift-wrapped presents of ash and sawdust to his door, while singers drove Campbell crazy with their endless rendition of "Hang Down Your Head, John Campbell." Finally Candy Boak and her Mothers Nazi Brigade showed up and tried (unsuccessfully) to drown out the singers with a ride-around lawn mower.

Santa arrived in Ukiah driving a bulldozer at the front of the "lighted log-truck" parade (I'm not making this up). Since it was Ukiah, the trucks were loaded with pecker-poles and chips. The only thing missing was the recently laid-off L-P employees, who should have been panhandling at the end of the parade.

But the year ended on a happy note, with the third Okerstrom feller-buncher going up in flames near Ukiah. That makes $1.5 million worth of feller-bunchers that have self-destructed in the woods of Mendo County.

Why I Am Not A Misanthrope

AVA, January 9, 1991

In the last EF! *Journal*, Chris Manes responds to the question "Why are you a misanthrope?" by saying, "Why aren't you one?" After all, humans have a 10,000-year history of massacres, wars, eco-cide, holocaust, etc., so the burden of proof is on us non-misanthropes.

I would like to respond to Manes' challenge, and my answer has nothing to do with humanism, anthropocentrism, or the belief that humans are a "higher" life form. Unlike Murray Bookchin, I reject that claim from the git-go. I believe in biocentrism, and think that all life forms are equal. I agree that human population is totally out of control. And I am as appalled as any misanthrope at the havoc that humans have wreaked on the natural world.

But I disagree with Manes' conclusion that the problem is "humankind." You cannot blame the destruction of the Earth on, for example, the Quiche tribes of Guatemala or the Penan of Borneo. These people have lived in harmony with the Earth for 10,000 years. The only way you could identify the Earth's destroyers as "humankind." would be to exempt such people from the category of "human." Otherwise you would have to admit that it is not humans-as-a-species, but the way certain humans live, that is destroying the Earth.

Manes briefly acknowledges that these ecologically sound human cultures exist, but he dismisses them as trivial because "the fact is most of the world now mimics our dissolute ways." This statement completely ignores the manner in which "most of the world" was forced to abandon their indigenous cultures or be destroyed. You cannot equate the slave and the slave-master. Only after massacres, torture, ecocide and other unspeakable brutality did the peoples of the world acquiesce to the conquering hordes with the culture of greed and destruction.

Technocratic man, with his linear view of the world, tends to see tribal societies as earlier, less evolved forms of his own society, rather than as alternative, simultaneously existing methods of living on the Earth. The presumption is that, given time, these cultures would somehow be corrupted like ours. But there is no evidence whatsoever that these ancient civilizations would have changed without our violent intervention. So it is not humans, but industrial-technocratic societies, that are destroying the Earth.

In the same manner that misanthropy blames all humans for crimes of the industrial/technocratic society, so does it blame all humans for the crimes of men. The list of atrocities for which Manes condemns the human race—massacres, wars, ecocide, holocaust—are not the works of women. Of course a few women can be found and paraded out who participate in the male power structure. But by and large, throughout history, wars and atrocities have been the territory of men, in the interest of men, and against the interests of women. By categorizing as "human" traits that are actually male, misanthropes are being androcentric (male-centered) instead of biocentric (life-centered) as they claim to be.

So misanthropy is not a form of humility, as Chris Manes says. It is a form of arrogance. By blaming the entire human species for the crimes of technocratic men, Manes conveniently avoids any real analysis of who is responsible for the death of the planet. Not surprisingly, Manes himself is a member of the group that most benefits from our consumptive society—privileged white urban men.

If the purpose of philosophy is just to play mind games, then misanthropy can be seen as provocative or enticing. But if the purpose of philosophy is to help us analyze the crisis we are in so that we can try to find solutions, misanthropy fails. It preserves the status quo by refusing to distinguish between oppressor and oppressed. It goes against one of the basic instincts of all life forms, preservation of the species. And, without contributing anything of value to an analysis of the problem, it alienates us from the people we need to work with to bring about change—people whose ideas are grounded in reality and experience, not in college textbooks.

Reply to Crawdad Nelson

The Truth About Earth First! and Loggers

AVA, December 26, 1990

Crawdad Nelson's analysis of Earth First! and the timber issue in his recent article "Ignorance Is Bliss" is both shallow and inaccurate. He starts by repeating the timber industry stereotype of Earth First!ers as lazy, unemployed hippies, and tells us to go do some real work if we want to ally with the loggers.

Crawdad knows many of us personally, and I don't know who he thinks he is to talk down to us like that. In Humboldt County where Crawdad lives, the vice president of the union at the Simpson Pulp Mill openly associates with Earth First!, and was recently re-elected to his union post. Of the 25 people at our last local Earth First! meeting, only two were students, and the rest hold jobs including carpenter, auto mechanic, child care worker, recycling center operator, office worker and logger. Many of us have children, and we cook, clean, grow our own food and homestead the land. Many of us also belong to local watershed associations and do regular unpaid stream restoration work in our neighborhoods. So we don't need Crawdad to tell us about work.

Crawdad's main point is that, instead of protesting the corporations' overcut, we should be setting up alternative logging operations. There are several things wrong with this idea. First of all, since most of us are working people, we don't have the capital to buy the logging and milling equipment we would need. This is the same reason the employees of Maxxam, L-P and G-P can't just quit their jobs and start doing things right. It's one of the basic laws of capitalism, and one of the ways the corporations maintain control.

Secondly, because the big corporations control the timber market, timber prices are based on a system that pays the workers as little as possible (including 85¢ an hour at the L-P Mexico mill), and gains efficiency at the expense of the long-term health of the forest. Non-destructive forestry is much more labor intensive than corporate logging, and alternative companies cannot compete in the corporate market.'

It is true that there is an alternative market—people who are willing to pay more for lumber that is logged in an environmentally sound manner, like we pay more for organic produce. But unlike the market for food, this market is limited by the fact that most people do not build their own houses, and therefore most lumber is bought by large development companies that are not willing to pay the higher prices. In fact, in some cases (Weyerhaeuser in particular) the timber corporations *are* the development companies.

Finally, setting up alternative logging operations will not in itself save the forest, because the corporations own much of the timber land. And, when they are finished destroying that, our government has shown itself only too willing to turn the national forests over to those same destructive corporations.

This is not to say that people shouldn't engage in

alternative forestry, or that we shouldn't support efforts such as those of Jan Iris to build the kind of logging operations we need to survive in the future. We can and must build the shell of a new society within the decadent old one. But we must recognize that these operations are limited in scope by the laws of corporate capitalism, and they cannot, by themselves, end the corporations' destruction of the Earth.

This is why, in addition to trying to live lightly on the Earth, we Earth First!ers continue to confront the corporations. Yet Crawdad actually claims that our protests are the cause of the greed logging we are demonstrating against. Earth First! didn't double Pacific Lumber's redwood cut to pay for Maxxam's junk bond takeover—but we helped make a national issue of it when Hurwitz did. And if Earth First! had not gone to Osprey Grove those trees would not have been saved. They would just have been cut down last July without the public outrage that arose over L-P's slaughter of Osprey Grove after our protests in September.

Just one year ago, I debated Crawdad Nelson in the pages of this paper when he blamed the workers for the destruction of the forest. Now he's a born-again worker and he's blaming Earth First! I don't know why Crawdad has so much trouble with this concept. It's not the loggers, it's not the environmentalists. It's the corporate millionaires like Charles Hurwitz and Harry Merlo who are pillaging the Earth. I don't know if we can build a strong enough coalition to stop them before the forest is destroyed. But the effort will not be helped by people like Crawdad promoting timber industry stereotypes and blaming the messengers.

Dave Foreman
Comes to Ecotopia

AVA, March 13, 1991

"I'm just a stupid guy," said Dave Foreman when asked to explain some of his stances at his Sebastopol appearance last week. "I'm an asshole." And so Foreman once again avoided addressing the hard issues or explaining the contradiction between his radical theories and conservative politics.

Dave apologized profusely for the article that had just appeared in the *Press Democrat* (written by Bleys Rose) titled "Earth First! Co-Founder: Time for Group To Take A Hike." It depicted him as saying local Earth First!ers should "butt out" and let the Sierra Club and Wilderness Society settle the timber issue. And considering Bleys Rose's record of writing vicious hit-pieces against both Earth First! and the peace movement, I'm sure Dave is telling the truth that he was exaggerated and misrepresented.

But apologizing at a small forum does not undo the damage done by that article. And this is not an isolated incident. Foreman has been saying things to discredit Northern California activists since last summer. His new book, which he was in Sebastopol to promote, calls us "anarchists and class-struggle leftists" who have "infiltrated" Earth First! and led it away from its true purpose. Not that there's anything wrong with anarchists or leftists, but Foreman uses the term in a derogatory, red-baiting manner, along with words like "kiddie stunts" and "feral ado-

Dave Foreman Comes to Ecotopia

lescents" to describe our work.

The most serious case of this public trashing came last summer. While I was still flat on my back recovering from the nearly successful attempt on my life, and front lines activists in Redwood Summer were getting beaten and shaved in jail or rammed on the picket line by a car driven by Pacific Lumber President John Campbell, when tensions were at their height and solidarity was essential to prevent violence, Foreman told the newspapers that we were "leftists, hippies and yippies" more interested in "class struggle than the rhetoric of ecology." These statements were gleefully and predictably exploited by Pacific Lumber, which put out its own press release saying Redwood Summer activists were so extreme that even our own leader disavowed us.

I don't think Dave Foreman deliberately said things to marginalize us last summer any more than I think he deliberately said things to discredit us last week. I just think he doesn't have a clue about what's really going on in Northern California. Foreman endorsed Sierra Club negotiations in last week's *Press Democrat* article without even knowing that Gail Lucas was in the process of trying to sell out the gains made by grassroots activists here, and that her "compromise" with the timber industry would allow 70% cuts in old-growth areas with 25-year re-entry. Quite a far cry from the local Earth First! position of "not one more old-growth tree cut down."

Foreman says he sees Earth First! as a catalyst group that brings attention to an issue so the mainstream groups can come in and negotiate. But that's not the way it's been up here. The changes that are taking place in redwood forest practices are coming directly from the activism of Earth First!, EPIC and other grassroots groups, without the intervention of the so-called professionals. This includes CDF suddenly "voluntarily" changing its policy and deciding to uphold the Tebbutts' lawsuit over cutting baby trees. It includes Gov. Pete Wilson and Congressman Frank Riggs coming out in support of saving Headwaters Forest, which was identified, walked, mapped, named and made an issue by Earth First!

And even the Wall Street analyst in the *Press Democrat* explained L-P's no-clearcutting announcement by saying, "If you were operating a business and you had extensive operations throughout the country, and you didn't want these people marching up to all your doorsteps wherever you are, you would obviously accede to some of their more reasonable demands. All redwood producers, if they want to avoid the wrath of God and the even worse wrath of environmentalists, have been moving towards selective harvesting."

It sure is strange to be given more credit by the *Press Democrat*'s Wall Street analyst than by the founder of your own group. But Foreman has lost touch with the grassroots. He still talks about demos that happened in 1983 because that's the last time he was out there on the front lines. He is unable to assess the success or failure of our tactics because he doesn't talk to us enough to know what's going on.

Dave Foreman has lost his vision. "I don't have any answers," he said in Sebastopol. "I've given up on changing the system." Those were not encouraging words to hear from someone who used to inspire people to action. But things have gotten heavier than any of us expected. I never thought I'd get bombed, and I'm sure Dave never thought he'd get set up and busted by the FBI. I don't blame anybody who steps back under these circumstances.

Foreman has officially quit Earth First!, and he says he is now running for the executive board of the Sierra Club. If that's where he feels more comfortable, then that's where he should work. But Foreman needs to recognize that his position as grand old man of Earth First! amplifies any statement he makes. It doesn't matter if he says he quit. As long as he is traveling around promoting a book called *Confessions of an Eco-Warrior*, featuring a cover photo of himself wearing an Earth First! shirt and looking like a Real Man, anything he says is going to reflect on the local Earth First!ers. And he may not like our haircuts or our politics, but we're putting our lives on the line to defend the Earth.

The Sierra Club Surrender

AVA, March 20, 1991

Things got a little out of hand here in the redwood region last year. People chaining themselves to logging equipment, throwing themselves in front of bulldozers, or marching 2,000 strong through Fort Bragg shouting "Earth First! Profits Last!" A local grassroots forestry reform initiative gaining statewide support and almost passing (but for the sabotage of the big money men, who are ultimately all on the same side). Lawsuits flying. Yellow ribbons waving. Feller-bunchers self-igniting and burning in the woods. Earth First!ers swimming in Harry Merlo's hot tub. Me getting bombed and having the audacity not to die. It was not an easy year for the timber companies. They managed to get out a record timber harvest, but at the expense of public opinion. Word got out that they are slaughtering the redwoods, and it's become a national, even international issue.

So the timber companies say they want to negotiate. They recognize that timber reform is inevitable, and they want to avoid another "costly initiative." They're afraid to even say the R-word, Redwood Summer, but you can be sure the protests are just as much on their minds. Anyway, in order to appear to negotiate without having to worry about actually changing their greedy timber practices, the money men have chosen Sierra Club State Rep. Gail Lucas to represent the environmentalists.

The Sierra Club Surrender

Lucas has little support, even among Sierra Club members. She sure doesn't represent the people who wrote the Forests Forever initiative, organized the Redwood Summer protests, or filed the grass-roots lawsuits. Lucas' salary as a negotiator is being paid by money man Hal Arbit. And from the results of her negotiations, it looks like Gail Lucas is a better representative of Sierra Pacific than Sierra Club.

Gail Lucas and the timber industry use all the right lingo in their "Forest Policy Agreement," as this sellout is called. This way, a casual observer would think the environmentalists had gotten what they wanted from the poor, beleaguered timber companies, so why are we still complaining? For example, they talk about preserving ancient forests, but the small print allows them to log all remaining old growth, as long as they take only 50% on the first cut, and eventually leave six "mature trees" per acre. They also call for sustained-yield logging, but define sustained yield in a manner that would allow 50-year rotations of redwood trees, whose natural lifespan is over 1,000 years, and who don't reach cone-bearing age for 100–150 years. Clearcutting is dealt with in a similarly deceptive manner.

And, of course, this agreement contains no provisions whatsoever for the workers who are being displaced by the timber companies. Not one word. Not even an acknowledgment that all this is causing social and economic devastation in our communities. And it certainly makes no attempt to get the corporations to make reparations. Compare this to the more locally based Mendocino County Forestry Advisory Committee. They proposed that, during a five-year transition period to sustained yield, any logging that exceeded sustained-yield rates would be subject to a "stumpage tax" of 20%. This tax would be used to form a relief fund for displaced workers.

Gail Lucas' blindness to the needs of the workers and our community is not surprising, considering her own fat salary and privileged position. But "environmentalists" who show so little concern for such basic social issues make it easy for the timber companies to turn the workers' just fears into hatred of environmentalists. And, as we know only too well, this often translates into vigilante violence.

About this time last year, Bosco, Keene and Hauser, the three-headed lapdog, met behind closed doors with timber barons Charles Hurwitz and Harry Merlo. They wrote up a "timber pact" on the back of a napkin which they said would settle the timber wars. Of course it did no such thing. And neither will Gail Lucas' backroom deal. Like Karen Smith said in last week's AVA, you can't negotiate the temperature at which spawning creeks cease to be a viable habitat for salmon or steelhead. The underlying determinant is biology, not economics or politics. And the timber wars will continue until the timber companies stop destroying the forest.

The PALCO Papers

AVA, March 27, 1991

Corporate millionaires are a vindictive lot. Take Charles Hurwitz, for example. When he's not busy raiding other companies, slaughtering ancient redwoods, or stealing the workers' pension plan, Hurwitz amuses himself by suing impoverished Earth First!ers. Thus it came to be that Pacific Lumber, also known as PALCO, is suing Earth First! activists Darryl Cherney and George Shook for $25,000 for the crime of sitting in a redwood tree.

Darryl and George have already paid their debt to society for this "crime" by serving 10 days in the Humboldt County jail. But the lawsuit asks for additional civil penalties. Of course Hurwitz knows that he'll never get any money out of Darryl or George, since neither of them owns a thing. The purpose of this lawsuit is bare-faced harassment. Such lawsuits are called SLAPP suits (Strategic Lawsuits Against Public Participation), and are a standard weapon in the arsenals of destructive corporations trying to avoid public accountability. They are filed against people for engaging in political activities that should be protected by the Constitution. And, although SLAPP suits often fail in court, they succeed in diverting the attention and resources of activist groups, and in intimidating people from challenging the rich and powerful.

Darryl and George first attempted to settle this suit out of court, but PALCO refused their generous offer to pay $100 each, and the lawsuit moved on to

One old growth redwood takes up a single truckload. That's the Pacific Lumber mill in the background. (photo: Daniel Baron)

the Justice Court of Fortuna. Fortuna is a town whose national anthem is "I'm a Lumberjack and I'm Okay," where the police chief last April instructed the good citizens not to talk to Earth First!ers. So Darryl and George, represented by lawyer Mark Harris (of Redwood Summer/Head Shaving Case fame) asked for a change of venue. And that's when the case got interesting.

Since they needed to prove that EF!ers can't get a fair trial in Fortuna, lawyer Mark Harris used the Right of Discovery to request all documents Pacific Lumber may have relating to Cherney or Earth First! The stuff he got back—mostly internal company memos sent from public relations director David Galitz to PALCO President John Campbell—shows a sneering, bully mentality worthy of any Mississippi good old boy. And it shows Pacific Lumber's complicity, at least in the role of official cheerleader, in the violence we are subjected to. I'm not making up a word of this. These are real Pacific Lumber memos, and are available for inspection.

The first memo is dated June 21, 1989, shortly after EF! organizer Greg King was punched and knocked to the ground by an irate logger at a non-violent demonstration in Calpella. Galitz sends this memo, along with a clipping from the *Press Democrat*, to Charles Hurwitz, John Campbell and others in Maxxam and PALCO management. It reads:

Subject: Earth First

Enclosed is an article on Cherney and King's latest stunt. As soon as we find the home of the fine fellow who decked Greg King, he has a dinner invitation at the Galitz residence.

David W. Galitz

The next memo we have is dated April 18, 1990, right around the time the timber companies began circulating false press releases claiming to be from unnamed Earth First!ers saying that we intended to use violence against loggers and mill-workers during Redwood Summer. Galitz writes to John Campbell:

Subject: Earth First
   Enclosed is a *Press Democrat* article on the environmentalists' internal split over Mississippi Summer. Also enclosed is a flyer with the Earth First logo, however, as Daryl's [sic] name is misspelled, we are not sure who put it out.
   The other "Hike in the Woods" was handed out by a New York crazy.

David W. Galitz

Galitz's acknowledgment that this press release was fake since it misspelled Darryl's name is particularly interesting. Because despite this knowledge PALCO continued to distribute the press release, through their public relations firm Hill & Knowlton, to city newspapers. In fact on April 25, 1990, Jane Kay of the *San Francisco Examiner* wrote an article criticizing them for having just distributed this "inflammatory" press release. A few days later, columnist Robert Morse wrote: "Things are getting pretty weird up there. Not only are the trees being clearcut, but dirty tricksters are turning them into fake press releases." Darryl then approached both

John Campbell and L-P's Shep Tucker to try to get them to stop the distribution of these fakes. Both company reps admitted to Darryl that the fakes were being distributed in their mills, and neither was willing to take any action to stop it.

On April 23, Galitz sent another memo to John Campbell, this time chuckling over the death threats I was receiving:

Subject: Earth First

How attitudes can change!! When the Earth First! put out the "wanted poster on Charles," one for $1000 and later at $5000 reward it was okay. Now Ms. Bari is upset she apparently has her own wanted flyer.

David W. Galitz

The "wanted poster on Charles" that Galitz refers to was an Earth First! flyer offering $1000 reward for the arrest and conviction of Charles Hurwitz for his illegal takeover of Pacific Lumber. Quite a far cry from the anonymous and obviously serious death threats I was receiving, including the rifle scope and cross-hairs superimposed over my face in a photo.

Since Galitz so enjoys seeing us threatened and attacked, it's not surprising that he would latch right on to the Sahara Club Newsletter. The Sahara Club is an organized hate group from Southern California that targets Earth First! and other environmentalists. They came here in person during Redwood Summer and gave workshops for the local Stompers on how to use dirty tricks against us, and they even got arrested planting a fake bomb in the Arcata Action Center. Anyway, back on April 27,

Galitz mailed copies of the Sahara Club Newsletter to Kevin Eckery of the Timber Association of California and Shep Tucker of L-P, with the following cover letter:

> **Dear Kevin,**
>
> Our Southern California sales people were kind enough to send the enclosed. It is so good, we had to share it. I may join if only to enjoy the writing style.
>
> Best Regards,
> THE PACIFIC LUMBER COMPANY
> David W. Galitz
> Manager, Public Affairs

Here is a sample of the "writing style" Galitz enjoys so much, taken from the Sahara Club Newsletter he was distributing last April:

> **Special Sahara Clubbers Division!**
>
> The Sahara Club needs about a dozen volunteers to form a special division—The Sahara Clubbers! All Volunteers should weigh at least 200 pounds and have a bad attitude. Big, tall, ugly desert riders preferred. We want to set up a few trucks with Sahara Club stickers in "certain spots" and see who might be tempted to break the law. Naturally, the Clubbers will be expected to honor all laws, but if some Earth First scum resist a citizens arrest in the process, it may be necessary to "subdue" them prior to turning them over to the authorities. If interested, contact us by mail. All names will be carefully checked via the off-road grapevine. Clubbers will be issued personalized walking sticks about the size of baseball bats.

This same issue of the Sahara Club Newsletter

includes a diagram of a bomb that they claim is from an Earth First! terrorism manual. The Sahara Club will send you this manual for five dollars. Of course, Earth First! never produced any such manual, and it is only available from the Sahara Club. But by distributing it as ours, they accomplish a dual purpose of getting info out on how to construct bombs, etc., while simultaneously inciting hatred against Earth First!

Of course PALCO execs shed no tears when I actually was bombed in May. May 29 found Galitz distributing this cheery note from State Senator Jim Nielsen:

TO: My Friends In The Forest
FROM: Jim Nielsen
The summer may be long and hot—not just due to the threat of fires!

Let's hope this explosion disposes "eco-terrorists" to cease their destructive, life threatening behavior.

The PALCO Papers that we have seen are probably incomplete. There are, for example, no memos concerning John Campbell ramming our picket line last August and careening down the road with protester Bob Serena plastered to his hood. I'm sure they got a belly laugh out of that, especially when Bob Serena went to jail and John Campbell went free. But even what we've seen shows an outrageous glimpse of corporate executives promoting and enjoying violence against Earth First!ers. And I think this is just the tip of the iceberg.

Darryl and George's dedicated (and pro bono)

lawyer Mark Harris submitted a Brittanica-sized brief to show the judge why EF!ers couldn't get a fair trial in Fortuna. It included the above memos, along with dozens of local newspaper articles and letters to the editor saying Darryl is violent, a terrorist, corrupting children, inhuman, ungodly, etc. It included newspaper clips from last April when the city council and police chief of Fortuna made public anti-Earth First! statements, saying we were violent because Fortunans threw eggs at us at a demonstration. It included the bumpersticker that says "Earth First!ers, America's Favorite Speed Bumps." But despite all this and more, Judge John L. Loomis ruled last week that he would not move the trial out of Fortuna.

Darryl and George are appealing this decision, of course. We don't know what the outcome of this suit will be, but so far, as a SLAPP suit, it has failed miserably. The info we have gotten as a result of this case far exceeds the hassle or intimidation it has caused.

Review

Dave Foreman's
Confessions of an Eco-Warrior

Harmony Books, 228 pages, $20. Reviewed in the AVA *April 4, 1991*

Last year when Northern California Earth First! was preparing to renounce tree-spiking, I called Dave Foreman to tell him what we were up to. Dave responded by writing me a letter stating emphatically and passionately why he disagreed with me. Then he said that, despite our differences, he respected my work and thought I was "a hero who will be remembered 100 years from now."

I don't know what happened to Dave Foreman in between that letter and the publication of his new book, *Confessions of an Eco-Warrior*. But the tolerance—indeed celebration—of diversity that has been the vitality of Earth First! since its inception seems to have gone too far for him. The "Rednecks for Wilderness" have been taken over by (shudder) hippies, and now Dave Foreman wants out.

There's no taking away from Foreman what he has contributed to radical environmentalism. Ten years ago, he helped change the face of the movement by introducing a revolutionary concept—biocentrism, or deep ecology. The idea that humans are not the crown of creation, but rather just another of nature's many species. And that (all species have a right to exist for their own sake, regardless of their usefulness to humans. And that wilderness must be preserved for the sake of biological diversity and evolution, not just to provide scenery for backpackers.)

It was through Dave's work that I and many others embraced these concepts. They are well explained in *Confessions of an Eco-Warrior*, but disappointingly, many of the chapters in this book are reprints of earlier articles. Still it is worthwhile to restate the basis of our activism.

But there is an inherent contradiction in Dave Foreman. His ideas are radical, even revolutionary, but he is politically and culturally conservative. I mean, the guy worked for Barry Goldwater. He proudly calls himself a patriot and a Republican. His heroes, mentioned repeatedly in this book, include white-man land rapers like George Washington, Thomas Jefferson, and John Adams instead of biocentrists like Chief Seattle or Vandana Sheeva (of the Chipko movement in India).

These contradictions become glaring when Foreman tries to translate the theories into political action. For example, he says Earth First! was never intended to include anti-corporate activism. He says it was founded on the issue of public land use only. "Most people in this country," he says, "myself included, respect the concept of private property." Well, wait a minute. If you really believe that nature is not here to serve humans, and humans are merely part of nature, how can you support the idea that humans can "own" the Earth? And what are we supposed to do if the 2,000-year-old redwoods we need to save for the sake of biological diversity and evolution happen to be on "private" land? And what if the reason they are being cut is to finance a junk-bond corporate takeover? Should our slogan be No compromise in Defense of Mother Earth on Public Land Only, And Only If We Don't Have to Confront the Corporate Power Structure?

Foreman's middle-class bias is also shown in his contempt for industrial workers. "We are inconsistent when we castigate Charles Hurwitz for destroying the last wilderness redwood forest, yet feel sympathy for the loggers working for him," he says. "Many loggers, or cat-skinners, oilfield workers, miners, and the like, simply hate the wild and delight in 'civilizing' it." Of course, many suburban professionals hate the wild too, but Foreman is much more generous toward them. It's okay for Foreman to support himself by writing books printed on paper made by applying toxic technologies to the trees that the evil loggers cut down, because "most of us still need to make a living that involves some level of participation in 'the system.'" Now, I don't hold any romantic views about the noble proletariat, especially after being the recipient of their fisticuffs, truck-rammings and pipe bombs. But I also know timber workers, oilfield workers and miners who love the wilderness and are trying to stop its destruction. And it seems to me that people's complicity should be measured more by the amount of control they have over the conditions of their lives than by how dirty they get at work. One compromise made by a white-collar Sierra Club professional can destroy more trees than a logger can cut in a lifetime.

Foreman defends tree-spiking in this book,

although he acknowledges the ethical problem posed by the near-decapitation of millworker George Alexander when a saw hit a tree spike at the Cloverdale L-P mill. Foreman says that the Cloverdale spiking was not done by Earth First! This is probably true, although I think it's irrelevant to the argument over tree-spiking's safety. But, says Foreman, "After the initial hoopla blaming Earth First! for the accident, several northern California newspapers issued apologies when it was learned that the Mendocino County Sheriff's Department's primary suspect was a conservative Republican in his mid-fifties who owned property adjacent to the logging site." In fact, the press had a field day vilifying EF! over that incident, and never retracted or apologized for anything. And the absolutely only paper that ever named the suspect or acknowledged that it wasn't EF! was the AVA. That kind of inaccuracy in recounting local events makes me wonder how much of the rest of this book is exaggerated for convenience of argument.

Another part of Foreman's book describes at length his proposal for how to reform the Sierra Club and other mainstream groups. The problem, he says, is that the big environmental groups are staffed by professionals who spend their time in front of computers instead of hiking in the wilderness. In order to restore that "wilderness gene," he wants all staff members of the "Big 10" environmental groups to be sent on a two-week wilderness vacation each year. I must admit that the idea of state Sierra Club rep Gail Lucas backpacking in the wilderness is pretty funny to contemplate. (Where would she plug in her hair dryer?) But there's no way that it would solve the problem of Sierra Club compromise. The Big 10 kowtow to the corporations because they are part of the system, and if they stop compromising, the corporations will stop negotiating with them. If a two-week wilderness trip really did change Gail Lucas, she would just be replaced by someone who had more of a "compromise gene."

Just as significant as the things Foreman says in this book are the things he doesn't say. There are no real "confessions" in this book. Rather than confront the hard, controversial issues, Foreman lobs vague accusations at us "class struggle social justice leftists" that he claims have "infiltrated" Earth First! He doesn't mention the controversial right-wing stances he has taken, such as advocating the starvation of Ethiopians and the closing of borders. He never analyzes the success or failure of tactics like Redwood Summer, and he proposes individual monkey-wrenching as a main strategy without discussing whether or not it has actually succeeded over the past 10 years. He barely mentions and never goes into any detail about his experience of being infiltrated by an FBI provocateur and busted for conspiracy to down power lines in Arizona.

Foreman also engages in some petty stuff. He lists the founders of Earth First! and omits Mike Roselle, who, although he is now on the outs with Foreman over these issues, was certainly a principal force in building Earth First! Foreman also lists the Earth First! musicians who have inspired him and conspicuously omits Darryl Cherney.

Finally, Dave Foreman concludes that we hippie anarchists have steered Earth First! away from its original principles, and it's time for him to quit. He says we have already accomplished what we set out to do 10 years ago. I certainly disagree with that. Sure, we've educated a lot of people, but they're still butchering the forest, and our country just destroyed Iraq. What I think we've been doing is putting the principles of biocentrism into practice in the real world. And the radical implications of the theory, as well as the repression we've encountered, have scared Dave Foreman off.

So I'll return the compliment you gave me last year, Dave. You're a hero who will be remembered 100 years from now. But the movement has passed you by, and it's time to step aside. Work elsewhere, where you feel more comfortable. But quit bashing those of us who are still on the front lines.

Notes From Hell

Working at the L-P Mill

AVA, April 17, 1991

"I've worked in the sawmill for 13 years, and every year the logs get smaller. Everyone knows L-P is leaving. It's just a matter of time," a Ukiah L-P millworker told me that last spring. Since that time L-P has laid off over one-third of its workforce in our area. They have closed or are closing their mills in Potter Valley, Covelo, Cloverdale and Calpella, and they have laid off the graveyard shift in Ukiah. Meanwhile, they have opened up their redwood planing operation in Mexico, using machinery that they took out of the Potter Valley mill. Yet despite all this, we have not heard a peep of complaint from the L-P workers. How does a company as cold and crass as Sleaziana Pacific keep their workforce so obedient? A look behind the barbed wire fence that surrounds their Ukiah mill might yield some clues.

"It's their little world, and when you step through the gate you do what they say or you don't stay in their little world," says one millworker. The work rules are designed to turn you into an automaton. There's a two-minute warning whistle, then the start-up whistle. You have to be at your work station ready to go when the start-up whistle blows, or you can be written up for lateness (three white slips in a year for the same offense and you're fired). You stay at your work station doing the same repetitive job over and over for two or two and a half hours (two hours in the planing mill, two and a half hours in the sawmill) until the break whistle blows. Then you get a ten-minute break, except that it takes you two minutes to walk to the break room and two minutes to walk back, so you only get to sit down for six minutes. And don't get too comfortable, because there's a two-minute warning whistle before the end of breaktime, then you have to be back at your station ready to go when the start-up whistle blows again. If you ever wondered what they were training you for with all those bells in public school, here's the answer—life at L-P.

In the Land of the Free, democracy stops at the plant gates. The Bill of Rights is supposed to protect against unreasonable or warrantless searches. But not at L-P. Their drug policy reads like the gestapo: ("Entry onto company property will be deemed as consent to inspection of person, vehicle, lockers or other personal effects at any time at the discretion of management. Employee refusal to cooperate in alcohol and other drug testing, or searches of other personal belongings and lockers are subject to termination [sic].")And, before you even get hired you have to submit to a urine test and sign a consent form to let them test your urine any time "for cause," again at the discretion of management.

Amid constant noise and visible sawdust in the air, millworkers do jobs that would shock people who are unfamiliar with factory work. Take the job of offbearer. As whole logs come into the mill they are stripped of their bark, then run through 9-foot-tall band saws to make the first rough cut. The off-bearer stands a few feet from these saws and uses a hook to grab the slices of log and set them up for the edgerman. There are no guards on the saw-blades, just exposed, high-speed, spinning teeth. The off-bearer must wear a face shield to protect himself from flying knots or metal debris from the logs, but that's not always enough to prevent injury. "It's even worse," says one experienced off-bearer, "because the knots are few and far between, so you're not on the alert. It can run cool for a week or a month, then wham!—something pulls the saw off."

This is what happened in the famous tree-spike case at the Cloverdale mill, when the band saw hit a metal spike and broke. Saw blade fragments went flying, and a 12-foot piece hit off-bearer George Alexander in the face, cutting right through his face guard and nearly decapitating him. That's why Northern California Earth First! renounced tree-spiking, and that's why no one in Earth First! will ever convince me that tree-spiking is safe or okay.

Loss of life or limb is a constant danger at L-P, but it doesn't happen every day. What does happen every day is the mind-numbing tedium of the job, and L-P's constant rush for production. Take the job of lumber grader. Rough cut lumber, 2x12 and up to 20 feet long, comes up on the chain, and the grader has to scan it, turn it over, decide the best way to trim it for length and split it for width, and put the grade marks and trim marks on the board. You have two to three seconds to perform all these tasks, while the chain keeps moving and the next board comes up. All night long. Back injuries, tendonitis, and shoulder strains, common among graders and other millworkers, are caused by turning over the heavy

Counter-demonstrator at Fort Bragg, Redwood Summer Rally. (photo by Nicholas Wilson)

lumber. But the company just wants its production quotas. "We broke a production record in our section," said one of my sources. "We used to get pizzas and beer for that, but this time they just got us one of those six-foot submarine sandwiches. We probably made them $200,000 in L-P's pocket that night, and they gave us a sandwich."

Of course in such a petty, dictatorial atmosphere, some petty dictators are bound to arise. And there is none better known at L-P than Dean Remstedt, swing shift foreman in the planing mill. Remstedt runs his shift with threats and favoritism, and is known as a racist. A few years ago he passed out a flyer making racist jokes about Jesse Jackson. It offended some of the millworkers so much that they took it to the *Ukiah Daily Journal* (anonymously of course). Remstedt denied that there was a problem. "It was something laying in the break room that we was laughing about," Remstedt told the *Journal.* But Hispanic workers, who make up about one-third of the shift, were not laughing. "To me, when I got that, that was from the company," one of them told the *Journal* reporter. And of course, L-P's upper management did nothing to change that impression.

Millworkers say Remstedt is "a fanatic about production" and that he "intimidates people into taking chances [with safety] for fear of being disciplined or of losing their job." He sets the example with his own reckless behavior, which has led to him having several on-the-job accidents himself. He once climbed onto an automatic lumber stacking machine that was not properly turned off, and he was knocked to the ground when the auto-cycle started up and the lumber moved forward, sending him to the hospital with minor injuries. Another time he stood on the forks of a forklift raised to a high position so he could reach something overhead. He fell off and knocked himself out cold. They wrote up the forklift driver for that one, but they never write up Remstedt, even though the injuries to others on his shift have been a lot more serious than his own, including a woman who lost her leg walking between roller cases on a machine that bands lumber.

So it's not surprising, considering his racism and his safety record, that it was on Remstedt's shift when Fortunado Reyes was killed. Remstedt was off that night, but he had long ago set the pattern of work practices on the shift. A few days earlier Remstedt had ridiculed Fortunado in front of his co-workers for pushing the emergency stop too much and slowing down production. "He called Forty a sissy, and that's not all," say his friends. No one knows exactly how he died because no one saw or heard it. But apparently Fortunado was straightening lumber on a tray when he was caught unawares by another moving tray of boards, and was crushed between the lumber and the machine's steel beams. Co-workers found him lying on the catwalk. "We looked up and Forty was lying there with his ear on the catwalk, like he was listening in. I said, 'Hey, what are you doing?' but he didn't answer. We poked him and he didn't move, and we knew something was really wrong. When we turned him over you could see the indentations from the lumber in his chest." Some of the millworkers, and later the ambulance crew, tried to revive Fortunado with CPR, but it was too late. "By the time the ambulance took him away he was already starting to bloat up," eyewitnesses said.

Fortunado's death outraged some of the millworkers, who were tired of Remstedt endangering people's lives for the sake of production. A few of them decided to break the silence and tell the truth to OSHA, even at the risk of their own jobs. As a result, L-P was cited for two safety violations, including the emergency stop policy, and fined the pitiful amount of $1,200 for taking a man's life. Remstedt was also ordered to give a safety talk on the proper use of the emergency stop. "But one week later he was doing it again like nothing happened, climbing all over the machinery," said a disillusioned worker.

Still some people didn't give up, including lawyers for Fortunado's widow, Maria. (L-P awarded Maria a total of $2,000 for "burial expenses" for Fortunado.) And last September, the Mendocino County D.A. surprised us all by filing criminal charges against L-P for Fortunado's death. This resulted in another slap on the wrist and another insultingly low $5,000 fine for L-P. Then, to add to the insult, L-P President Harry Merlo himself wrote a memo to the Ukiah millworkers blaming "inflammatory claims by a few groups of rabid preservationists" for the "negative atmosphere" leading to the criminal charges.

It takes a real stretch of the imagination to blame environmentalists for anything having to do with Fortunado's death, but Harry Merlo is an imaginative guy. And the timber industry has been wildly successful so far at convincing the workers that it's the environmentalists, not the companies, who are to blame for their woes. "It's the only thing that gets a rise out of them," one man said of his co-workers' hatred of environmentalists. "Their heartbeat gets faster and their eyes light up." How can people be so brainwashed to overlook the Mexico operation, the miles of clearcuts, the shrinking logs and the closing mills, and blame us instead of L-P? I asked several workers that question, and this was their reply: "Let's say you're a big macho logger, and you know something is wrong. You could blame L-P, but then you're powerless. Or you can blame Earth First! and then you can punch 'em."

Interestingly, the workers who talk to me (obviously a select group) often explain their own awareness in terms of L-P's environmental destruction. "I've always been environmentally conscious," says one. "My dad took us camping when we were in diapers. I've been backpacking since I was nine years old." Another says, "I went hunting at my favorite spot in the Yolla Bolly Wilderness, and it was gone. It looked like a nuke hit it because of L-P's clearcuts." "I like to take my son fishing," says another, "but L-P's wrecked the fishing in this county."

So what are the chances that the L-P workers will wake up before it's too late? Pretty slim. "The money's too good, and there's nothing else to do," a sawmill worker told me. L-P millworkers start at $7.00 an hour, but the top of the pay scale is $13.51, or over $14 with night premiums. "Most people are just crawling in their holes, hoping the mill will keep running," my sources said. There's a lot of discontent under the surface, and a lot of people don't like the company. The people who talk to me all express the same feelings, and they all assume that no one else shares their views. So I guess there is some theoretical chance that some day something will make people mad enough to stand up to L-P. But the most common attitude at the Ukiah mill is "Gotta go to work" and "Don't make waves."

L-P employees have no say over company policy, and they work under conditions that privileged college kids and yuppie professionals can't even imagine. (Environmentalists who blame them for the destruction of the forest are just as stupid as workers who blame environmentalists for the loss of their jobs.) Some of the more conscious millworkers will try to find a way to get out, and these are the people most likely to ally with us. But most will try to keep working until the last pecker pole runs through the chipper. Then they'll drive off into the clearcuts, cursing the environmentalists for the loss of their jobs, while Harry Merlo counts his cash and moves on to the next killing field.

Why I Hate the Corporate Press

AVA, April 24, 1991

Last Sunday the *San Francisco Examiner* printed an Op-Ed article by me in answer to the outrageous "ex-CIA agent" attack on Earth First! that
they ran the week before. Basically the article came
through as I wrote it. But the editors couldn't just
let it be. They made subtle and not-so-subtle
changes that brought the words printed under my
byline more in compliance with their own biases.
Here is the article, with the changes marked:

San Francisco Examiner Op-Ed Page, 4/21/91
'Tabloid attack' on Earth First
by Judi Bari

When I looked at my Sunday paper last week. I
thought I had accidentally picked the *National
Enquirer*. But no, it really was the *Examiner*, running a supermarket tabloid-style article called "Tale
of a Plot to Rid Earth of Humankind."

"It's a strange story," the article begins. And
indeed it is. Apparently an ex-CIA agent claims that
Earth First, has "small organized clandestine cells"
of highly educated scientists working to develop a
virus that will wipe out the human race while spar-
ing other species.

Not only is this claim preposterous, it is also
unsupported by any evidence. The ex-CIA agent who

is the source of the story offers no details or proof. The best the author of the article can come up with is an anonymous letter-to-the-editor from a 1984 edition of the *Earth First Journal*, carefully excerpted for maximum shock value

The *Examiner* does not take responsibility for the views of every screwball who writes a letter to the editor, and neither does Earth First. Did the article's author pore over 10 years of tiny print in the journal's letters column to find this "gem," or did the ex-CIA agent point it out as his own source?

Lacking evidence to support the "mad-scientist" theory, this article then goes on to try to discredit Earth First by associating us with violence. It says Earth First co-founder Dave Foreman is under federal charges of conspiracy to "blow up" power lines.

This is false. Earth First doesn't advocate use of explosives. *It has never been involved in their use— except as a target in the car bomb attempt on my life last year.* [I wrote "except as a *victim* in a car-bomb *assassination attempt* on me last year." (Assassinations are political, attempts on people's lives don't have to be.)]

The charges against Foreman stem from a $2 million FBI program to infiltrate and disrupt Earth First. In May 1989, *three people led by admitted FBI provocateur Michael Fain* [I wrote "three people, *not including Foreman,* and led by admitted FBI provocateur Michael Fain..."] were arrested for supposedly trying to cut down, not blow up, a power-line tower in Arizona, *that was allegedly part of a plot to sabotage lines from nuclear plants.*[*I did not write this sentence!!!* They inserted it without my knowledge. I would never say such a thing, because there was no "plot to sabotage power lines from nuclear plants." That's an FBI lie, and I don't repeat FBI lies, even with the word "alleged" in front of them. How dare the *Examiner* put their words in my Op-Ed.] Foreman was arrested for conspiracy, but there's no real case against him.

The view of Earth First as isolated and violent flies in the face of reality. We have actually been in the forefront of the environmental movement, seeking to protect the Earth from the ravages of this destructive society. This doesn't mean we want to eliminate humans, but we feel that we must drastically change the way we live or we will destroy the ecosystems that support all life.

(Who needs a virus to kill humans when real mad scientists have given us nuclear holocaust, toxic waste, deforestation, ozone holes and the greenhouse effect?)

The real reason Earth First is being targeted by ex-CIA agents and FBI provocateurs is that we are effective.

Earth First is involved in a political struggle for logging reform. [I wrote "Earth First! is involved in a *legitimate* political struggle for logging reform."] It was Earth First that identified, mapped, named and made an issue of Headwaters Forest, which Gov. Wilson now cites as a top priority for preservation. We brought thousands of nonviolent demonstrators to the north coast for Redwood Summer last year, and made a national and international issue of redwood destruction. The forestry reforms now being proposed by both the timber industry and the mainstream groups follow our activism.

Several spokespersons for Earth First are based

in Northern California. The *Examiner* knows us and knows how to get in touch with us. Why is it buying crackpot articles about us from second-rate news services?

This would be no more than an annoyance if it weren't for the intensity of the struggle. Tales of secret plots to wipe out humans may sound like a joke, but people in the rural timber-dependent areas are being deliberately led to believe they're in danger from Earth First. The more marginal we can be made to appear, the easier it is to incite hatred against us. And, as I certainly know, this hatred often translates into violence.

* * *

And by the way, our name is Earth First! with an !, and the *Examiner*'s refusal to print the ! is petty and prejudicial. The ! is there to convey the urgency of the situation, and the fact that we are a direct action group, not a lunch-with-the-bureau-crats group.

About 20 people recently picketed the *Examiner* offices to protest the printing of the ex-CIA article. As a result, some of them are now meeting with the *Examiner*'s editors to discuss these problems, including the changing of my Op-Ed piece. I must admit that, looking back over last summer's clip-pings, the *Examiner* slandered me less than most "mainstream" press, and I hope they will make some amends now. But, as Bruce and Rob [Anderson] keep saying, there's no such thing as objectivity of the press, and we will never get our message out by filtering it through the lens of the corporations.

Community Under Siege

AVA, May 8, 1991

Speech given at the Cinco de Mayo/May 5th gathering in Boonville.

I came of age during the Vietnam era, and I've known for a long time that the system is enforced by violence. Some of my earliest political experiences were of 20-year-old national guardsmen beating my 18-year-old non-violent friends senseless and bloody. I didn't think I had any delusions about how thin the veneer of civility is in this country. But I have to admit that I was totally unprepared for the sheer horror of being bombed and maimed while organizing for Redwood Summer last year.

The bombing represented the end of innocence for our movement. Sure, we had seen violence before, but this was different. The logger who broke Mem Hill's nose, the log truck driver who ran me off the road—these people were victims of the timber industry themselves who, in the heat of the moment, took their anger out on us. But whoever put that bomb in my car was a cold and premeditated killer. And the FBI's attempt to frame me and Darryl for the bombing made us realize what we are up against. Not only are they willing to use lethal force to protect their "right" to level whole ecosystems for private profit, they are backed by the full power of the government's secret police.

The man in charge of my and Darryl's case at the FBI is Richard W. Held, chief of the San Francisco office. He went on TV last summer to say that Darryl and I were the only suspects in the bomb attack that nearly took my life. Richard Held became notorious during the 1970s for his active role in COINTELPRO, an outrageous and illegal FBI program to disrupt and destroy any group that challenged the powers-that-be.

COINTELPRO's method was to foment internal discord in activist groups, isolate and discredit them, terrorize them, and assassinate their leaders. The best known example of this was Black Panther Fred Hampton, who was murdered by the FBI and police as he slept in his bed in a Chicago apartment in 1969. And there were many, many others.

But back to Richard Held, the man in charge of my bombing case. His personal role in COINTELPRO began in the early 70s in Los Angeles, where he ordered insulting cartoons to be drawn and sent, supposedly from one faction to another, in the L.A. Black Panthers. This heated up antagonisms between the factions so much that, with a little help from FBI infiltrators, they erupted into shooting wars that left two Panthers dead.

One of Richard Held's most famous targets in the Black Panther Party was Geronimo jiJaga (Pratt). Geronimo, a Panther leader from Los Angeles, was framed for supposedly killing a white woman on a tennis court in Santa Monica over an $18 robbery. The FBI's own wiretaps prove that Geronimo was 400 miles away at a Panther meeting in Oakland at the time of the killing. But he was convicted anyway, based on the perjured testimony of an undercover FBI agent. Geronimo is still in jail today, despite the massive "Free Geronimo" campaign of the 1970's. He is internationally recognized as a political prisoner, and his defense team names Richard Held as one of three FBI agents directly responsible for the frame-up.

Held was also on hand in Pine Ridge South Dakota in 1975, to help his father, Richard G. Held, direct the FBI's reign of terror against the American Indian Movement. In this case the FBI took advantage of existing divisions in the native community to hook up with a vigilante group called GOONS, or Guardians of the Ogalala Nation. These local thugs were armed by the FBI and guaranteed that they would not be prosecuted for crimes against AIM members. They attacked over 300 AIM people and killed 70 of them. Not one of these crimes was solved because, said the FBI, they "didn't have enough manpower." The Pine Ridge campaign ended with a military sweep of the reservation by 200 SWAT trained agents, and with the framing and jailing of Leonard Peltier.

Another of Richard Held's accomplishments was in San Diego, where he was instrumental in organizing an FBI-funded right-wing paramilitary group called the Secret Army Organization (SAO). The SAO bombed the Guild Theater, a black community project, and tried to assassinate Peter Bohmer, a radical professor at San Diego State University. They missed and severely wounded his associate, Paula Thorpe. By the way, the assassination symbol of the SAO was the rifle scope and cross-hairs.

In 1978 Richard Held was transferred to Puerto

Rico, where he oversaw the FBI's execution of two Independentista leaders, Arnaldo Dario Rosada and Carlos Soto Arrive, who were made to kneel, then shot in the head. Held stayed on until 1985, when he stage-managed an island-wide SWAT assault by 300 agents who busted in doors and rounded up activists.

For all his good work, Richard Held was then promoted to be in charge of the San Francisco FBI, where he still works today. And I don't know if the FBI had anything to do with putting that bomb in my car, but I know for certain that they tried to frame me for it and made sure the real bomber wasn't found. They blowtorched out my whole floorboard and front seat and sent it to their "crime lab in D.C.," thereby destroying the evidence that would prove they were lying about the location of the bomb. And they lied about finding nails in the car that matched the nails in the bomb. And when someone calling himself the Lord's Avenger wrote a letter describing the bomb in exact detail and taking credit for it, their "investigation" consisted of raiding my house once again to try and find a typewriter to match the letter, which of course they didn't. And through the whole thing they kept putting out selected press releases so the highly cooperative press could make me look like a bomber when they knew perfectly well that I was the victim of an assassination attempt.

So with this knowledge of how the FBI operates, when I look at what's going on in our movement I can only conclude that we are under attack by a COINTELPRO-type operation. Earth First! is definitely a target. We know that the FBI has spent at least $3 million to infiltrate and disrupt Earth First! in Arizona and Montana, not even including what they've done in Northern California. In Arizona, admitted FBI agent provocateur Michael Fain infiltrated their group for two years, winning the activists' trust and friendship. Then he led them to try and drop a power line, and got them busted for it by the FBI. This is the supposed "Earth First! plot to destroy nuclear power plants" that the mainstream press keeps talking about. There was no plot. Just some naive people who were misled by the FBI. And Dave Foreman wasn't even there. They arrested him in his bed at 5 a.m. and led him out in his underwear.

In Montana the FBI targeted an environmental studies professor named Ron Erikson, saying he and his Earth First! students were responsible for a tree-spiking incident. They raided people's houses and forced them to give fingerprints, handwriting and hair samples. Yet even after a grand jury investigation, they found no evidence at all to link Erickson or his students with any tree-spiking. But they discredited him professionally and terrorized the Earth First!ers.

So I would be crazy not to assume that the FBI has had its hand in the events up here, both before and after the bombing. But whether it's the FBI or just the timber industry, I know for sure that the techniques of COINTELPRO have been used here in an attempt to disrupt us, discredit us, create a climate of fear, and derail our attempts to save the redwoods. Here are some examples of standard COINTELPRO practices that have shown up in our community:

Black Propaganda—This term refers to information that appears to come from one source (EF!) but actually comes from another source (FBI or timber). The fake press releases that were distributed before the bombing fit this category. They claimed to be from Earth First! and called for violence against timber workers, but one had no contact name or number at all, and the other spelled Darryl's name wrong. An even scarier example of black propaganda came from the right wing anti-environmental group the Sahara Club. In April 1990 they printed a diagram of how to make a bomb, claiming it was from an Earth First! terrorism manual. Of course there is no such manual printed, distributed by, or legitimately associated with us. But by distributing it as an EF! manual, the Sahara Club could simultaneously get info out on how to make bombs while inciting hatred against EF!

Gray Propaganda—This term refers to damaging information whose source is not clear. Under this category I would place the recent front-page article in the San Francisco Examiner in which an "ex-CIA agent" claims, with no evidence or details whatsoever, that Earth First! has "clandestine cells of highly educated scientists" working to develop a virus to wipe out the human race.

Intimidation—This certainly describes the many death threats we activists have gotten, including the SAO-style rifle scope and cross-hairs threat that I received a month before I was bombed. Or the man who walked up to Darryl Cherney in Arcata and said, "Get a good look at my face, because I'm the one who's gonna kill you." Even a 15-year-old Willits High School anti-war organizer got a call saying, "We know you had Judi Bari speak at your rally. We're not afraid to kill someone, you know."

Harassment—This includes harassment of community people who support us, and is designed to drive those people away. Not only was my house red-tagged by the building department following an anonymous complaint after the bombing, but so was my landlord's. A non-activist friend who let me stay at her house had the FBI visit her work and talk to her boss. And my entire neighborhood was threatened with having their houses burned down when I moved back here last August.

Surveillance—The purpose of surveillance is as much to create paranoia as to gain information. And in case I had any doubts that I was still being watched, a few weeks ago an Oakland cop (the FBI's front men) told a reporter that he knew I had just returned from U.C. Santa Barbara, and that he presumed a series of pipe bombs that mysteriously appeared on campus a few days before I got there were connected to me.

Vigilantes—Although certainly on a smaller and less lethal scale, the FBI and local law enforcement have used similar tactics to those used against AIM in Pine Ridge South Dakota. They have encouraged vigilantes by sending a clear message that crimes against Earth First!ers will not be prosecuted, including the bombing of me. At least a dozen Redwood Summer people were assaulted (and I'm not counting incidents at the demonstrations), and two were beaten into unconsciousness and left in remote areas. Several gyppo logging companies paid hourly wages for armed men to lie in wait in the woods for EF!ers last summer, hoping to catch us sabbing equipment. They had instructions to shoot, with a bonus to be paid if they got one of us. Retired logger Ed Knight described it on KQED as "vigilanteism at its worst."

Local Police Complicity—This includes Mendocino County D.A. Susan Massini, who wouldn't prosecute for Mem Hill's broken nose or for me being rammed by the log truck. And Sheriff Shea, who tried to whip up fear and hatred of Earth First! by calling for an emergency ordinance to restrict the size of our picket signs, using a video of a Palestinian student demonstration in Beverly Hills 10 years ago to "prove" how we would use our signs as weapons. And Sgt. Satterwhite who, like the FBI in Pine Ridge, told me he "didn't have the manpower to investigate" the death threats against me. And the Ukiah police who, just one month ago, refused to apprehend a man who came to the Mendocino Environmental Center and threatened Gary Ball with physical violence, said he was going to burn down the MEC, and raged in biblical terms saying I deserved to be bombed and should be bombed again.

Local Government Complicity—This includes Mendo County Supervisor Marilyn Butcher, who promoted the lynch-mob mentality last year when she publicly responded to the death threats against me by saying, "You brought it on yourself, Judi." And it includes Humboldt County Supervisor Harry Pritchard who, just a few weeks ago, called us terrorists and said one of us would get killed if we didn't stop "taking food out of people's mouths." And it includes the city governments of both Ukiah and Willits, who recently bypassed all public channels to allow the apparently permanent installation of yellow ribbons on our public streets, a not-so-subtle message of intimidation to anyone who would oppose the timber industry or the New World Order.

There are many more examples, but the patterns is clear. John Muir once said, "Tug on anything in nature and you will find it is connected to everything else." I would say that the same is true of the corporate state. Because all we ever tried to do here is save a few trees and protect our communities from the ravages of a few out-of-town corporations. And we have found this incredible array of forces lined up against us with the timber industry. So as the new logging season gets under way, with tensions rising again, we had better figure out how to deal with this COINTELPRO-style assault we are under. Of course one of the first things we should do is to educate ourselves, and that's why I'm saying all this. But we also have to counter their attempts to marginalize, isolate and intimidate us.

It's important to remember why Earth First! is targeted, and that is because we are effective. In spite of our shock and horror at the bombing last May, we didn't back down. Three thousand people from all over the country came to Redwood Summer and chained themselves to logging equipment, hugged trees, blocked logging roads and marched through timber towns. Sure we made mistakes. But in spite of incredible provocation we maintained our presence and non-violence throughout the summer. The Forests Forever voter initiative made a statewide issue of redwood slaughter, but Redwood Summer made it national and international. Together we are the cause of the current political push to save

Headwaters Forest and reform logging practices.

People in the environmental movement who are not Earth First!ers should remember that we are all affected. If you allow us to be isolated, if it's not okay to be an Earth First!er this year, then next year it won't be okay to be in the Sierra Club. Don't believe the incendiary stuff you read and hear about us in the corporate press. You know us. We are your neighbors, and we are ready to work with you and talk to you any time.

Our entire community is under siege, and that includes the forest itself, not just the people who defend it. If we back down to timber and police terror, they will continue to destroy the redwood forest and its life support system. We are already seeing the climate changes that go with deforestation, including the five-year drought and killing frosts. How much longer can they cut like this before the ecosystem collapses?

If we stand together, I think we can make the difference. In Humboldt County, Maxxam is on the verge of financial collapse from its own junk bonds. And L-P and G-P are almost done in Mendo County. They've cut the good stuff, and now they're fighting to take 20-year-old baby third-growth trees in a last mop-up operation before they leave. How much is this chip-cut worth to them? Economically those trees barely pay their way out of the woods. But biologically they mean the difference between whether the forest can ever recover, or whether it will end up converted to vineyards, subdivisions, or desert.

That's why we're not backing down. We're tired and we're scared, but the timber industry is tired too. And the darkest hour is just before the dawn.

Who Bought Steve Talbot?

AVA, May 29, 1991

Review of the KQED documentary "Who Bombed Judi Bari," by Steve Talbot

Steve Talbot has a unique talent. He used to be a child actor on the *Leave It To Beaver* show. He played Gilbert, one of the Beav's friends, and when Talbot smiles that little smile, it gives people this subliminal comfortable 1950s feeling. He can get cops to tell him state secrets and hippies to show him their marijuana patch. So we had high hopes for his documentary, "Who Bombed Judi Bari?" Bruce Anderson even promo'd it in advance as "The Definitive Mendo Movie." Talbot had us all convinced that he was a leftist and a supporter, and that he was going to produce a piece that would finally tell the truth about what's going on up here.

He should have left it to Beaver. Because instead of the hard-hitting expose he had promised, Talbot produced a liberal piece in the format of *Unsolved Mysteries*, that focuses in on the activists and little people while completely ignoring the timber corporations and letting the FBI and police slide by.

Talbot does a good job establishing my and Darryl's innocence, and I guess we should thank him for that. Thank you, Steve. But he lets the FBI and Oakland police off easy for their role in lying about the evidence and covering their lie. He shows the bombed-out car with the entire seat and floorboard removed, but he doesn't mention that they are missing because the FBI blowtorched them out and sent them to D.C., thereby concealing the evidence that would have proved they were lying about the bomb's location. He also fails to mention that the Oakland police left the car out in the rain unprotected for 10 days, destroying its value as evidence.

Talbot questions the FBI with kid gloves on. When the FBI spokesman lies in his face and says they are not investigating environmentalists, Talbot shows the viewers evidence that the FBI has actually been investigating and disrupting Earth First! for 10 years. But he never confronts Mr. FBI Liar with this evidence. And he never, in his entire discussion with or about the FBI, mentions the fact that the man in charge of our case is Richard Held himself, grand old man of COINTELPRO, famous for causing assassinations and frame-ups of leaders in the Black Panthers, American Indian Movement, and Puerto Rican Indepententistas. That's a pretty incredible omission, considering how similar the tactics used against us here are to those used by Held in other COINTELPRO operations.

Another equally incredible omission in Steve Talbot's documentary is any mention of the timber corporations in whose interest I was bombed. In fact, to watch this show you would think that all we have up here are mom and pop loggers. And it is 34 minutes into the show before Talbot even talks about them. The word Maxxam does not come up once in this entire documentary. Georgia-Pacific is mentioned only as the site of one of our demos, and

Louisiana-Pacific only as the victim of a pipe-bomb attack at their mill. Nowhere is their role in inciting a lynch-mob mentality against us even hinted at. And Talbot certainly had the info to do it.

Steve Talbot had in his possession a series of internal Maxxam Corp. memos known as the Palco Papers (see AVA 3/27/91). We got them from a discovery motion in a lawsuit, so we know they are authentic. They are from Maxxam corporate executives right before and after the bombing, and they show them applauding violence against Earth First!ers and sneering at the death threats against me. Imagine the impact of this documentary if it had shown some of these memos on screen, highlighting their incendiary language and the fact that they were received by Maxxam Pacific Lumber President John Campbell. Then cut to a scene (we have the video footage available) of John Campbell ramming our picket line during a Redwood Summer protest and careening down the road with a protester plastered to his hood. We have never been able to get the mainstream press to print the Palco memos, because they are too incriminating of timber corporate executives. Steve Talbot assured us that he would air them. His decision not to was one of the most cowardly things he did in the making of this show.

Talbot touches on but fails to adequately establish the rising tide of violence in our community and how it was whipped up by timber and police. He mentions me getting rammed by the logging truck but skips the Whitethorne demo when logger Dave Lancaster broke EF!er Mem Hill's nose, and Mendo County D.A. Susan Massini refused to prosecute despite complaints, demos, and a lawsuit. He also skips Greg King getting decked at the Calpella demo while police stood by and watched, then refused to arrest his attacker. These were pivotal events that established not just an incident, but a pattern of violence against EF!ers, and non-enforcement of laws to protect us.

Talbot does mention the fake press releases that were put out on Earth First! stationery in the months before the bombing, calling for violence against loggers and millworkers. But he just says they "appeared in the community." He doesn't mention that they were distributed to the workers in the mills and in logging towns with at least the full cooperation of the timber companies, and probably with their actual sponsorship. Talbot also does not mention that Hill & Knowlton, a PR firm hired by Maxxam (and more recently hired by the Kuwaiti government to run the $11 million disinformation campaign on the Iraq war) distributed one of these fake press releases to city newspapers even after it had been well established locally that it was a fake. S.F. Examiner reporter Jane Kay even chastised Maxxam for their deceit in a newspaper article one month before the bombing. But Talbot passed right over timber's role in the disinformation campaign.

The lengths to which Talbot goes to avoid showing corporate involvement can only be appreciated when you know what he left on the cutting room floor. He does a surgical edit of the Mendo County Board of Supes meeting where Marilyn Butcher has a temper tantrum and walks out. It shows me holding up the death threats and Marilyn saying, "You brought it on yourself, Judi." Then it's kind of confusing, and Marilyn walks out. That's because Talbot cut it up and spliced it back together to take out my response to Butcher, which was, "Well, L-P and G-P brought it on themselves." He also edits out the part where Sheriff Shea stomps out after I accuse right-wing radio host Charlie Stone of conducting a hate campaign against me on "radio K-KKK" in Ft. Bragg. And he edits out the part where Doug Goss, head of L-P security in Ukiah, spews hatred as he shouts, "We want to hear from someone besides this woman."

None of these events make much sense anyway, because Talbot has never established the political context in which they are taking place. Never is it shown that the timber corporations consider me a threat, or why. He mentions Redwood Summer briefly, and shows a few tree-sits. But no hint is ever given about my timber worker coalition building, or the fact that I was organizing an IWW union local in Ft. Bragg with both timber workers and Earth First!ers as members. Or that I was officially representing five G-P workers in an OSHA complaint after they got PCBs dumped on them at work, and both the company and the sell-out AFL union tried to cover it up by saying it was just mineral oil.

Talbot also omits a colorful and dramatic video clip we gave him of a Board of Supes meeting in April that year in which we responded to L-P's announcement of mass layoffs by appearing in public for the first time with our worker-environmentalist coalition. We showed up with Earth First!, IWW, and L-P employees to demand that Mendo County use its power of eminent domain to seize all of L-P's corporate timberlands and operate them in the public interest. We were taken seriously enough that one supervisor met with us publicly to discuss how this could be accomplished. And someone else apparently took it seriously too, because the death threat campaign against me started right after that meeting. In fact, the photo of me in the famous rifle-scope and cross-hairs death threat is taken from a newspaper story about this meeting.

All this is light-years away from Steve Talbot's shallow treatment of the whole thing as a murder mystery. When he gets into his "America's Most Wanted" list of suspects, I again have to wonder at the ones he left out. Five of his six "suspects" have nothing to do with timber. Why didn't he investigate Candy Boak, organizer of pro-timber groups We Care and Mother's Watch? Candy actively harassed and threatened me before the bombing. For the past few years she has been sabbing Earth First! by bringing hostile counter-demonstrators to our actions, impersonating me to the press by phone and giving out false information, publishing fake Earth First! literature, and openly surveilling our meetings and our organizers.

Why didn't Talbot investigate the Sahara Club, a right-wing anti-environmental group that puts out a monthly hate letter which regularly includes violent and insulting references to Earth First! in general and me in particular. One month before the bombing, the Sahara Club published a diagram of how to make a bomb, which they said was from an Earth First! terrorism manual. Of course no such manual is published by or available from Earth First! But the Sahara Club offered copies of the supposed Earth First! manual for $5, which enabled them to simultaneously incite hatred against us and distribute information on how to make bombs. The Sahara Club, which is based in Southern California, actually came to Redwood Summer and joined with Candy Boak to teach a "dirty tricks" workshop to pro-timber groups. A Sahara Club member was arrested in August when EF!ers caught him planting a fake bomb in the Arcata Action Center.

And why didn't Steve Talbot investigate Charlie Stone and Thomas Loop, rightwing activists from Ft. Bragg, where the G-P mill is located? Charlie Stone is the radio host who whipped up hatred against me by name daily on his radio show in the month before the bombing. He also organized the logger lynch mob that confronted me at the Board of Supes meeting where Marilyn Butcher walked out. Thomas Loop is a rabid anti-abortionist and pro-timber woodcutter who gave the most raging and hateful speech of all at that same Board of Supes meeting. He was involved in the logger meetings in Willits at which the Lord's Avenger claims to have placed the bomb, so he would have known my whereabouts. Both Thomas Loop and Charlie Stone are involved with public fascist sympathizer Jack Azevedo in various right-wing groups.

Yet Talbot's focus in choosing his list of suspects is always to avoid obvious signs of conspiracy and look at the little people and the lone assassin. Even his exposé of Irv Sutley as a probable police informant who tried to set me up is flawed in that manner. Talbot's exposé of Irv is probably the best accomplishment of his investigation, and I don't want to belittle it. After the bombing, Ukiah police released a photo of me holding an Uzi, that they say was sent to them

Who Bought Steve Talbot?

anonymously. Irv Sutley is the owner of the Uzi, and the person who persuaded me to pose with it. Talbot got hold of the letter that was sent to the Ukiah police with the Uzi photo, and it is from an admitted police informant, trying to set me up for arrest. The particular combination of information and disinformation in this letter indicated to me that it most likely was written by Irv Sutley. Talbot shows this in the documentary, but never poses the question, if Irv is an informant, who does he work for? From what we know about the history of FBI disruption of EF!, it is certainly not unreasonable to suspect that the answer may be the FBI. The reason this is so significant is because, as shown in documentary, the letter to the Ukiah police appears to match one of the death threats I received. Not just the same layout, but apparently the same typewriter. So if the death threat came from an FBI informant, does this mean that the FBI was involved in the set-up that preceded the bombing?

But rather than face these hard questions, Talbot zeroes in on the personal and apolitical. The most outrageous of his charges is that my ex-husband, Mike Sweeney, may be the bomber. Talbot has only the most wildly circumstantial evidence to make him think Mike Sweeney could possibly be capable of making a bomb. He has no evidence that Mike is crazy enough to try and kill the mother of his children. My ex-husband and I have a cooperative relationship in our divorce, and he has no motive at all to bomb me. Mike was taking care of our children at his girlfriend's house when the bomb was planted, and she can verify that Mike did not leave her house at any time when he would have had an opportunity to place the bomb. And I know my ex-husband didn't do it, because he couldn't look me in the eye if he had.

But none of this was enough to convince Steve Talbot. He conducted a hostile investigation, trying to turn up anything he could against Mike, while refusing to pursue leads that would exonerate him. Then he wastes six minutes of the documentary on a wild goose chase that tries but fails to link Mike Sweeney to the bombing. In the course of it, he brings out a man who charges that my ex-husband and I burned down his airport 10 years ago. Although they admit there is no evidence of this, I have to answer this totally extraneous charge. Talbot tries to verbally exonerate me (but not Mike) from the fire. But of course on television the visuals are more important than the words. And there are photos of this spectacular airport fire (somehow associated with me and my ex) that parallels earlier photos of feller-bunchers burning (which have also been falsely associated with me).

Why does Talbot drag me through the mud just so he can make this unconvincing charge against Mike Sweeney? I think Steve Talbot actually convinced himself that, in the midst of this incredibly heated political situation, in which timber and police were cooperating to set me up like a bowling pin for assassination, my ex-husband stepped in and did the job for personal reasons. I don't think anyone would have even considered this type of scenario if the assassination victim were a man. Talbot would never have had the audacity to go to Brazil and conduct a hostile investigation of Chico Mendez's ex-wife. But men seem to have a hard time taking a woman seriously enough to consider her a political target instead of a personal/sexual target. To prove in his documentary why my ex-husband should be a suspect, Talbot brings Mr. FBI Liar out on screen again to say that 90% of all homicides are committed by a spouse or close friend. Well, this wasn't a homicide. It was an assassination attempt. And 90% of assassinations of political dissidents in this country are committed by the FBI.

I probably wouldn't be so disappointed in Steve Talbot's documentary if I hadn't actually believed that he was going to produce a real exposé, rather than just another corporate piece. Instead, a little bit of new information came out, but the corporations and police got by while my family and I had to endure yet another false charge being blared around the media. So I guess I haven't learned my lesson yet. If Steve Talbot were really ready to take on the FBI and the big timber corporations—a combination that has already proved itself capable of murder—he would probably be an activist, not a journalist. So, after all the time we spent with him, "The Definitive Mendo Movie" has yet to be produced. And I guess we activists are going to have to tell this story ourselves. No one else has the courage.

Scenes from
the Revolution

AVA, June 5, 1991

Redwood Summer II got an unexpected early start last week, and it's not looking good on the law enforcement end of things. Our non-violent protests were met with discrimination and excessive force by the Mendocino County Sheriff's Department, and if we can't get Sheriff Tuso to do better than that, it's going to be another hard summer indeed.

Things got going Thursday a week ago, when we got a midnight call from a sympathetic Caltrans employee. He told us they were going to cut five old growth redwoods on Highway 20 the next morning. We're so close to the end of the forest in Mendocino County that we're defending the old growth tree by tree, and these were the same five trees that Earth First!-Eco-trans had saved from the chainsaw last fall. They are also part of a much larger Caltrans plan to widen Highway 20 and take out that whole corridor.

By the time the tree-falling crew got out on the road the next morning, six EF!ers were already there. They climbed one tree and hugged the others, while the fallers moved in as quickly as they could. Anna Marie Stenberg jumped in front of a logger who was trying to girdle a tree with his ax. When he continued chopping around her, endangering her life, Anna Marie grabbed his loggers ax and threw it down a ravine. Now someday, when people finally realize how precious these last few old growth trees are, Anna Marie will be remembered as a folk hero. But the stunned logger just exclaimed,"Hey, that's a $35 ax!" and punched her. By 10 a.m. about 15 people had arrived. Mendo Sheriff Berle Murray—one of the two deputies who responded to the death threats against me last year by saying, "If you turn up dead, then we'll investigate"—showed up and began arresting the tree huggers, who by now were standing in front of moving chainsaws to stop the cutting. When they put up passive resistance, Berle quickly deputized a Caltrans employee to help haul the EF!ers off the tree.

In spite of the impropriety of deputizing hostile partisans to help arrest EF!ers, no disasters ensued this time. They handcuffed four EF!ers and got them away from the trees. Then an amazing thing happened. Berle Murray came up to Anna Marie and asked her if she wanted to make a citizens arrest of the logger who punched her. That's the first time in the history of the timber wars in Mendo County that they've let us arrest one of them, no matter what they did to us. Anna Marie said sure, and, with her hands still handcuffed behind her back, turned to the logger and said, "You're under arrest."

Despite the drama, four of the trees went down that day. Biocentric attorney Rod Jones responded by filing a lawsuit against Caltrans for wrongful death, in the name of Dead Redwood #1, Dead Redwood #2, Dead Redwood #3, and Dead Redwood #4. And, for the weekend tourist traffic, EF!-Ecotrans came back at night and poured red paint over the stumps, with signs sticking up saying, "Redwood Murder." When Caltrans tore down the signs, EF! came back and hung a banner across the highway saying, "Stop Caltrans Redwood Murder— Ecotopia Earth First! Ecotrans." That sign stayed up for the rest of the holiday weekend.

But Tuesday morning Caltrans was there to take down the banner. Only Ecotrans was there first. They raced each other to the trees, and while the Caltrans climber was putting on his spurs Naomi (a grandmother of two) free-climbed ahead of him. "It felt like Jack and the Beanstalk, with these hairy arms coming up behind me," she said. Naomi got to the banner first and untied the guy line so that Dave, who was up the tree on the other side, could reel in the banner.

Meanwhile a Caltrans climber was going up Dave's tree. And just when he got up and tried to grab the banner, Dave tossed it down to another pro- tester on the ground, who is also named Dave (as are all Ecotrans men). Berle Murray was also at the base of the tree. When he saw Dave catch the banner, some ancient reflex from high school football snapped in and, without giving an order to stop or anything, he tackled Dave. CHP officer Fred Shearer piled on too, and Dave went down, breaking his front tooth. Murray wrapped construction twine around Dave's wrists and used pain compliance holds to jerk his hands behind him and handcuff him.

So, having totally blown the arrest, Berle Murray did what all police do in this situation—he charged Dave Mullin with assaulting an officer. They hauled him down to Ukiah and booked him on this totally bogus charge, and, as far as we can see, they actually intend to prosecute. In fact, both Sheriff Tuso and D.A. Susan Massini went on local TV to

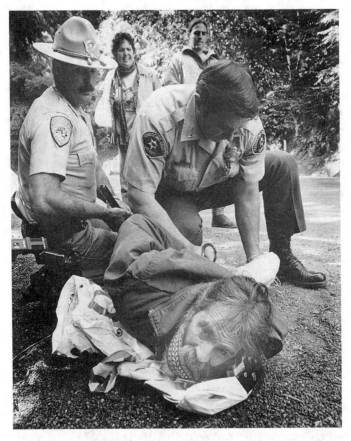

Dave Mullin, 50, in the act of assaulting two county police officers. Mullin is carrying out his attack from the prone position, beneath his two victims. (photo by Evan Johnson)

denounce our charge of excessive force. This is particularly improper since (1) neither of them has talked to the victim, Dave Mullin, to get his side of the story, and (2) nobody has even filed a charge against the Sheriff's Department yet.

But hey, nobody ever said law enforcement in Mendo County was fair or logical. The problem is, though, that sometimes these situations can be deadly. The action in Anderson Valley over the Hiatt cut this past weekend was one that could have been disastrous. Bruce describes this action elsewhere in this AVA, so I won't go into details. But at one point the EF!ers were locked to the cattle guard on the road, when a man in his 70s came by on his way to church and decided to run over some hippies with his pickup truck. People pleaded with him to stop, telling him that the protesters were locked down and couldn't move out of the way. Two EF!ers stood in front of the truck to get it to stop, and they were both pushed down under the grill. The only way the truck was finally stopped, inches from the legs of the people locked down in the road, was that Deputy Squires jumped in and removed the keys. The man and his wife were both ranting to the EF!ers that "people like you" should be killed.

So there's no question about it, Deputy Squires saved our people's asses. But then they let the guy go without arresting him! Not only had he just assaulted us, he was continuing to threaten us right in the presence of the Mendo sheriffs. They say they have filed an incident report, and he may be prosecuted. But compare his treatment to that of Dave Mullin, who broke no laws and was non-violent. The sheriffs sure didn't tackle the old man in Boonville or use compliance holds to restrain him. They said they would only arrest him if the EF!ers would make a citizens arrest, then they proceeded to arrest the EF!ers without making Hiatt make a citizens arrest. Why couldn't they arrest a man who had just committed a violent crime in their presence?

I suspect that this policy of forcing us to make citizens arrests comes not from Deputy Squires, who, by all accounts behaved fairly and professionally, but from Sheriff Tuso. And I guess it's an improvement over last year, when the Mendo sheriffs wouldn't assist us no matter what. But it's still not enough. We need equal protection of the law in this highly volatile struggle. We're non-violent, but not going to go away and let the trees go down. And if the Sheriff's Department won't do their job, we are afraid someone may get killed on the front lines this summer.

Exposing the FBI

AVA, June 12, 1991

About 20 years ago, when I was a young and naive student at the University of Maryland, I exposed an FBI informant who was spying on the campus radicals. His name was Tom Hyde, and he was a big, kind of gross, kind of redneck guy. He was offensively sexist, even to my inexperienced ears, and the main political idea I ever heard him espouse was that we should have naked demos and fuck on the mall. He was older than most of us, and he had no visible means of support. He also liked guns and violence, and kept several rifles at his house, which he liked to show off to the student revolutionaries. I don't remember what kind of guns they were. Not Uzi's.

Tom ran with the top student leaders in the riots. He had been involved in one instance where a piece of construction equipment was burned (there were no police cars handy) and in another rock-throwing incident where people got caught in a blind alley and rounded up by the cops. Tom escaped the sweep. But mainly I would see him always working the literature tables, doing the less glamorous, and therefore much less popular, drudgery work of the movement.

I was not really a campus radical yet. I was just beginning to get interested and go to meetings, but mostly I was still into the cultural side of the revolution. In other words I spent a lot of time hanging out in the dorms smoking pot and trying out all these new exciting psychedelic drugs that had suddenly appeared on campus.

One of the people who hung out with us was Bill Hyde, Tom's younger brother. Bill was totally apolitical and a total druggie, but he was a lot nicer than Tom, and we got to be friends. One day he told me he had a confession to make. He said his brother Tom was working for the FBI, and that Tom had gotten all those campus radicals busted in the rock-throwing incident in the blind alley. Bill didn't know what to do about it, but his conscience was bothering him, especially since I was beginning to spend more time with the politicos, and Tom was still spying on them.

No problem, I thought. I'll just expose Tom to the campus radicals, and they'll kick him out. After all, Tom wasn't really one of us, culturally, and his behavior was so crude and discrediting that everyone would immediately see him for what he was. Hah. When I went to the campus radicals with my info, they were very concerned. But, they said, how could they believe me? I was just a druggie from the dorms and Tom had been in the group from day one. Besides, he did all that work at the literature tables. So they couldn't just take my word. If I really thought Tom was an FBI agent, I would have to confront him face to face, in front of key members of the campus radical group.

Like I said, I was still young and naive. So I agreed, and the meeting was set for a week later, at Tom's apartment. But meanwhile, brother Bill got busted with a lot of drugs and, having no fixed address, was released into the custody of FBI brother Tom. So when I went to the big confrontation,

The famous uzi photos of me and Irv Sutley.

both Tom and Bill were there. Bill looked scared and Tom looked pissed. But I stood up to him and made the charges, and naturally he denied everything. Bill wouldn't say a word, but finally, when Tom stepped out of the room for a minute, he turned to the campus radicals. "Look," he pleaded, "Tom's my brother, and I have nowhere else to go." Then Tom came back in and Bill shut up again.

All this was not enough for the radicals. They decided that I was a druggie and not trustworthy, but Tom was a long-term member of their group, so they believed him. A few weeks later, Bill, who had somehow managed to move out of Tom's apartment, called me and apologized for being too scared to back me up. I said I understood, and Bill came over to visit and get high. He had some new guy with him, and he brought two pounds of pot, which he offered to front us. Late that night, Bill called again and said, "Hey, that guy with me—I think he's a narc. You'd better clean up." I said I would do it first thing in the morning.

But 6 a.m. the next morning I was awakened by a pounding on my door, and when I opened it, six cops crashed in with guns drawn, pushing me up against the wall and scaring the shit out of me. They tore my place apart, looking for "drugs," and laughed when I got upset at them ripping the posters off my walls. All they found was the pot and some radical books and papers. They arrested me and my boyfriend, who was a member of the campus radical group.

That same day, Tom Hyde left town. The campus radicals put out a "Wanted For Crimes Against The People" poster with his photo on it, but he was never seen again in that community. As for me and my boyfriend, we were fortunate that the arrest took place in Maryland, a state who's government is so openly corrupt that if you are white, all you have to do is hire the right lawyer and you can get things "taken care of." We got off with probation without a finding of guilt.

Of course, all this comes up in reference to Irv Sutley. Irv is now being accused of being the informant who sent the Uzi photo of me to the Ukiah police and offered to set me up for a marijuana bust. Although we admittedly don't have positive proof, there is certainly overwhelming circumstantial evidence. The gun belongs to Irv, and he posed me with it. He also has photos of other activists with the same gun. And the letter that was sent to the Ukiah police along with the Uzi photo is entirely composed of information that is known to Irv, most of which can be traced back to conversations from the same weekend when he took the photo. Irv claims innocence, saying that a third party, probably the FBI, must have done it. He says the FBI must have been surveilling CISPES in Santa Rosa and overheard him talking on the CISPES phone. He says he probably casually mentioned taking the photos of me, and the FBI decided to sneak into his house, steal a photo, and mail it to the Ukiah police.

This is quite a leap of logic, especially when you consider that I was a full-time carpenter at the time, and not so active or well known yet. The FBI would have had to anticipate my future EF! stardom to be that interested in me that early. And, in order to believe Irv's story you would have to believe that not only did the FBI steal the picture from Irv's house without him ever being aware of it, but then they wrote this letter that just happened to be composed of stuff Irv would know. Then this unknown agent offered to set me up for a drug bust, an offer unlikely to be made by someone who doesn't have direct contact with me. And finally even if you can believe all that, Irv admits that three months later, he sent the same photo (slightly different pose) to the AVA without my permission, apparently completely unaware that the Ukiah police had the photo too. That's quite a coincidence, isn't it?

People on the Peace and Freedom Party Central Committee (of which Irv is a member) have asked me to confront Irv with these charges. They say they've known him for a long time, and they just can't believe this. After my experience at the University of Maryland, I have no intentions of confronting him face to face. And I think that in most cases we can never really prove who's an FBI agent and who's not. Even Tom Hyde.

Last Ditch Logging

AVA, July 10, 1991

One thing about working in the woods in Mendocino County is that there just isn't much wood left. The once mighty old growth is gone, and even decent second growth is getting hard to find. You can see how a logger in Humboldt or Del Norte could be fooled into believing there is enough forest left to sustain this logging assault. But here in Mendo County, the land of the baby redwood, it's getting harder and harder for the loggers to ignore what they're seeing with their own eyes.

"I can't live here anymore. I've seen too much of the woods destroyed," a twenty-year veteran Mendo logger told me. "It's a paradox. You love the wood, you're with it all day, and you're killing it." A younger woods worker, born and raised in Mendo County, says he's "fed up with doing the damage. It's not right. That's why so many loggers are drunk. It's not natural to whack up that much shit in one day."

It's not easy for a logger to admit that his job is destroying the forest, and the fact that a few are beginning to come forward and do so is an indication of how bad things really are out there. Unlike millworkers, and unlike most industrial workers, loggers have a legendary pride in their occupation. "The whole idea of being a logger," says one of my sources, "is that it's not something you do, it's something you are. While you're out there, your cursing it. It's 100 degrees, there's flies, there's mosquitoes, there's dust and dirt all over the place, and those chokers are heavy. But it's a good job for someone who likes to work."

A choker setter is the perfect example of that. After the trees are felled, his job is to scramble up and down the hillsides carrying up to 100 pounds of metal cables, which he wraps around the cut trees so they can be hauled in to the landing. He has to dodge moving equipment, trees and cables to do it. For this he gets paid $9 or $10 an hour, and most local gyppo companies work a ten-hour day. Equipment operators get up to $13 an hour, and fallers get paid piece work, usually amounting to $150 or $200 a day, out of which they must buy and maintain their own equipment.

L-P has never had union loggers in this county, but G-P loggers used to be covered by the IWA union contract. "Back then we did pretty good," said an ex-union faller. "We got an hourly wage plus a production bonus." But in 1985 IWA union rep Don Nelson agreed to a contract that cut out the woods workers from union protection, and now all the loggers in Mendo County work for gyppo firms. L-P and G-P contract out to the gyppos, and the job goes to the low bidder who is willing to cut the most corners. Competition among the gyppos is intense, and the corners they cut include quality of logging, equipment maintenance, wages, and worker safety.

Logging is the most dangerous job in the U.S., according to the U.S. Labor Dept. The death rate among loggers is 129 per 100,000 employees, compared with 37.5 for miners. Charlie Hiatt's father, Kay Hiatt, was killed in a logging accident when a stump rolled down a hill and crushed him. His son-in-law had his back run over by a loader. "I've been hit over the head by trees four or five times, twice without a hardhat," one choker setter told me. "Once I got hit in the face by a cable," says a logger, "I woke up two days later."

Okerstrom has one of the worst safety records of the Mendo gyppos, with three deaths and a neck-down paralysis in three years. In 1986, Okerstrom and L-P knowingly sprayed Garlon over an area where a logging crew was working near Juan Creek, poisoning 12-15 people. The loggers' skin turned beet red, they had severe headaches, diarrhea and nausea, one man threw up blood and another man's wife had a miscarriage after handling his clothes. The company maintained that the loggers just had the flu. When they tried to complain and to document the poisoning, Okerstrom fired two longtime good employees, Tom Fales and his son Frank, and threatened them with a lawsuit if they caused any more trouble.

But the Garlon spraying, like the PCB spill a few years later, was the exception in that it aroused opposition from the workers. Mostly loggers just accept the danger as part of the job. "These are tough guys," a logger told me. "Guys who will cut their hand off and put the glove back on with the hand in it and go back to work." So when these same guys, who rarely complain about damage to themselves, start complaining about damage to the forest, you know how close we must be to the end. "There's very little logging going on out there. There's a lot of trashing," says an R&J logger. "We'll log an area and move on to the next landing, and R&J flies over it with a helicopter to check it for any trees we might have missed. That's when I realized how fucked it was." In cat logging jobs like these, the tractor is driven as close as possible to the logged area. A main cable is attached to a winch on the tractor, and five to seven choker cables are hooked on the end of the main cable. Each choker cable is wrapped around a felled tree, and when you pull five to seven trees at once, you're going to knock down a lot of small trees, says my source. "Oaks are no expense—if they're in your way just mow 'em down. In between skids I sit on a bald mountain looking at another bald mountain. The yarder is crashing, whistles blowing, trees swinging around, branches flying off like missiles, dust flying—it's all death and destruction."

Cable logging is used in places where the slope is too steep for a tractor. It does less damage than tractor logging because the cables lift one end of the log off the ground as it is dragged up the hill. But cable logging enables them to log slopes that are too steep to sustain the damage. "I've seen canyons in this county that are 1000 feet straight down. And we logged them!" says an experienced Mendo logger.

A lot of the actual logging practice is in the hands of the guy on the cat. "I've seen roads built where they pushed the soil right into the creek," says a Hiatt logger. Even when done according to the forest practice laws, you are allowed to log right up to a stream. You don't have to leave any shade at all on a Class 3 (seasonal) stream, and you can take 50% of the shade in a Class 2 (year-round tributary to a fish-bearing stream). If there's a canopy left you can take all the conifers, and in the past, logging practices have been so sloppy that they have counted the fog as a canopy. "Really, I've seen it written into plans. It's horseshit," said a longtime coast logger.

But the most urgent complaint I heard from the Mendocino County loggers I talked to was the cutting of baby trees. Before the 60s, they didn't even take the second growth, they considered it junk. Now L-P's limit for a sawlog is 6 inches by 8 feet. Out of this they claim they can get two 2x4s, one 1x2, and chips. Things have gotten so bad that last year in Comptche some of the timber fallers actually walked out on a cut because the trees were too small for them to make any money at their piece-work rate.

R&J is one of the prime offenders at cutting baby trees. "There was one cut on the Garcia last year where they needed 40–50 more years for the trees to grow. They were cutting trees 15 inches at the stump," said one source. Another told of an R&J cut in Manchester where they took 12-inch trees. A decent second growth cut will yield about 70,000 board-feet per acre. The trees in Manchester were so small that they yielded only 2,500 board-feet per acre.

Hardwood logging is another new policy from L-P. There's no legal requirement to leave the oaks, but redwood loggers didn't used to bother with them. Now L-P takes it all, as Harry Merlo promised, leaving our hills even more denuded and subject to erosion. They chip the oak and send it to their pulp mill in Samoa, or ship it to Japan to make fax paper. The chip market is always good, even in winter, and L-P wants every timber dollar they can get their greedy hands on. In a recent timber harvest plan for 1,100 acres near Covelo, L-P broke new ground in the field of liquidation logging by including the digger pines and manzanitas in their cutting plans. That's what Harry meant when he said he logs to infinity -chipping up scrub trees and bushes to extract the last bit of biomass off the dying Earth.

It's a far cry from the giant redwood and fir trees that used to cover our area. "The way I see it," says a lifetime Mendo resident working in the woods, "we're missing out on about 80% of what used to be here. Not just 80% of the forest, but 80% of the whole ecosystem." That number, deduced from life experience, is strikingly close to the numbers that Hans Burkhardt worked out on his computer. Hans figures that the standing volume of timber left in Mendo County is only 10% of what it was 140 years ago, before cutting began.

"It used to be, you'd go out to Navarro or Ray Gulch and there would be trees. Now it's all clearcuts," laments a local logger. "I grew up around Fort Bragg, and every place I ever loved is gone," says another. "Anderson Creek, Indian Creek and Rancheria used to be loaded with steelhead. I remember one hole where they all met, and there'd be 250 fish in the hole, stacked three deep. Now we haven't had a run in four years."

Along with no trees comes no jobs, and between the recession and the overcut my sources estimate that unemployment in the woods is 50% this year. Some people are waking up. They can't help but see that there's hardly any loggable timber left in Mendo County But most of them are "too scared to admit the truth, even to themselves. When I talk about it they say yeah, but they refuse to take it seriously. They just put their heads in the sand and blame who they're told to blame." And that means us.

There's a lot of anger out there, and my sources

were all afraid for our safety. "It's part of loggers' pride to attack Earth First!," said one. Last year some of the gyppos hired armed guards to watch their equipment. One guy who works for Hiatt tried to get people to meet at his house and go after EF! with clubs when we were camped at Navarro Beach around the time of the Osprey Grove demo. Luckily, we moved the night before, so we don't know if it was just talk or if they would have done it. But there was peer pressure on the job for people to join in. Comments like, "I'll kill one of them" are heard on the job all the time. And this week's violence in Headwaters Forest has shown us once again the kind of hatred we're up against.

("It's going to be a war. It's going to be the biggest social change in our lifetime," one of the loggers told me. "But we're going to have to change, otherwise we're not going to have a place to live. If we keep destroying our home, we're going to run out of home. The problem is that the system is based on consumption.")

The problem in the forest is both biological and sociological. But there is a solution to both problems, according to the woods workers who talked to me. "Put the loggers to work doing restoration," said one after another of them. "I'm sure they can handle planting trees for $12–$15 an hour." "Why can't all these loggers drive their cats and four-wheelers and haul things out of the creeks? It's full-time work to replace what we've destroyed." Of course the corporations are in no hurry to finance restoration. They're already in the run phase of cut-and-run. But, for example, when someone like Congressman Pete Stark sponsors a bill to tax old growth at 75%, that money should be earmarked for hiring displaced loggers to do restoration. "Loggers don't want welfare or relief funds," said my sources. "They want to work."

Last week I went to the EF! Rendezvous in the Siskiyou Mountains. It's all public land there, and it's checkerboard clearcuts. Not as bad as Mendo yet, but heading the same way. Some of the local loggers from the nearby town of Happy Camp came up to our rendezvous and told me their story. Lots of people got laid off after the election last year, just like they did here. One of the men I talked to lost his mill job and tried growing pot, but got busted and was losing his house. Another man was a logger who also got laid off but had a temporary job building a house for his boss. Both families—four adults and eight kids—had moved into the logger's house together. But now they were all getting kicked out of there too, because the landlord had sold the house to a yuppie who wanted to use it as a vacation home. "We're going camping, I guess," said the logger's wife. Born and raised in the mountains, they are determined not to be driven into the city, where many displaced timber workers are going. "We're going to Idaho. There's work there for sure. There are places where you can stand on a mountaintop and not see a clearcut." I've heard other people say they're going to Oregon, but loggers in Oregon are leaving, and the problem is the same all over.

Last January, the Happy Camp loggers told me, they had a demo against the Forest Service to protest the unemployment. It was organized by the yellow ribbon people, and 450 Happy Camp timber workers and their families rallied in Yreka at the fairgrounds. When I asked if it did any good, they said no. "It barely made the Yreka papers. Then we went home and we were still unemployed." And it occurred to me that yet another purpose of the timber management-sponsored yellow ribbon campaign is to prevent real or effective local organizing. Imagine what could have happened if, instead of just protesting the unemployment, the displaced timber workers had demanded jobs restoring the clearcuts. It's public land. Every environmental group in the country would have backed them up, and they just might have gotten funding.

But if we keep going the way we are now, the forest and the loggers have had it.

Redwood Summer II (July 1991). Demonstrators gather at dawn after burying a Pinto in a logging road in Mendocino County. Prepared for the worst after being beat up at every demo for a week, this action turned out peaceful and successful due to careful planning and self-criticism. (photo by Chris Calder)

Redwood Action Week

AVA, July 14, 1991

You'd never guess it from reading the mainstream press, but during the past few weeks Ecotopia Earth First!ers have chained themselves to bulldozers in Headwaters Forest, streaked through the State Capitol rotunda dressed as wild mud women, buried a Pinto in a logging road, and generally raised hell in defense of the redwoods. We pulled off seven demos in a row and, although there were some serious blunders at the beginning, we stuck with it, corrected our mistakes, and ended up with successful actions.

We had planned Redwood Action Week to be from July 5-12, but reality is rarely that orderly. So when Pacific Lumber started a week early—clearcutting right up to the border of Headwaters Forest—14 Earth First!ers decided to hike in and stop them. The action started in typically chaotic fashion, with the EF!ers getting dropped off in a remote location in the dead of night. Just as the van pulled off, rifle shots rang out and the EF!ers realized they had been dropped off in the wrong place.

Somehow everyone managed to get the hell out of there and figure out how to get where they were supposed to be. This is no mean feat, nor is the 10-mile nighttime hike they took to get to the old growth that was being cut. "It was prehistoric," one of the EF!ers told me. "Giant ferns and 1,000-year-old trees, so straight they would make Charles Hurwitz salivate." Log and slash barricades began to appear, and a trench dug itself across the haul road. Then, just before dawn, three women krypto-locked themselves to a bulldozer, with a Save Headwaters banner across the dozer blade.

By the time it got light, the Pacific Lumber security truck and six or seven loggers had shown up. The security guard radioed for help and the loggers, deputized by the company, grabbed some of the EF! support people and handcuffed them with Pacific Lumber plastic handcuffs. They ripped the banner, grabbed a camera, and threatened to cut one of the men's hair. The dozer driver jumped in the cab, started the motor and blasted the horn with the women still chained to the machine. Normally, krypto locks take a long time to remove because they must be cut with a diamond-bladed saw, which is not standard equipment on a logging site. But Palco was ready for them this time, and the second security van that drove up had the saw. Six EF!ers ended up getting arrested.

Although this action was not a total disaster, the level of hostility encountered by the protesters should have tipped off the organizers that 10 miles into Palco property is not the best place for a confrontation. Unfortunately, at this point, testosterone poisoning took hold and we began to blow it.

By now, base camp had been set up at Honeydew, Seeds of Peace was feeding us, and out-of-towners had begun to arrive. Most of them were young and inexperienced at woods actions. Most were from California college towns, but some were from as far away as Massachusetts or North Carolina. So when two young men in camo from our local EF! group started setting themselves up as experts, people (including me) just deferred. The plan they had come up with was a military fantasy. Now that we had more "troops," they planned to have two columns advance from opposite sides and ambush a "convoy" of logging equipment 10 miles into Palco property at Headwaters. A front blockade and a rear blockade would jump out and stop the logging equipment from moving in or out, thereby bringing the logging to a grinding halt.

There were many flaws in this plan besides the needless complexity, including the fact that not everyone was in good enough physical shape for such a grueling hike, and not everyone was prepared to get arrested. But no informed discussion was ever held because of "security" requirements for secrecy. Suggestions for alternative blockade sites were brushed off, and people were led to believe that they could participate in an action in the middle of Palco property and still be in a "low-risk" category for arrest by planning to run into the forest when the cops came.

With this kind of setup, it's not surprising that disaster ensued. The two columns, comprising about 40 people, somehow managed to meet up, although one was an hour and a half late. They hid near the road waiting for the mythical logging equipment convoy to show up, at which point the advance team would radio back on their walkie-talkies and the two blockade groups would jump out. But the batteries went dead on the walkie-talkies, and the loggers and equipment came in separately, not in a convoy. One kid jumped out on his own and started flailing his arms to stop a truck, then ran back in when no one followed him. Finally about 20 people succeeded in stopping a log truck, and a few of them locked themselves to the truck's axles.

A grader came up behind the truck and charged the blockaders. People would have gone under the blade if they had stood, so the line broke and the grader got through. Then Palco security chief, Carl Anderson, wearing his "Spotted Owl Soup" T-shirt, drove up with a van full of hostile loggers right behind them. They jumped out and started roughing up the protesters, punching one man in the temple and throwing others in the ditch. Pandemonium followed as the rear blockaders, who were "not committed to getting arrested" decided to flee. Never in my experience with Earth First! have people run away when others were locked down and being assaulted. The people chained to the truck decided to unlock and get out before they got killed. And soon afterward, the same macho man who organized this disaster was ordering people to flee, and was himself hurling big rocks into the road to slow down pursuing Palco vehicles as he ran, thus further endangering the other protesters.

People were pretty fed up with the "leadership" at this point, but most were unable to even find their way out of the woods without a guide. At one point they revolted and sat down in a clearcut, refusing to take orders any more. The sheriff had arrived and joined in the chase, and some of the EF!ers were picked off and arrested. "We were the lucky ones," they said. "We didn't have to walk out." Others made it to the old growth to hide, but the loggers had stolen some of their gear. They were cold and hungry when they finally made it out the next day, and one person got separated and spent an extra day alone in the forest before getting busted.

When they did get out of the forest, the EF!ers were supposed to wait for the pick-up van near a ranch house. But the ranchers came home and saw them, and pretty soon four of the same fallers who had roughed people up in the woods showed up at the ranch house and wailed on one of the EF!ers, leaving him punch-drunk and with a big black eye for a souvenir. Twenty-two EF!ers were arrested all in all, and when some of them asked to make citizens arrests of the loggers who assaulted them, the Humboldt sheriff and Palco security just ignored them.

When people finally straggled back to base camp, the full trauma of what had happened began to sink in. The plan had failed. Boys playing soldier had seriously endangered the whole group. People were exhausted from the 25–30 mile trek they had gone on in order to avoid a simple misdemeanor arrest. And the whole process of consensus decision making had broken down and been replaced by a de facto hierarchy. Things looked pretty bad for Earth First!, and it wouldn't have surprised us if people had given up and left.

But they didn't. Instead they wrote the whole incident into a song (see page 176) and spent the next three days meeting, analyzing, and regrouping. Some people had to go home, but a significant number decided to stay and try again, correcting the mistakes we had made. One last attempt at a banner hanging on the Avenue of the Giants convinced us to take our actions out of Humboldt County. Even though the banner was on public land, Pacific

Lumber security chief Carl Anderson took the lead in getting the banner down and arresting the protesters. With CHP's cooperation he jerked one man up by the hair while hostile loggers cut a climber's rope and threatened others. It's pretty clear that Pacific Lumber runs Humboldt County outright, and their zero-tolerance policy toward us includes the use of violence, intimidation, and a complete blurring of functions between law enforcement and company thugs.

So we did two things. First, we corrected our own internal processes to restore democratic decision making and recommit to non-violence. If that means more people have to know the plan and we can't have as tight security, so be it, but we're not going on any more odysseys without knowing what we're getting into. And we moved our actions to safer locations. We went to Bohemian Grove, Sacramento and Mendocino County, where we could protest the slaughter of the Redwoods without getting slaughtered ourselves.

The first of these actions was at Bohemian Grove, one of the last little clumps of redwoods left in Sonoma County, where the nation's most powerful government and corporate criminals were having their annual retreat. The first day, EF!er Anna Marie Stenberg got arrested with BGAN activists at the gate, trying to make a citizens arrest of the corporados. But the second day, four EF!ers hiked through the backwoods and got all the way into the encampment to witness the famed Cremation of Care ceremony. They were only 20 feet away, hiding in the brush, when the ceremony began. Rich white men in maroon KKK outfits solemnly announced the cremation of care, when suddenly voices cried out from the trees, "Earth First! Profits Last!" It was the corporados' worst nightmares come true. Not only was the ceremony disrupted, but it took the rent-a-cops twenty minutes to catch the culprits, while they continued to shout, "You can burn your care, but you can't burn your guilt!"

That was Sunday. On Monday, thirty EF!ers showed up in Sacramento, where the State Assembly was pondering the purchase of Headwaters Forest and various sellout timber bills. Suddenly two wild mudwomen streaked across the rotunda, while two respectable-looking men in business suits chained themselves to the statue of Columbus. A woman with green hair chained herself to the governor's door, and two EF!ers rappelled down the Capitol dome to hang a banner that said, "Save Headwaters Forest, Last Redwood Wilderness." Howls echoed through the rotunda, and the frightened officials delayed the start of the assembly session while they arrested eight EF! terra-ists.

Meanwhile, back in Mendocino County, we were getting ready for a woods action. Since our encounters with police and vigilante violence in Mendo County earlier this year, we had done a lot of groundwork with the sheriff. We had set up Citizen Observers and met with law enforcement and county supervisors, and Sheriff Tuso had ended up putting out a statement acknowledging our right to protest and setting up guidelines for how to deal with us. So a lot of what went right in Mendo County was because of the background political work that was done before the action even started. But we also thought up a simpler, safer plan. A

(Ford Pinto that had spent its life polluting the Earth volunteered to atone for its sins by burying itself in a logging road.) Only the locals knew which logging road, but everyone in the action knew the plan. Nobody had to use their body to stop a logging truck, and the blockade was set up at the intersection of the logging road and the county road, so there would be no long hike and no mandatory trespass. Instead of scared commandos, we could be merry pranksters.

The spirit of this demo was what was most memorable. Darryl was great, like he used to be before the bombing, and we sang and danced the whole time. The issue was baby tree logging, and even the loggers had to laugh when we started singing about "Okerstrom the Fellerbuncher, Jerry Philbrick Forest Muncher." When the truckers came, Darryl started singing trucking songs, changing the words as he went along. "I used to haul one log on my semi/That tree was a thousand years old/Now, I'm a-hauling 30/And every one a pecker pole."

Most of the loggers wouldn't say much to us, but at least they didn't punch us. And one truck driver asked Naomi if we would keep off his truck if he drove it up to the blockade, because he thought his load of tiny trees would look good in the newspaper photo. The Mendo sheriffs came and observed cheerfully, then after a while they asked if we wanted to get arrested. We said no, so they read us an order to disperse. We stood on the side of the road and sang and cheered while we watched them disassemble our handmade blockade with their killa-godzilla machine. The logging operation was blocked for most of the day, and the issue of baby tree logging was given a boost.

That demo was so much fun that people wanted to do one more before they broke up base camp. So Friday morning, as the Skunk Train pulled out of Willits, the tourists were greeted with a singing band of EF!ers, passing out brochures and pointing out the narrow corridors of trees surrounding the Skunk line on our 3-by-5-foot blowups of Mendo clearcut photos. Then, as they rode the train to Fort Bragg, they saw nine different Earth First! banners in the trees at various places along the way, reminding them that all is not well in the redwood forest.

So that was it for Redwood Action Week, and like I said, we recovered from our mistakes and pulled it off after all. But the lack of mainstream press coverage brings us back to the age-old philosophical question: If an Earth First! demo happens in the forest and nobody writes about it, does it really exist? I know the lack of press coverage is discouraging, but I think we need to take a more long-term view. The reason they aren't covering us this year like they used to is not because we are not powerful enough to get their attention. It's because the corporados have concluded that our message is too powerful to publicize without jeopardizing their privilege.

It's harder to reach new people and raise money when they don't put us on the front page of the paper. (But part of the Ecotopian secessionist movement is to build our own society apart from the death culture. That is our success, and that's where our future lies.)

Protest Was Over Liquidation Logging

Ukiah Daily Journal, Op-Ed
Reply, September 1991

Recently the *Ukiah Daily Journal* printed an editorial about the Earth First! blockade of a baby tree logging operation on Sherwood Road. In it you first misrepresented Earth First!'s position, then ridiculed us based on that misrepresentation. I would like an opportunity to set the record straight.

The reason Earth First! was on Sherwood Road that morning was to protest the liquidation logging of the Noyo watershed. As you stated, that particular site had already been logged five times. And it certainly showed. Once a climax redwood forest, it had been high-graded and overcut until all that was left was some scraggly tan oak with a few baby redwoods and firs mixed in. Yet here they were, clearcutting it all, regardless of age and regardless of species, trying to scrape one last round of profit off the exhausted hillside.

But Earth First! was not just protesting that particular 80-acre cut. We were protesting the cumulative impact on the whole trashed-out watershed. This point was made very clearly at the demonstration, since we carried two 3-by-5 foot color enlargement aerial photos of the Noyo, where the cut was located. These photos are shocking proof of how depleted the forest really is in Mendocino County. Together they show 26,400 acres (36 square miles) of adjacent clearcuts. You don't need a degree in biology to know that this is destroying the soil and the rivers, changing the microclimate, and threatening the ability of the forest to ever recover. If you don't believe me, just take a drive down Sherwood Road from Willits to Fort Bragg and see for yourself.

The sad truth is that there just isn't that much timber left in Mendocino County. The loggers certainly know this. They are cutting junk now that they would never have bothered with a few years ago. According to Hans Burkhardt of the Mendo County Forest Advisory Committee, the standing volume of timber in our county is only 10% of what it used to be.

In 1975 a FRAPP report predicted that, if harvest rates continued, by 1990 there would be a timber gap, where there would not be enough mature trees to sustain the area's economy. Instead of slowing down to save the trees and jobs, the timber industry kept right on cutting full steam ahead. Now the timber gap is here. But instead of letting the forest recover, the industry's unconscionable response is to cut immature trees for chips.

Chip logging is not even an economically wise use of the land. While a good stand of second growth will yield around 70,000 board feet per acre, these chip cuts are only bringing in 2,500–5,000 board feet per acre. And of course chip fodder is worth a lot less than sawlogs. Because the value of the timber is so low, gyppo operators cannot afford to pay the kind of wages loggers used to make. Not only is the industry degrading the forest, they are degrading the job as well.

175

The justification Mr. Matthews gave for the Sherwood cut was that they were removing the oaks so they could plant conifers and convert the forest back to sawlogs. If the timber industry were really interested in converting to conifers and providing for the future, they would not be clearcutting the last of the forest. Instead they would plant now, wait a generation, then let their children thin (not clearcut) the oaks so the conifers could grow. The only thing another clearcut is going to convert the land to is yuppie subdivisions. What irony that the gyppos blame us for taking their children's jobs. They are taking their own children's jobs.

The timber crisis in Mendocino County is not caused by environmentalists, it is caused by overcutting. And instead of hurling insults at each other, we need to find a solution that will save the forest and serve the community as well. The problem is how to make the transition to saner logging methods, and still feed our families in the meantime. Some forward-thinking loggers have been considering this very question at the Institute for Sustainable Forestry in Briceland. They have found that if you select-cut the tan oak and mill it on site, rather than shipping it off to chip, you can get about the same value out of a pickup load as they now get from a log truck load. I don't know if this "value added on site" approach is enough to get us past the timber gap, but it seems to be a move in the right direction.

The *Ukiah Daily Journal* has repeatedly printed the accusation that I don't know the difference between an oak and a redwood. Of course this is ridiculous. We are defending the redwood ecosystem, not just the redwood trees, and the fact that the forest is now down to the tan oak is a measure of how desperate the situation is. I would like to see Mr. Matthews and his sons be able to continue logging in the Noyo. But the only way they will be able to do that is to stop liquidation logging and convert to restoration forestry. Otherwise both the forest and the jobs will soon be gone.

Nice and Radical

AVA, September 18, 1991

A recent AVA included a letter from Beryl Blackmore complaining that Earth First!ers are helping to make "environmentalism" a bad word in the Mattole. As evidence she drags out an old story claiming EF!ers chained themselves to logging equipment that was needed to fight a forest fire, and "many acres" of trees were lost as a result. It's too bad Beryl, in her haste to condemn us radicals and establish herself as a nice person, didn't bother to check her story out. If she did she would have found that it is not only untrue, it is based on a deliberate lie by Pacific Lumber Company, which cranks out lies through its propaganda department headed by the PR firm of Hill & Knowlton. Hill & Knowlton knowingly distributed the famous fake press releases (supposedly from Earth First!, calling for violence against loggers during Redwood Summer) to out of town press after we had firmly established locally that they were phony. Hill & Knowlton is also the same PR firm that had an $11 million contract with the Kuwaiti government to produce disinformation during the Iraq war, and brought us such gems as the supposed chemical weapons facilities disguised as baby formula factories.

At any rate, this particular Hill & Knowlton/P-L lie about the fire refers to an EF! action on August 8, 1990, in Murrulet Grove near Headwaters Forest. EF!ers were indeed chained to a bulldozer the same morning that a fire broke out elsewhere, but none of the equipment at that logging site was used for the fire. The EF!ers were only locked down to one bulldozer for one hour, and after they were cut off, the bulldozer resumed logging, not firefighting. P-L tried to make political hay out of the situation by falsely claiming we blocked their firefighting efforts, and therefore "it is time for Earth First! to end their summer protests." The *Press Democrat* dutifully printed the lie, and the nice people dutifully wrung their hands and condemned us, while turning their heads to the wholesale slaughter of the redwoods so they could concentrate on their much more genteel restoration projects.

I don't have anything against restoration projects. We need to restore every acre that can still be restored. But people working on restoration should not be so quick to condemn the front lines activists who literally risk their lives to stop the slaughter of the forest. The loss of one old growth grove can negate a lifetime of restoration, as the lack of fish in the "restored" Mattole should indicate. Yet in order to be "allowed" to continue doing this work for free, the nice people try to separate themselves from us by buying corporate lies and blaming us for the outrageous repression that is used against us. Beryl objects to our characterization of yellow ribbons as "the swastika of the '90s." Yellow ribbonism is an organized right-wing program to whip timber workers into a lynch mob mentality against environmentalists so they won't notice that they are the victims of the same corporations they are thugging for. Sounds a lot like brownshirts to me. And hey, Beryl, don't forget they nearly killed me last year for doing exactly what you advocate—allying with workers rather than blaming them. Of course it's a lot easier to put a happy face on the situation when you conveniently ignore the fact that these corporations are willing to lie and even kill to protect their "right" to level whole ecosystems for private profit.

The most shameful example of this attitude occurred at the Roll on the Mattole last summer, when nine local stompers showed up wanting to beat up Darryl Cherney. Darryl, who had been asked to play music at the event and was even paid $50 for performing, was escorted out the back way by the brave organizers of this event who didn't want all this nastiness in their watershed. There were 200 hippies at the event, and surely they could have escorted out the stompers instead. By taking the action they did, they endorsed and encouraged vigilantism. Two of them, including local teacher Dan Faulk, even went on KMUD and actually blamed Darryl for the incident, saying he was "trying to increase his martyr status," and that he had "crashed" their happy little watershed party. You can be sure they didn't win any respect from the stompers this way. And if it's not okay to be Earth First! this year, it won't be okay to be Mattole Restoration Council next year. Contrast this reaction to that of my community in Willits, where our entire neighborhood was threatened with having their houses burned down when I moved in. Instead of backing down, they proclaimed that I had a right to live anywhere I wanted. They held a "Welcome to Willits" party for me; held a fund-raiser in town; and logger Walter Smith's wife, Karen, wrote a letter to the Willits News condemning the threats and publicly offering to let me and my children live with her family for protection. As a result, not only can I walk around openly in Willits without fear of harassment, but the political climate is safer here for all parts of the spectrum of activism.

The Texas Chainsaw Chancellor

AVA, October 9, 1991

Things are not going well at the California State Universities. Barry Munitz, vice president of redwood raping, pension-stealing Maxxam Corp., has recently been appointed chancellor. And as one of his first official acts he is spending one-half million dollars to remodel and staff the new $1.2 million Mediterranean-style mansion that the university just bought him in Long Beach. The kitchen and living room are being enlarged, the closets updated, and a stained glass window is being installed over the tub in the master bath.

Coming at a time of serious budget crunch, when the CSUs have just raised fees by 20%, laid off 1,000 faculty and canceled 4,000 class sections, some people think Munitz's redecorating project is in bad taste. But Munitz, who is used to living high, doesn't see what the fuss is all about. He says his mansion is cheaper than the last chancellor's mansion, and anyway he needs to be able to entertain important people there. Alan Wade, a professor at Sacramento State disagrees. "I don't think our chancellor needs to live like a sultan while we turn away students and lay off faculty. What's he going to do, entertain in the bathtub?"

But the Munitz mansion is, of course, just the tip of the iceberg. The real controversy around Barry Munitz involves his incredible background. While most chancellor wannabes were plodding along in the halls of academia, Munitz was making millions in private industry, bankrupting an S&L in a junk bond scam and looting the redwoods for Maxxam.

Den of Thieves

For the past 10 years, Barry Munitz has served as right-hand man to corporate raider Charles Hurwitz. They conduct their sleazy business deals from behind a complex veil of interlocking companies. Hurwitz owns FDC, which has Munitz as vice president. FDC owns Maxxam with Hurwitz as president and Munitz as vice president. FDC also owns UFG, whose chief executive used to be Hurwitz but switched to Munitz. If this sounds confusing, it's supposed to be. But it wasn't confusing enough to hide what Hurwitz and Munitz were up to. In common terms, it's called bank robbery.

One of the companies Hurwitz and Munitz control is United Savings Association of Texas, a savings and loan bank. They bankrupted this company by investing $1.4 billion of its funds in Michael Milken's worthless junk bonds. In other words, they just gave the bank's money to Milken. This was no skin off Hurwitz or Munitz, though, because the taxpayers had to finance the bailout of United Savings when it failed. It was the fifth-largest S&L bailout in history. And, in exchange for all this generosity, Milken helped Hurwitz finance his junk-bond takeover of Pacific Lumber.

The Maxxam takeover of Pacific Lumber reads like a star-studded chapter of Who's Who in Corporate Crime. Michael Milken, Boyd Jeffries and Ivan Boesky (all of whom have since been convicted of felony stock manipulation and fraud) helped Charles Hurwitz by buying stock for him or transferring it to him. So by the time Pacific Lumber got to vote on whether to sell the company to Maxxam, Hurwitz already controlled 65% of the vote. He paid only $150 million in cash (which he got from Milken in another junk bond scheme) and got Drexel-Burnham to float more junk bonds for the rest of the $900 million purchase price.

Shortly after the takeover, Hurwitz told a group of stunned Pacific Lumber employees that he believes in the golden rule: "Those who have the gold, rule." And to prove it, he immediately began to liquidate the assets of the company to pay off his debt. Unfortunately, in this case the assets of the company include the last of the ancient redwoods. Maxxam doubled the rate of cut and, despite EPIC lawsuits, Earth First! tree sits and blockades and a near civil war in the redwood region over the issue, 1,000-year-old trees are still falling to pay off Maxxam junk bonds.

Another particularly sleazy aspect of the takeover was the looting of the workers' $90 million pension plan. Maxxam took the money from the P-L pension and used it to pay some of their junk bonds. Then they bought a new pension plan for much less money from Executive Life Insurance. But Executive Life was itself a junk-bond financed company. In fact, it just happened to be the largest buyer of the Drexel-Burnham junk bonds that funded Maxxam's takeover of P-L, owning one-third of the company's debt. Of course you can't play this shell game forever, and last year Executive Life went bankrupt, leaving people who spent their lives working for Pacific Lumber with no secure pension. Right now, due to pending lawsuits and political pressure, Maxxam is making good on the pension payments, but the future does not look good for P-L workers.

Meanwhile, having gotten control of Pacific Lumber, Hurwitz and Munitz went on to bigger things. Maxxam's next target was Kaiser Aluminum. This time they worked their deal with Marc Rich, a man Forbes Magazine labeled as the "Champion Sleaze" of the business world. Rich lives in Switzerland and cannot return to the U.S. without facing jail for tax evasion and fraud. But he still does business here through people like Hurwitz and Munitz. Rich put up the cash for Maxxam's Kaiser takeover in exchange for control of the aluminum Kaiser produces. Adding this to his other aluminum holdings, Rich now has enough of a corner on the market to manipulate world aluminum prices.

One more example of Munitz's business style showed up when a Maxxam development company headed by Munitz decided to build a Ritz Carlton Hotel on a bighorn sheep lambing ground in Rancho Mirage in Southern California. Rancho Mirage is so rich that they call it "The Playground of Presidents." Opposition to Munitz's building project came from such powerful people as Frank Sinatra, and the wealthy residents of Rancho Mirage actually voted to stop the hotel from being built in their pristine back-yard. But Barry Munitz was not to be stopped. He filed a $240 million lawsuit against the city council for interfering with his business, and the Ritz Carlton Hotel got built, showing that Munitz and Hurwitz are equally capable of screwing the rich as well as the poor.

Hostile Takeover of CSU

So why did the Regents appoint someone like Barry Munitz to be chancellor of the California State University system? You can be sure it wasn't as a model of integrity for the students. The answer can be found in the budget crisis. Munitz's plan is to use his contacts in the business world to bring corporate money to the CSUs for research funding. He says the "short-term controversy" over his background will be more than made up for by his ability to get corporations to fund University research.

Up until now, 90% of the CSUs' funding has come from the state. If corporations control research funding, they will also control what research is done, and they will own the results of that research. For an example of the kind of research Maxxam is interested in, a 1990 report from one of their board members praises the University of British Columbia for its progress in developing square trees, which would create less mill waste and be easier to stack on the log decks.

So, having already taken over a redwood company, an aluminum company, a development company and a bank, it looks like Hurwitz and Munitz are now taking over a university system. Meanwhile Sen. Barry Keene, Maxxam's lap dog in the state legislature, is already using the Munitz chancellorship as an excuse to try to increase timber corporation control over state environmental rules. Keene's latest outrageous proposal is to appoint Chancellor Munitz as mediator for a special state arbitration panel on environmental disputes. At Sacramento State, where opposition to Munitz is strongest, the student newspaper put this proposal in its proper perspective. Appointing Munitz to arbitrate environmental disputes they say, is like appointing Pete Rose to head the Gaming Commission, Guns & Roses to run a pharmacy, Imelda Marcos to work at Kinneys, Colonel Sanders to be in charge of the Audobon Society, or Ted Kennedy to run SAFE RIDES.

Actually, one good thing has come out of the Munitz appointment as chancellor, and that is the rise of student activism. At Sacramento State they collected 600 signatures in two days on a petition asking for Munitz to be recalled. They are also attempting to pass a resolution of their student government opposing him being chancellor. Maxxam has gotten away with an awful log of sleazy doings. We hope its latest takeover of the California State University system will ignite the opposition it deserves.

Church First!
Goes To Trial

AVA, October 30, 1991

Mendocino County District Attorney Susan Massini has done it again. She reduced charges against Walter Rowe, the Anderson Valley good old boy who tried to run over Earth First! demonstrators with his pickup truck on his way to church, to misdemeanor disturbing the peace. Mr. Rowe was given a firm slap on the wrist and sent home secure in the knowledge that it's okay to assault EF!ers as long as Massini is around. Even deer have more protection than we do in Mendo County...at least there's a season on deer.

The Church First! incident took place last June at the Charlie Hiatt baby tree logging operation near Boonville. Lawsuits had been filed against the cut and, expecting a court restraining order, Charlie hired 20 fallers and tried to take down all the trees over the weekend. So EF!ers Robert Parker and Brian Wiatt chained themselves to a cattle guard on the road to the logging site and shut down the operation for the day.

Around 10 a.m. Walter Rowe and his wife drove up in their pickup truck on their way to church. They were incensed to find the road blocked by about a dozen protesters. Rowe stopped briefly, and the protesters explained what was going on. Although there was an alternate route out, Rowe apparently decided that no damn Earth First!ers were going to make him late for church. He revved his motor and lurched forward toward the cattle grate where the men were locked down.

Horrified, the EF!ers surrounded his car screaming "No!" and pleading with him to stop before he ran over Robert and Brian. Rowe revved his motor and lurched forward again, and Polly and Naomi jumped in front of the truck, desperately trying to stop him. But he kept going, knocking Polly into a ditch and pushing Naomi down under the bumper. Just in the nick of time, Mendo Deputy Sheriff Squires got there and managed to reach into the truck, turn it off and grab the key. The truck was stopped literally inches from the place where Brian's leg was chained to the cattle grate. Mr. Rowe was ranting and sputtering as the sheriffs took him out of his truck, and there is no reason to believe he wouldn't have run over Brian, Robert and Naomi if Deputy Squires had not stopped him. Deputy Squires wrote this all up in his police report, corroborated by statements from six witnesses. He called it a felony assault with a deadly weapon.

But all this was not enough for Susan Massini, the timber industry's dream D.A. Massini, of course, is the one who refused to prosecute logger Dave Lancaster for breaking EF!er Mem Hill's nose. She also refused to even investigate, much less prosecute, when Donnie Blake rammed my car with his log truck and ran me off the road less than 24 hours after we had blockaded him at an Earth First! demo. In both cases, after being denied access to the criminal courts by Massini, we sued in civil court and won judgments of $26,000 and $34,000 against our attackers.

We realized we were going to have trouble with

Massini again on the Church First! case when she tried to cancel her first meeting with the victims. Massini called Naomi the morning of the meeting to say she "woke up with a terrible feeling in the pit of (her) stomach" and was having "flashbacks" to the time we took over her office to protest her inaction in the Mem Hill case. She didn't seem to notice that she was talking to people who have to fear for their lives, not just their careers, as a result of her actions. But Naomi maintained her reputation as Ecotopia's politest Earth First!er by assuring Massini that she wouldn't do anything to scare her.

Massini began the meeting by saying she had checked the police records of Naomi, Polly, Robert and Brian to see if they were "clean victims." She hadn't bothered to check the record of their assaulter Walter Rowe, and she couldn't understand the EF!ers' fundamental objections to her approach. Three meetings were held in all, and each time Massini had new reasons for reducing the charges. They slid from assault with a deadly weapon to assault with intent to do bodily harm, to misdemeanor assault, to disturbing the peace. This is a test, Susan Massini. What charges do you think you would have brought if an Earth First!er had come inches away from running over an old-timer and Deputy Squires had had to jump into our truck and pull out the keys?

Naomi had one last phone conversation with Massini right before the court date to try to convince her of the seriousness of the crime. What I like about Susan Massini is that she doesn't let professional decorum get in her way. She gets right down in the mud and flings it. So, after a hostile conversation, she insulted Naomi's family and slammed down the phone. And this is the woman who's supposed to be representing Naomi in this case.

With that lead in, we weren't surprised at what happened in court. There were only about 12 of us there, and we weren't doing anything except sitting there. But court security forces were totally nervous. They were overheard in the hall making plans to fan out and close off the building if we did anything. Don't forget that there has never been a single act of violence committed by an Earth First!er in the entire history of the timber wars here. But there have been many acts of violence against us, including the one we were there for the trial of, and including the still unsolved car bomb attack that nearly killed me.

Anyway, they needn't have worried. Massini never appeared, and the trial was never held. She passed it off to assistant D.A. Hickock two days before trial. He wasn't even familiar with Deputy Squires' police report, but he met in private with Mr. Rowe and worked out the deal. Naomi and Polly were lied to about what was going on and were not allowed in nor allowed to submit their written statements. Later Hickock told them his excuse (a new one) for reducing the charges. He said Mr. Rowe was a confused old man, and was probably too deaf to hear the people screaming for him to stop and too blind to see them throwing their bodies in front of his truck. In which case you would have to wonder why they didn't take his driver's license away.

Massini thought she had gotten away from us. But when she showed up at the Courthouse Bakery on her lunch break, there we were sitting at a table eating our lunch. When Massini got in line to order hers, we all decided to get up and order seconds. We surrounded her in line and told her what we think of her brand of justice. And it was a small consolation, but at least we got the satisfaction of ruining her lunch.

But Massini's nightmare was not over yet. A few hours later she got word from the coast that Anna Marie, Roanne and Tom had just been arrested for occupying the Veterans Building in behalf of the homeless and were being held in the Fort Bragg jail. I guess the very thought of a run-in with Anna Marie gave Massini more flashbacks and bad feelings in the pit of her stomach, because she sent back word to the coast to drop the charges and let them go.

Now I'm sure that, in her twisted little mind, Susan Massini thinks she committed an act of fairness and evened the score with us by letting the coast protesters go. But that's not the way it is. Walter Rowe's crime was an act of life threatening violence against us, while that of the protesters was simply a non-violent civil disobedience. Massini's continued tolerance of violence against EF!ers (and against native people, Latinos and homeless people) is responsible for the climate of fear and lawlessness in Mendocino County. She helped create the conditions that led to the bombing. And through her continued corruption of the justice system she will be responsible if more violence occurs.

FBI Still Covering Up Bombing Case

Ukiah Daily Journal, Op-Ed
Reply, January 29, 1992

Recently Congressman Riggs put out a press release about the car-bombing assassination attempt on me in 1990. He said the FBI has assured him that they are conducting a "thorough and unbiased" investigation and that, although the FBI was "aware of Earth First! and Redwood Summer" before the bombing, they had conducted no prior investigation of me, Darryl Cherney, or Northern California Earth First!

It's too bad that neither Congressman Riggs nor the *Ukiah Daily Journal* bothered to talk to me before putting this in the paper. If they had, they would have found out that the FBI lied again, this time right in the congressman's face, and that we have documents to prove it.

Through the Freedom of Information Act, we have obtained the FBI files of one of the Northern California Earth First! organizers. These files show that the FBI was indeed investigating Earth First! before the bombing. This investigation included a warrantless search and seizure of Darryl Cherney's car in April 1990, and the FBI documents that we have seen even include a reference to the contents of a travel bag that they illegally seized from Darryl.

As for the FBI's claim that they are conducting a fair and thorough investigation of the bombing, excuse me while I stop laughing. They have never talked to either me or my lawyer about it. They have failed to follow obvious leads or interview key witnesses. They even canceled a meeting with Betty Ball, of the Mendocino Environmental Center, because they were "busy with the war in Iraq." They did not reschedule when the war was over.

Through our own investigation, and with the help of the Willits Police, we have discovered that one of the death threats I received before the bombing was typed on the same typewriter as a police informant letter about me that was sent to the Ukiah police in 1989. I believe I can identify the author, and have said so publicly. The FBI was handed these matching documents on TV almost a year ago, yet they have never even attempted to contact me about it.

The questions Frank Riggs asked the FBI about their handling of the case were way too mild. It's not just that they didn't investigate. They arrested me and Darryl, and declared us the only suspects, based on false statements by FBI agents. The bomb expert declared that the bomb was on the floor of the back seat, therefore we should have seen it and knew we were carrying it. But news photos of the bombed-out car clearly show the frame buckled right under the front car seat with the back seat still intact. Any fool could see that the bomb was hidden under the front seat, and meant to kill me. Weeks later, the FBI admitted they were "mistaken" about the location of the bomb. But they did not remove me from their "only suspect" list. Similar charges about matching nails also proved completely false.

The *Ukiah Daily Journal* certainly trivialized my experience when they wrote "Bari and Cherney were briefly detained and named as suspects, but were never formally charged." For eight weeks my name was smeared through every paper in the area, as I was declared guilty of the crime that nearly took my life. I cannot even describe the terror of finding myself in agony in the hospital, crippled for life, reading headlines like "BOMB MADE AT BARI'S HOUSE" and fearing that I would spend my life in jail and not get to raise my two small children.

The FBI and other police agencies involved have committed massive violations of my and Darryl's constitutional rights—false arrest, presumption of guilt, etc. We are currently suing them for these abuses, a fact conveniently overlooked by both Riggs and the *Ukiah Daily Journal.*

I think this community has a hard time admitting what really happened in 1990. I have heard a lot of people, ranging from Ed Kowas of KMFB to Steve Okerstrom of Okerstrom Logging, say that "nobody got hurt" in Redwood Summer. Ahem. I was nearly killed, then blamed for the crime. And to this day no adequate investigation has been done, and the bomber is still at large. It is a disgrace that a hate crime of such magnitude could be committed in our country, and nothing be done about it.

Showdown at the Earth First! Corral

AVA, March 3, 1992

Early this month, fifteen of us Ecotopia Earth First!ers went to a national conference of Earth First! activists. The conference had been called to deal with some problems we were having with the EF! *Journal.* A few months ago the *Journal* had printed an article that, in very thinly veiled language, advocated dressing up as a hunter and going out shooting other hunters. In eleven years of Earth First! history, nobody has ever advocated such a position. This disturbed us so much that Ecotopia EF! wrote a letter denouncing the article, and withdrew our names from the contact list in the *Journal* until the matter could be resolved.

Our letter drew some interesting replies. We got a few letters of support, but most were negative. "Bingo," who is listed in the *Journal* as the Santa Monica EF! contact, wrote, "If you are not tough enough for Earth First! then I suggest you join the Sierra Club or the Audobon Society. If that is too radical, try the Green Party. Have a nice day!" But Dave Wheeler, listed in the *Journal* as EF! contact from Sugarloaf, California, took the cake with his reply. He called our concern that printing articles advocating shooting hunters would endanger EF!ers "humanist nonsense! Of course a few humans are endangered. So what! Plenty of damn humans here. The death of a few activists is not important in the evolution of Gaia. Are you warriors or whiners? I'd trade a hundred of you for one spiker."

I was beginning to wonder what I'm doing in a group that allows assholes like this to be listed as EF! contacts, even though there is no evidence that they represent an actual EF! group. But soon Orin and Ann, two real live respected EF! activists from Vermont, put out their own letter supporting our call for an activist conference to deal with the problems at the *Journal.* Other prominent EF!ers agreed, and Portland EF! took on the task of sponsoring the conference.

After all this, you would think that the *Journal* would lie low for a while and not print any more incendiary stuff, at least until the conference. Instead they kept it up. In the next issue they printed two editorials affirming the *Journal* staff's support for the shooting hunters article. The most outrageous of these editorials was written by someone who identified herself only as "Sprout, a Midwestern Trans-plant." Sprout expressed puzzlement as to why people would "overreact" to the shooting hunters article. The only thing she could see that could "create such fear and anger" was that the article advocated shooting *humans.* "Yet," says Sprout, starting from a false premise and concluding with acrobatic leaps of logic, "support within our movement for shooting humans is nothing new. I doubt there is any opposition to anti-poaching patrols in Africa shooting poachers to protect non-human animals." So, she concludes, the problem is that we must be racists because "shooting people of color has always been accepted and even encouraged," and apparently she thinks we only object because the hunters are white.

This editorial was so perverse and provocative that it naturally caused a storm of controversy. But the *Journal* staff wasn't done yet. One more issue of the paper came out before the conference, and this time they included a cartoon of a developer being lynched from a tree with the caption, "Another thing trees are good for, Kill a developer." So by the time we got to the activist conference, I thought it was pretty obvious that we had a serious problem with the way the *Journal* was being run. Certainly their editorial policy did not resemble anything *I* had ever known as Earth First!

When we left for Portland, our Ecotopia group discussed the fact that the FBI was certain to be at the conference. They have spent over $3 million that we know of in the past few years infiltrating and disrupting Earth First! in Arizona, Montana and Northern California. Four EF!ers are now in jail in Arizona after their group was infiltrated by FBI agent provocateur Michael Fain. Fain won the EF!ers trust and friendship over a two-year period, got them to try to drop a power line, then got them arrested for it. The Arizona EF! trial revealed that at least four FBI agents and informants worked the group for years. At one point the FBI circled Dave Foreman's house with an airplane, recording the conversations inside with a high-powered directional microphone. All this certainly indicates that the FBI has more than a casual interest in disrupting Earth First!

In Missoula, Montana, where the EF! *Journal* is now based, the FBI conducted a disruption campaign against the local EF! group in 1989. They targeted an environmental studies professor named Ron Erikson, saying he and his Earth First! students were responsible for a tree-spiking incident. They raided the EF!ers houses and forced them to give fingerprints, handwriting and hair samples, then conducted a six-month grand jury investigation, but found no evidence to link Erikson or the EF!ers to any tree spiking. If the FBI had this much interest in Missoula, Montana Earth First! in 1989, does anybody really believe that they *left* Missoula in 1990 when the national Earth First! newspaper moved there?

And of course, here in Ecotopia, there is no question that the FBI is still very interested in our activities. They actively and publicly tried to frame me and Darryl when we were bombed in 1990. Now we have filed a lawsuit against them for violating our civil rights, and we are getting enough legal, physical and monetary support to pursue it seriously.

The FBI agent in charge of my and Darryl's case is Richard Held himself, master strategist and Grand Old Man of COINTELPRO. Richard Held helped develop the COINTELPRO techniques of using fake documents, death threats, infiltration, surveillance and assassinations in order to foment internal discord in activist groups, isolate them, discredit them, terrorize and destroy them. Richard Held was directly involved in framing and jailing Black Panther Geronimo (Pratt) JiJaga *and* American Indian Movement leader Leonard Peltier. He helped direct the reign of terror against AIM in Pine Ridge South Dakota in 1975, and was in charge of the US-sponsored death squads in Puerto

199

Rico that attacked and assassinated Puerto Rican Independentistas in the early 1980s. One week before the Earth First! activist conference, I stood on a stage at LaPena in Berkeley arm in arm with representatives of the Black Panthers, AIM and Puerto Rican Independentistas and denounced Richard Held and the FBI. The event was organized by our group, the WBI (Wobbly Bureau of Investigation), and I am certain that Richard Held is not real happy with me these days.

So when I went to the EF! conference, I fully expected it to be infiltrated and disrupted. But I was still unprepared for the intensity of what went down. As I tell this story, I want to make it clear that I'm not accusing any individual of being an FBI agent. Just because someone is disruptive doesn't mean they're an agent. Hey, I was one of the most disruptive people there, and I know *I'm* not an agent. But what COINTELPRO does is foment real, existing divisions within groups until they get us fighting each other. That's what I think happened, and I think we (and I) fell for it hook, line, and sinker.

Over 100 people showed up at the EF! conference from all over the country, but mostly from the west. There was an underlayer of tension and hostility among this group that I had not seen at other Earth First! gatherings. Of course this was related to the purpose for which the meeting had been called. But it was not helped by the fact that free kegs of beer were made available during the entire gathering, including meeting time as well as party time. Nine kegs were consumed over the weekend.

The first thing we did was a go-around where people told about their local work. There was an encouraging level of activity, but a discouraging number of EF!ers who are now working under names other than Earth First! The next agenda item was harassment and disruption of Earth First! We did another go-around on that one, and even I was surprised at the level of violence, intimidation, and weird shit being heaped on Earth First!ers all over the country. Besides the better-known stories of Arizona, Montana and California, here are some of the others:

Los Angeles—Sahara Club hate campaign, including surveillance, phone death threats, and the publication of EF!ers addresses, phones and license plate numbers.

Vermont—An obvious break-in at an EF!ers' house, but the only thing the burglars did was unload the EF!ers gun. Death threats. An inside sab job at a pulp mill that released raw sewage was blamed on EF! A provocateur posed as an ally from the Abernaki tribe and used intimidation to detain an EF!er against her will. Several PAW (Preserve Appalachian Wilderness) activists' houses burned down.

Southern Oregon—Provocateurs at demos, death threats.

Montana—A fake letter was sent to the Ku Klux Klan, supposedly from Earth First!, baiting the KKK with provocative language.

Washington—A prominent EF!er who was the target of a police harassment campaign died a suspicious death. Police told his wife it was a drug overdose, but blocked her access to his body. She saw him lying in a pool of blood and asked why. Police told her it was his body decomposing, even though he had just died.

Iowa—EF! activist was turned in to cops on a false charge of domestic violence. Cops came to his house and rousted him from bed.

Washington—An EF! group in Bellingham was virtually destroyed when the largest local newspaper ran a hit piece that listed quotes from Eco-Defense and alleged related local sabotage jobs. They then ran photos and biographies of key EF!ers, listing their home addresses and places of work. EF!ers lost jobs and businesses and had to leave town.

Southern Illinois—EF! demo was sabbed when a person who signed up to organize the carpools failed to show up at the designated meeting place.

When it was my turn I told about the bombing and the campaign of terror that surrounded it. I passed around the police informant letter about me that was sent to Ukiah police in 1989 along with the photo of me holding an Uzi. I passed around the Uzi photos of me, Darryl and Pam (all EF!ers), and of Irv, who owns the gun, posed us for the photos, and apparently wrote the police informant letter. I passed around death threats, fake press releases and hate mail, and I passed around FBI COINTEL-PRO directives that outlined instructions for FBI agents to use exactly these kinds of tactics to disrupt activists in the '70s.

I also told the story of how Richard Held caused a split in the Black Panther party by sending insulting cartoons and letters, supposedly from one faction to another, targeting individuals that the FBI, with their hierarchical mindset, saw as the key leaders. I held up a flyer that was being anonymously circulated at this very Earth First! conference. The flyer had a cartoon map on one side showing Ecotopia as a tiny province compared to the huge areas of East, Southwest, etc. The leaflet asked, if you live in one of the "less important" areas "are you willing to devote your energy and resources to a major campaign in a more important one?" The back of the leaflet had an EF! "Membership Application" that asked questions like, "Have you been to Redwood Summer? Do you respect those who have suffered for the movement enough to put aside petty criticisms and disagreements? Don't you understand the basic solidarity of workers and environmentalists? But doesn't it make sense to you that resource extractive jobs and wilderness go together? Will you swear yourself to the uncompromising defense of Wilderness, even if you have a different agenda?"

I said that this leaflet was the perfect example of what COINTELPRO does. Not that the FBI necessarily wrote it, but its effect is to inflame existing divisions in EF! by holding me and Ecotopia up to ridicule and attempting to divide us. I said maybe the leaflet was just a joke, but I wanted to know who put it out. Dead silence. No one claimed it. Then a man from the Montana group lit into me. "All you ever care about is personalities!" he said. Another Montana man chimed in, saying he didn't have anything to do with the leaflet, but "when you see something like this, you should take it as a criticism, because it's *your* behavior that's causing this to happen!"

After some more group discussion, some of which was sympathetic, I said that I felt I was being deliberately isolated and discredited within the EF!

movement, and I thought the reason for this was that I was suing the FBI. I thought the EF! *Journal*, whether knowingly or not, was contributing to my isolation by failing to publicize either Ecotopia's activities or our struggle against the FBI. At every turn in this discussion people from the *Journal*/Montana group disagreed and argued with me. Several activists from other areas said they didn't even know we were suing the FBI, and I began to get frustrated. Someone said we should consense on supporting the lawsuit, but someone else said we should just howl instead. Quite a few people failed to join the howl, including most of the Montana contingent.

The next morning's agenda was supposed to start with a critique of the *Journal*. But Naomi, Ecotopia's formerly politest EF!er, wasn't going to let them get away with that howl. She started the meeting by demanding a formal consensus on support for the lawsuit. But when she called for concerns, seven or eight hands went up. Some said they didn't have enough information, but quite a few said that, although they support our fight against the FBI, they don't support my local work.

I have to admit that it is galling to hear people blithely dismiss the work for which I was horribly maimed and nearly killed. And I have to admit it started to get to me. This will probably be a surprise to the people outside the Earth First! movement, but there is a significant segment of EF! that considers Redwood Summer to have somehow betrayed the principles of Earth First! They consider it a failure or a joke. In real life, Redwood Summer made an international issue out of the slaughter of the redwoods and has been instrumental in saving the last redwood wilderness, Headwaters Forest. But the purebred EF!ers are still writing letters to the *Journal* trashing us two years later. They say we would have saved more redwoods by spiking trees. And they have never forgiven me for renouncing tree-spiking.

Part of the reason for this is just the perversity of the collection of white, privileged individualists who make up much of Earth First! They don't give a damn about working people, and they oppose mass organizing on principle. But another reason for EF!s' failure to claim their own victory over Redwood Summer (and it was their victory, not mine—I spent the summer in the hospital) is the Earth First! *Journal.*

The *Journal* has never accorded me (or Redwood Summer, or Ecotopia EF!) a shred of respect. In December of 1990 I wrote an article taking a feminist stance against the theory of misanthropy. It was a serious article, and it elicited serious responses from EF! author Chris Manes and noted social ecologist Murray Bookchin. But the *Journal* failed to print those responses. Instead, they printed a vile misogynist attack by Ken Shelton, a non-activist from Southern California. Shelton called my article "an excementicious piece of eco-femme idiocy." He called Redwood Summer "a truly maggot-gagging, ignominious display, effective in saving precisely zero old-growth redwood trees." He concluded: "Give us a break, Bari. Behind every aggressive white male stands a pampered female, wheedling, whining, and conniving, clamoring for more comforts and commodities. If you take any group of civilized people and set them down in the jungle with instructions to live like the Guatemalan Quiche, the women will set up such a din of bitching and caterwauling that the men will be forced to pave over the jungle and invent refrigerators and automobiles just to shut them up!"

A lot of people wrote in and spoke up in my defense over that one. But I was still in a wheelchair at the time, weak and devastated, and it was a hard blow for me. I have never seen the *Journal* print anything near that insulting about anyone else.

The *Journal* also butchered, buried or rejected other articles I sent them. They refused to print anything sent by Darryl. And, due to a series of "misunderstandings" they canceled the Ecotopia EF! insert that we were scheduled to have in the *Journal* last fall. This was to be a four-page insert, prepared by us, that would have reported on our Summer '91 action campaign. Finally, it got so hard to deal with the *Journal* staff that I gave up on submitting articles at all.

When we had the go-around about the *Journal*, though, it was clear that the problem was way more widespread than Ecotopia or me. Person after person related stories of "misunderstandings" with the *Journal* staff. Bay Area EF!'s article about their San Bruno action got edited beyond recognition or accuracy. Pat's article about population got axed. Vermont EF!'s article about the alliance they are building with the Abernaki tribe was not printed. Iowa EF!'s article was not printed. Lone Wolf, a longtime EF! activist and artist doing EF! roadshows, said he no longer gives out the *Journal* as an organizing tool. Earth First! singer Dana Lyons, who is also touring for the movement, said the *Journal* is an embarrassment.

But for every complaint, the *Journal* staff had an excuse. They would not acknowledge or accept any of the criticisms at this meeting. For one thing, nobody accepted responsibility for anything. The *Journal* has a pretty amazing structure, which I call the MX Editor system. The editorial collective is composed of a constantly rotating staff, with varying numbers of semi-permanent and temporary members. Outgoing editors choose the incoming editors, and no one's name is attached to any editorial decision. Don't complain to Tim, because he used to be the permanent editor but he's leaving next issue. And don't complain to Erik, because he's the new permanent editor but he wasn't here before. Allison is off this issue but on the next, but she's boycotting this meeting because she doesn't want to be "harassed." And Sprout has disappeared completely. This system was devised to prevent anyone from gaining dictatorial control. But they couldn't have come up with an easier system to infiltrate and disrupt if the FBI had set it up themselves.

Finally, after all the complaints, it was time for proposals. Karen Wood, a longtime respected activist from Southern Oregon, made a proposal to immediately elect three editors, who would take control until the Rendezvous in July, when a long-term solution would be voted on. This was a reasonable proposal, and I think it would have passed if the meeting had proceeded normally. But at this point things began to get weird.

Instead of discussing Karen's proposal, the facilitator said, "Okay, that's one proposal, now let's have another." And she recognized another person with another proposal, then another, then another. If someone tried to just make a comment, the facilitator said, "Let's turn that into a proposal," until finally there were 23 proposals simultaneously on the floor, and the entire group was thoroughly confused. Proposals ranged from Karen's serious one to things as trivial as the *Journal* sending out a postcard if they reject your article.

At some point in this discussion some real EF! activists (not FBI agents) started speculating as to whether it is inconsistent with the philosophy of deep ecology to oppose shooting humans. I responded that I didn't care if it was inconsistent or not. If we advocate shooting humans we are becoming an armed struggle group, and I'm not willing to be in an armed struggle group. And even if at some point EF! was to decide it was time for armed struggle, such an important decision should be consciously decided by the group, not just put out in our name by someone called Sprout, a Midwest Trans-plant.

Meanwhile, I was getting increasingly exhausted and frustrated. What looked to me like a serious problem (possibly a life-and-death issue for me at least, and I don't really think that's paranoia) was being met with minor reforms and massive denial of the obvious. At one point two *Journal* staff members rose and recited in unison, in response to my criticism of the *Journal*'s treatment of me, "We have never printed anything detrimental about Judi Bari or Ecotopia Earth First!" No one refuted this, and I was not allowed to respond. I felt embattled and, as anyone who knows my personality flaws could have predicted, I began to talk out of turn and get contentious.

And in this state, I made my biggest mistake of

the weekend. I announced that people didn't seem to understand how serious this was. It wasn't just bad editorial decisions, it was that our national newspaper seems to be being manipulated by a classic FBI COINTELPRO [operation]. And if the *Journal* didn't get taken out of the control of the Montana editorial staff, I could not stay in Earth First! Then people were really mad at me. And someone I consider a friend announced that, "The problem with this meeting is that Judi is too hostile to Montana."

The meeting adjourned for lunch shortly after that, and I was devastated. I was nearly horizontal at this point, and too weak to walk back to the lodge where lunch was being served. Someone had gone to get me some lunch, and several Ecotopians were standing nearby, when this woman Kathy came up to talk to me. Kathy was a new EF!er from Portland, and the new girlfriend of a longtime activist. I had just met her the day before, but she had been solicitous of me, seeking me out and even once giving me a long back massage.

Kathy said she was going to be the facilitator for the next meeting, at which we were supposed to make our decision on what to do about the *Journal*. (Facilitators at this conference rotated like *Journal* editors.) She said she wanted me to know her biases—that she was on my side and in fact she already knew the outcome. Montana would agree to give up the *Journal*, but only if I would step back and trust the process and not try to interfere. One of my friends responded with a basically supportive statement, and suddenly Kathy lit into her with surprising venom. "Don't you tell Judi what to think! Your job," she said with a gesture that took in all my friends nearby, "is to be nurses. You need to treat Judi like a patient. Worry about her food and her comfort. Don't be putting ideas in her head!" So in this total loony bin, I have now been defined as the patient. And I have to admit that this interaction affected both my and my friends' view of my competence.

The next meeting was the showdown, and it was the biggest meeting yet. We had moved from the trees to the meadow, and someone had arranged the circle with my couch (I can't sit on a regular chair because of my injuries) directly opposite the facilitator's blackboard. Kathy announced that she and Harry were the new facilitators, and they had a firm facilitation style. We would make good, clear decisions, but everyone had to cooperate with the process. After the confusion of the last session with the 23 simultaneous proposals, people were relieved to hear this.

What followed was the most amazing meeting I have ever seen in 22 years of activism. It was like someone threw a tab of acid in the middle of the group. The outgoing facilitators said they had combined the 23 proposals into a few key decisions, and the incoming facilitators would write them on the blackboard, so we should all focus on the board to stay clear. Then Kathy quickly wrote four proposals, of which I remember two: "Will there be three editors or will there be two? Will the editors rotate on a six-month basis or a yearly basis?" These proposals had little to do with the long discussion we had just had, and they certainly did not speak to the real decision we had to make.

The facilitators then recognized a huge stack of

people to make comments. The order of the stack was in reversing circles—from the blackboard halfway around to Ecotopia clockwise, skipping us and going back to the blackboard and halfway around counter-clockwise, then getting to us. People were recognized in rapid succession, and the very first person called on, Renee from Seattle, sowed immediate confusion by saying: "Wait a minute! We can't vote on these proposals! We haven't even agreed to make a change!" Every so often someone else would say something like that, which totally negated whatever progress we had made. "We can't vote on editors. We haven't even decided to *have* editors!" Or, "We can't vote on what to do about the *Journal*. We don't even have a vision of what the *Journal* should be!"

At the first comment, Kathy erased the proposals from the board and began writing quickly as people spoke. Then, having told us to focus on the blackboard, she proceeded to draw total chaos. She wrote one thing horizontal, one diagonal up, one diagonal down. She drew arrows from one point to another. And, the crowning artistic touch, when the person said the bit about visions, Kathy said: "Right! Visions! Let's have a 15-minute brainstorm on visions!" And she wrote VISIONS diagonally and drew a big cloud around it.

The visions go-round was also a huge stack of people recognized in quick succession. But this time the circle went all the way around clockwise, including us. Then Kathy did something I've never seen a facilitator do. She started stalking aggressively around the circle counter-clockwise and pointing at people, saying, "Someone here has a proposal, I know they do." By this time I was in despair. I was completely horizontal now, and at one point I even pulled my sleeping bag over my head to try to keep from bursting out. And when I finally got called on and spoke (no more coherently or incoherently than anyone else at this point), a friend turned to me and said it was my fault the meeting was breaking down.

That was the last straw, and I got up and storm-ed out. People perceived me as having lost it, but I think it was the only sane thing to do at that point. I said, "You all are not taking seriously anything you've heard here. You've watched me deteriorate. I can no longer participate effectively. I'm out!" The last thing someone did was try to bait me into calling people FBI agents. "If you think this meeting is dis-rupted, name the agents!" I somehow, on pure instinct, managed to reply, "I don't have to name the agents to recognize disruption when I see it."

As I stormed off to my cabin, the meeting col-lapsed. Naomi said she objected to the facilitation, and tried to seize the floor, but was shunted aside. Then someone said the problem is that "Judi is psy-chically damaged from the bombing," and Naomi lost it. "Bullshit! *You* are psychically damaged if you can't see what's happening!" she yelled. And the meeting broke apart into small groups of people yelling at each other and arguing.

Meanwhile, as soon as the meeting disintegrat-ed and nobody was paying attention anymore, Kathy, the Facilitator from Hell, slipped away and followed me to my cabin. She came in soon after I collapsed on my bed and demanded of my two friends there with me, "I want access to Judi." "She's right here, ask her yourself," they replied. "I want access to Judi alone," said Kathy. And, because my friends thought Kathy was someone I'd known for a long time (due to the massage and the familiarity she had shown earlier), and because I was too weak to resist, we let her lead me out to the back porch alone.

"Look," said Kathy when she got out there. "I know the outcome. Montana will give up the *Journal*, but only if you come back to the meeting right now." I could hear people screaming at each other out in the meadow, and no way was I going back there. Kathy argued for a while, then finally left. But before I could even turn around, Renee from Seattle showed up on the porch, also trying to pull me back to the meeting. "Montana has agreed to mediation with you," said Renee, "but you have to come back out there and mediate with them. Just you," she added, since my friends had by now joined us on the porch.

By this time I was near total physical and emotional collapse. And it was pure survival instinct, not logic or ability to reason, that made me make the right decision to break away. Meanwhile, out in the meadow, an informal consensus had been somehow reached. The *Journal* would stay in Montana, with the same editors and the same rotating collective structure, but Mike Roselle would move out there and work with them until the Rendezvous. Then a decision would be made in a "fishbowl" meeting about what to do.

So the FBI won, and I certainly played my role in helping them do it. I ended up isolated and discredited, and the *Journal* ended up, except for the addition of Roselle, in the hands of the same people who had turned it from a national newspaper to a national embarrassment. Lots of people seem to think this was just a case of clashing egos in a dysfunctional group. But as eight of us drove home the next day (leaving a day early) and compared information and analyzed what had just happened, we could not help but conclude that this meeting had been professionally disrupted. Yes, Earth First! is a dysfunctional group. Yes, there are real political differences. And yes, I fucked up. But the FBI doesn't make up the divisions in a COINTELPRO operation. They inflame real divisions to bring down the whole group. And they target individuals to be broken down by what they call PSY-OPS (psychological operations), which is what I think happened to me. And this isn't some anonymous FBI agent I'm talking about who is famous for using these tactics. This is Richard Held.

So draw your own conclusions. I've drawn mine. And I'll even leave open the possibility that I'm wrong, and this was just a big misunderstanding that will be cleared up at the Rendezvous in July. But I doubt it, considering what we know about the FBI, COINTELPRO and Earth First! And because I've chosen to stand up to Richard Held over the outrages that were committed around the bombing. I have to err on the side of caution here.

People in Earth First! say they don't want to focus on the FBI. They want to get back to direct action. Contrast this to the Wobblies, who in both word and deed have told us, "An injury to one is an injury to all." But I'm not even asking national Earth First! to do anything directly to support Darryl's and my lawsuit against the FBI. All I'm asking is that they take some basic precautions to protect Earth First! from the obvious disruption campaign that is trying to isolate, discredit, and destroy the movement, just like they did to the Black Panthers, AIM, and the Independentistas.

I can't be in a group that provides for beer but not facilitation. I can't be in a group that recites horror stories one day, then gets amnesia the next day when the same techniques they have just discussed show up in their own meeting. Or that has academic discussions about the theoretical purity of advocating shooting humans while Earth First! activists are being targeted for assassination.

And even without the FBI, I have to admit that my relationship with Earth First!, outside Ecotopia, has always been strained at best. I certainly believe that the Earth comes first. I don't think that is an opinion, I think that is a law of nature, and our society's refusal to recognize it has brought us to the brink of collapse of the Earth's life-support systems. But I don't think you can separate the way our society treats the Earth from the way we treat each other. And that includes feminism, and that includes support for labor and oppressed peoples. At a time when we need to make connections and build coalitions in order to stand up to an unprecedented right-wing anti-environmental assault, Earth First! is becoming more isolated and more single-issue.

I'm tired of apologizing for my labor background. That's who I am. I was a union organizer for longer than I was an Earth First!er, and I think an environmental group should be glad to have someone with my background, rather than act like I'm not a "real" Earth First!er because of it. And I'm tired of arguing about tree spiking. I'm against it for moral as well as strategic reasons, and I need to work with people who share those values. And I'm very tired of arguing about Redwood Summer. If Earth First! doesn't know how to claim a victory and build on it, I need to find people who do.

So I'm absolutely clear that I've had it with Earth First! *Journal* and the macho, beer-drinking, privileged bullshit it represents. This doesn't mean all Earth First!ers. Some are great, and I love them and hope to keep working with them. I also recognize and appreciate that many "rank and file" Earth First!ers are not involved in any of this, and have already shown their support of Darryl and me by contributing to our lawsuit. But after what happened in Portland, I would feel imperiled to go to any more Earth First! national gatherings.

Unfortunately, it's not as easy as just disassociating, because locally, Ecotopia Earth First! contains some of the finest activists I've ever worked with. It's *our* name, and it represents *our* history, no matter what we may call ourselves tomorrow. We have gone through hell to earn the good reputation we have in our community, and people aren't about to just throw that away. Fortunately, one thing we have in Ecotopia Earth First! is respect for each other and a functioning group process. So the decision of what to do is being made collectively, and we're not done discussing it yet. Unfortunately, I'm in a different position than most of the group, and continuing to use the name may be more of a liability for me than for others. But whatever I and we decide, you know where my heart is. Earth First!

Murderville

AVA, April 22, 1992

A few weeks ago about 50 people held a peaceful demo outside the Simpson offices in Arcata to protest the spraying of herbicides on the Yurok tribal lands on the Klamath River. Simpson has been spraying Garlon-4 for years, despite the Yurok's increasing health problems including birth defects, colon cancer and miscarriages. The demonstration was led by the Native Basketweavers and Gatherers Association, whose gathering grounds are being poisoned by the spraying.

At one point in the demo, a Simpson employee drove his pickup through the crowd and, in classic Stomper fashion, sideswiped one of the basketweavers, a 45-year-old woman named Susan Burdick. Susan (who was shaken but not hurt) pounded on the side of the truck and yelled, "Hey, hey!"

Humboldt sheriffs soon arrived on the scene and walked right past the demonstrators into the Simpson grounds to talk to the company. When Susan Burdick and Margaret Robbins (another native basketweaver) tried to follow them past the gate to make the sheriffs listen to their complaint, two deputies threw them to the ground, handcuffed them and arrested them for trespassing and resisting arrest. Three Greens who were at the demonstration were also arrested for trespass. The sheriffs refused to question or arrest the driver of the truck.

Susan Burdick and Margaret Robbins are members of the same Klamath River Yurok tribe that Alexander Cockburn wrote about in the AVA a few weeks ago. Cockburn cited a massacre of Yurok people on an Indian island that was carried out by a vigilante gang in 1860 and described by a reporter of the time. "'Out of some sixty or seventy killed on the island, at least fifty or sixty were mercilessly stabbed and their skulls crushed with axes...old women wrinkled and decrepit, covered by weltering blood, their brains dashed out and enveloped in their long gray hair. Infants scarcely a span long, with their faces cloven with hatchets.' Though there was quite an uproar in the press, and though Eureka was referred to for a while thereafter as Murderville, no one was ever brought to justice. The names of the killers were known."

Susan Burdick and Margaret Robbins will be arraigned at 1:30 p.m. April 27 in the Arcata Justice Court, just down the highway from Murderville. They are unlikely to receive much more justice in this court than their ancestors did. And the genocide of Simpson Timber's Garlon spraying is just as deadly as the massacre in 1860. Only slower.

The Feminization of Earth First!

Ms Magazine, May 1992

It is impossible to live in the redwood region of Northern California without being profoundly affected by the destruction of this once magnificent ecosystem. Miles and miles of clearcuts cover our bleeding hillsides. Ancient forests are being strip-logged to pay off corporate junk bonds. And bee-lines of log trucks fill our roads, heading to the sawmills with loads ranging from 1,000-year old redwoods, one tree trunk filling an entire logging truck, to six-inch diameter baby trees that are chipped for pulp. Less than 5% of the old growth redwood is left, and the ecosystem is disappearing even faster than the more widely known tropical rainforest.

So it is not surprising that I, a lifetime activist, would become an environmentalist. What is surprising is that I, a feminist, single mother and blue-collar worker, would end up in Earth First!, a "no compromise" direct action group with the reputation of being macho, beer-drinking eco-dudes. Little did I know that by combining the more feminine elements of collectivism and non-violence with the spunk and outrageousness of Earth First!, we would spark a mass movement. And little did I know that I would pay for our success by being bombed and nearly killed, and subjected to a campaign of hatred and misogyny.

I was attracted to Earth First! because they were the only ones willing to put their bodies in front of the bulldozers and chainsaws to save the trees. They were also funny, irreverent, and they played music. But it was the philosophy of Earth First! that ultimately won me over. This philosophy, known as biocentrism or deep ecology, states that the Earth is not just here for human consumption. All species have a right to exist for their own sake, and humans must learn to live in balance with the needs of nature, instead of trying to mold nature to fit the wants of humans.

I see no contradiction between deep ecology and eco-feminism. But Earth First! was founded by five men, and its principle spokespeople have all been male. As in all such groups, there have always been competent women doing the real work behind the scenes. But they have been virtually invisible behind the public Earth First! persona of "big man goes into big wilderness to save big trees." I certainly objected to this. Yet despite the image, the structure of Earth First! was decentralized and non-hierarchical, so we had the leeway to develop any way we wanted in our local Northern California group.

Earth First! came on the scene in redwood country around 1986, when corporate raider Charles Hurwitz of Maxxam took over a local lumber company, then nearly tripled the cut of old growth redwood to pay off his junk bonds. Earth First! had been protesting around public land issues in other parts of the West since 1981, but this was such an outrage that it brought the group to its first "private" lands campaign.

For years the strategy of Earth First!, under male leadership, had been based on individual acts of daring. "Nomadic Action Teams" of maybe ten people would travel to remote areas and bury themselves in logging roads, chain themselves to heavy equipment, or sit in trees. There were certainly brave and principled women who engaged in these actions. And a few of the actions, notably the Sapphire Six blockade in Oregon, even had a majority of women participants. But by and large, most of the people who had the freedom for that kind of travel and risk-taking were men.

I never consciously tried to change Earth First!, I just applied my own values and experiences to my work. I have nothing against individual acts of daring. But the flaw in this strategy is the failure to engage in long-term community-based organizing. There is no way that a few isolated individuals, no matter how brave, can bring about the massive social change necessary to save the planet. So we began to organize with local people, planning our logging blockades around issues that had local community support. We also began to build alliances with progressive timber workers based on our common interests against the big corporations. As our successes grew, more women and more people with families and roots in the community began calling themselves Earth First!ers in our area.

But as our exposure and influence grew, so did the use of violence to repress us. And in this far-flung, rural, timber-dependent area, it was easy to get away with. At one demonstration an angry logger punched a 50-year-old non-violent woman so hard that she was knocked cold and her nose was broken. In another incident, my car was rammed from behind Karen-Silkwood style by the same logging truck that we had blockaded less than 24 hours earlier. My car was totaled and my children and I and the other Earth First!ers who were riding with us ended up in the hospital. In both these cases, as in other incidents of violence against us, local police refused to arrest, prosecute, or even investigate our assaulters.

Earth First! had never initiated any violence. But neither did we publicly associate our movement with an overt non-violence code. After all, that would contradict the he-man image that Earth First! was founded upon. Yet I did not see how we could face the increasingly volatile situation on the front lines without declaring and enforcing our non-violence. And, considering the rate at which the trees were falling and the overwhelming power of the timber corporations, I did not see how we could save the forest with just our small rural population and the small group of Earth First!

So, drawing on the lessons of the Civil Rights Movement, we put out a nationwide call for Freedom Riders for the Forest to come to Northern California and engage in non-violent mass actions to stop the slaughter of the redwoods. We called the campaign Redwood Summer, and, as it became clear that we were successfully drawing national interest and building the infrastructure to handle the influx, the level of repression escalated again.

As Redwood Summer approached, I began to receive a series of increasingly frightening written death threats, obviously written in the interest of Big Timber. The most frightening of these was a photo of me playing music at a demonstration, with a rifle scope and cross-hairs superimposed on my face and a yellow ribbon (the timber industry's symbol) attached. When I asked the local police for help they said: "We don't have the manpower to investigate. If you turn up dead, then we'll investigate." When I complained to the county Board of Supervisors they replied, "You brought it on yourself, Judi." Finally, on May 24, 1990, as I was driving through Oakland on a concert tour to promote Redwood Summer, a bomb exploded under my car seat. I remember my thoughts as it ripped through me. I thought "This is what men do to each other in wars."

The bomb was meant to kill me, and it nearly did. It shattered my pelvis and left me crippled for life. My organizing companion, Darryl Cherney, who was riding with me in the car, was also injured, although not as seriously. Then, adding to the outrage, police and FBI moved in within minutes and arrested me and Darryl, saying that it was our bomb and we were knowingly carrying it. For eight weeks, they slandered us in the press, attempting to portray us as violent and discredit Redwood Summer, until they were finally forced to drop the charges for lack of evidence. But to this day, no serious investigation of the bombing has been conducted, and the bomber remains at large.

There were indications in advance that the attack on me was misogynist as well as political. For example, one of the death threats described us as "whores, lesbians, and members of N.O.W." But soon after the bombing, a letter was received that left no doubt. It was signed by someone calling himself the Lord's Avenger, and it took credit for the bombing. It described the bomb in exact detail and explained in chilling prose why the Lord's Avenger wanted me dead.

It was not just my "paganism" and defense of the forest that outraged him. The Lord's Avenger also recalled an abortion clinic defense that I had

223

ago. "I saw Satan's flames shoot forth from _____th her eyes and ears, proving forever that this was no Godly Woman, no Ruth full of obedience to procreate and multiply the children of Adam throughout the world as is God's will. 'Let the woman learn in silence with all subjection. But I suffer not a woman to teach, nor to usurp authority over the man, but to be in silence (Timothy 2:11).'"

Other misogynist hate literature about me was also distributed while I lay devastated in the hospital. The worst was from the Sahara Club, an anti-environmental group that wrote in its newsletter: "BOMB THAT CROTCH! Judi Bari, the Earth First bat slug who blew herself halfway to hell and back while transporting a bomb in her Subaru, held a press conference in San Francisco. ...Bari, who had her crotch blown off, will never be able to reproduce again. We're just trying to figure out what would volunteer to inseminate her if she had all her parts. The last we heard, Judi and her friends were pouting and licking their wounds."

Meanwhile, out in the forest, Redwood Summer went on without me. Before the bombing I was one of a very few women who had taken a prominent leadership role in Earth First! But after the bombing, it was the women who rose to take my place. Redwood Summer was the feminization of Earth First!, with 3/4 of the leadership made up of women. Our past actions in the redwood region had drawn no more than 150 participants. But 3,000 people came to Redwood Summer, blocking logging operations and marching through timber towns in demonstrations reminiscent of those against racism in the South. And despite incredible tension and provocation, and despite the grave violence done to me, Earth First! maintained both our presence and our non-violence throughout the summer.

Being the first women-led action, Redwood Summer has never gotten the respect it deserves from the old guard of Earth First! But it has profoundly affected the movement in the redwood region. It brought national and international attention to the slaughter of the redwoods. The 2,000-year-old trees of Headwaters Forest, identified, named and made an issue of by Earth First!, are now being preserved largely due to our actions. The legacy of our principled and non-violent stand in Redwood Summer has gained us respect in our communities, and allowed us to continue and build our local movement. And our Earth First! group here, recently renamed Ecotopia Earth First!, is probably the only truly gender-balanced group I have ever worked in, now equally led by strong women and feminist men.

I believe that the reason I was subjected to such excessive violence was not just what I was saying, but the fact that a woman was saying it. I recently attended a workshop in Tennessee on violence and harassment in the environmental movement. There were 32 people in the circle, drawn from all over the country. As we each told our tale, I was struck by the fact that the most serious acts of violence had all been done to women. And of course this is no surprise. Because it is the hatred of feminine, which is the hatred of life, that has helped bring about the destruction of the planet. And it is the strength of women that can restore the balance we need to survive.

Louisiana-Pacific Blows an Easy One

AVA, June 3, 1992

L-P president Harry Merlo, the Snidely Whiplash of corporate executives, has outdone himself again. Not content with blitzing the forest, silting the rivers, poisoning the aquifer, closing the mills and laying off the workers, Harry has now decided to sue the people who are protesting these outrages. Two weeks ago L-P filed a SLAPP suit against the protesters at Albion (now in our sixth week of continuous actions!), naming Friends of Enchanted Meadow, Earth First!, Albion River Watershed Association, fifteen individuals and 100 John and Jane Does. This suit is in addition to the restraining order they have already gotten against our protests, and the injunction they are now seeking.

L-P process servers have been chasing us around trying to serve the restraining order papers on anyone who has been seen at a demo. When you get served, you also get sued. One process server even crashed a private party in Willits, disguised as a party-goer, and began serving papers on the people there until the real party-goers ran him out. Most people that I have seen get served have refused to take the papers, and the process servers have dropped them at their feet. This, we are told, is legal.

The best response we could think of to all this was to call another demo in support of the people who had just been sued, and so that people brave enough to defy L-P could deliberately trespass, get arrested, and get sued too.

The day started early, when Pardini and his logging crew showed up at 6 a.m. and found that a travel trailer with Ohio license plates had somehow fallen over on its side right in front of the L-P logging gate. Albion Nation/Earth First! demonstrators sat on the trailer, which was painted to say "L-P Get Out of Our Neighborhood." Pardini (who coincidentally is the same logging contractor who slaughtered Osprey Grove a year and a half ago) was not amused. Nor was L-P security chief Frank Wiggington, who called the sheriff. The sheriffs finally showed up two hours later, but declined to arrest anyone, since they were not trespassing. At this, Wiggington wigged out and shouted at the sheriffs, referring to the demonstrators, "They're making us look like fools! They're making the system look like a fool!"

Meanwhile at 9 a.m,. people started gathering at the Y, a road intersection near the logging gate that has become our traditional meeting place. The trees were festively decorated with anti-L-P banners fluttering in the wind. We started with a non-violence training and a discussion of the legal ramifications of violating a restraining order. The whole time, the process servers were running around serving people with court papers, which we promptly piled up in the middle of our circle and set ablaze. By now over 100 people had arrived, so we had a short rally, then set off walking down Slaughterhouse Road toward the L-P property line.

Slaughterhouse Road, recently renamed Slaughtertree Road, has been the community's access road to the river for over 100 years. But because L-P's disastrous old-growth cut lies down this road, the company has attempted to close it to the public. So there can be no doubt about it, L-P spray-painted a neon-orange line across the road. And when the people got there, they found L-P's orange line defended by cops, Pinkertons, and L-P security. Some people in the crowd tried to cross the line, but the cops didn't want to arrest that many and blocked their way. Nine walked through, though— local people with land at risk and a stake in the community. Polly and Val, who are already named in the suit, defied L-P and crossed the line again. Bruce Anderson also crossed the line, saying he'd burn his house down before he let L-P get it with their lawsuit.

The sheriffs locked their prisoners in an unventilated police van, and about 50 of us waited around, singing and playing music, planning to cheer the arrestees when they got taken out, then go home. Around that time Darryl Cherney, late as usual, showed up for the demo. He got out of his car and walked up to the front, but before he could sing a note, an L-P security man took one look at him and lost it.

"Take him, he's violating the restraining order!" said Doug Goss. And even though Darryl was doing nothing illegal and nothing different from the other 49 of us, the cops came into the crowd, grabbed Darryl, and hauled him over to the L-P side of the line and arrested him. Then Goss pointed at Howie Seidell and Beth Bosk. "Take him! Take her!" And the goon squad sprang into action, hauling them across the line, dragging Beth's feet.

Wait a minute, I thought. This isn't El Salvador.

They can't do this. They can't just grab us out of the crowd and haul us away for nothing. So I got up and walked up to Goss and told him to stop, that it was perfectly legal to be where we were. "Take her!" yelled Goss, totally gonzo by now. "Citizens arrest! Take her!" And the cops came after me.

Because of my injuries from the bombing, including a dislocated lower backbone and para- lyzed foot, I have deliberately not risked arrest in any of these demos. Goss, the cops, and everyone else knew that. But L-P gives no quarter to the crip- pled. I was pushed back and forced to the ground, then lifted up by two cops, one on each arm, and force-walked across the line, just like the others. This was the last straw for the crowd, which sat down in the road, blocking the police vans from removing us.

Now L-P had really blown it. They had tried to keep the arrest numbers down, and there was this whole crowd that they would have to take to jail. But while they were pondering how to transport that many people to Ukiah, along comes Norm DeVall with the court papers showing that our actions real- ly were legal, and it really was a false arrest. Relieved to have a way out, the sheriffs released us on "insufficient evidence," while we entertained Goss with tales of the false arrest lawsuit we were going to file against L-P, and what we would do with the money we were going to win.

The next day was our court hearing in Ukiah, over whether L-P's temporary restraining order against us should be changed to a permanent injunction. We argued that it is L-P, not us, who needs to be restrained, and three witnesses told of

Goss' D'Aubisson-style crowd management, while L-P's dour lawyer, Cindee Mayfield, squirmed in her seat. The next witness was a local Albion rancher/logger who had come out to see what was going on in front of his house one day and been put in a compliance hold, arrested and sued, threatening his home and land. "But," said a flustered Cindee, "we told you we would look into taking your name off the suit." "I know," said the witness, his voice dripping with contempt for Mendo County's inland hell-hole that only a Coastie can fully appreciate, "but you made me come to *Ukiah* today!"

At that point Cindee gave up and conceded the point, agreeing that L-P should be restrained from harassing us at the demonstrations. That's a pretty amazing concession, considering that L-P came to court looking for an order against us, and they were leaving with an order against them.

But that's the way this whole action has been going. The idea of suing us, we've been told, came straight from Harry Merlo himself. And Harry just doesn't understand how broad our support is in this community, and how much this whole county hates L-P. They've taken the forest, they've taken the jobs. No way are we going to let them take our houses. A longtime Albion resident named Neal said it best at our demo last week, "Harry Merlo, you really stepped in shit this time! You think you've got us, but now you've got the Albion Nation on you. And we have you surrounded."

What the L-P Memos Really Mean

June 10, 1992

During last week's courtroom drama over the Albion logging protests, I attempted to testify about the L-P Memos. These memos, sent by L-P top-level executive Bob Morris to L-P president Harry Merlo, show the seedy underside of this depraved corporation's local practices. I say that I *attempted* to testify because L-P lawyer Cindee Mayfield objected to every word out of my mouth, and Judge Luther upheld most of her objections. No way did they want this information out on the streets. But that's why we have the AVA. So, Judge Luther, this is what I would have said if you had let me testify.

The L-P Memos were leaked to the press last January. They are a series of memos written over a three-year period from 1988 to 1991 in which L-P Western Division Resource Manager Bob Morris becomes increasingly critical of Harry Merlo's business practices, until Harry finally fires him. At the time the memos became public, there was much oohing and aahing over the fact that L-P insiders were shown admitting privately what they were denying publicly: that L-P has vastly overcut the forest in the redwood region. But that's about as deep as the analysis of these memos ever went, and that's only half the story. The L-P memos are not environmental documents. They are economic documents, and they show that Harry was in it up to his

231

ears.

The very first memo, titled "Long-Term Timber Purchase Agreement," describes a plan for Harry Merlo to pull off a private takeover of L-P similar to the Maxxam takeover of Pacific Lumber. The plan was devised by Morris at Merlo's request. It called for Merlo to buy out part of L-P's Western Division, so that ownership would go to Harry Merlo as an individual, instead of the L-P stockholders as a public group. Apparently Harry was not satisfied with being president, CEO and chairman of the board of L-P. He wanted it all.

The takeover plan called for Harry to buy off the sawmills while leaving the timberlands to the stockholders. This would be easy to pull off, speculates Morris, because the stockholders will think they're getting the good end of the deal by keeping the timberlands, and will therefore sell the sawmills off for cheap. Of course, as in all sleazy business deals, they would have to move quickly once they got their ducks in a row. Otherwise an outsider (known as a "white knight" in corporate takeover parlance) could come in and snatch up Harry's deal by offering the stockholders more money. As Morris puts it: "The timing of a management-led buyout must be of short duration. It will focus attention on the company and this, coupled with our liquidity and low debt position, may attract outside participants."

"Objection!" piped up Cindee Mayfield when I got this far in my court testimony. "The witness cannot prove that this takeover plan was ever implemented." Naturally Judge Luther upheld the objection and I never got a chance to finish. But this is the whole point of the L-P Memos. Morris' disillusionment with L-P came as he watched Merlo set the stage for such a takeover, even though the final step of the buyout was never taken.

After this first memo was written, Merlo upped the logging rates to liquidate the timber lands, thereby stripping the value of the part of the company that the stockholders would end up with. Because the actual inventory and cut rates were considered proprietary information, the stockholders would not have to know that the woods had been looted and the trees were gone. At the same time, Merlo invested large amounts of money in the new mill equipment, then closed down the mills, thereby increasing (and hiding) the value of the part of the company that he himself would own.

It took Morris a while to figure out what was going on. But by March of 1990, he definitely smelled a rat. Why, he wondered, was L-P losing money in the mills while cutting their own timber while other smaller companies were making money milling timber that they bought on the open market? Morris called these strange money losses "red flag warnings" that something was wrong.

Specifically, Morris cites the Oroville mill, where they had sawed 67 million board feet (mbf) of their own timber at a loss of $2 million. If they had sold just 5 mbf of that timber on the open market instead of milling it themselves, they would have made a profit without overcutting. So why was L-P cutting so fast, and why was it that the more they milled the more money they lost?

Morris also cites other examples of puzzling financial losses in the mills, including the Calpella chip mill, which he calls "an economic disaster."

The costs of operating the Calpella yard, where baby trees were stored and chipped, were as great as the costs of logging and trucking those trees to the yard. At the time, Morris wrote it off to "inefficiency." But over the next year, as Merlo closed down mill after mill because of these supposed financial losses, Morris finally got it. This was not a case of avoidable business losses. This was a case of deliberate liquidation of the mill infrastructure.

In August 1991, Bob Morris wrote his final memo. In it, he decries the "decimation" of the Western Division, which violates not only good forestry but also sound business principles. "The hopes, dreams and inspirational motivation of hundreds of dedicated employees have been shattered," he writes. He notes the "inordinate proportion of milling capacity closed by L-P versus the (lack of such closures) by other less financially sound or resource rich companies." These include "Red Bluff, Potter Valley, Cloverdale, Inyokern, Lakeview, Carlotta, one shift at Oroville, one shift at Ukiah, one shift at Willits, and soon to close, Covelo and Big Lagoon." "The management of L-P owes its stockholders, longtime employees, their families and the dependent communities a better legacy than is now unfolding," Morris says.

Why did L-P invest $6 million in state-of-the-art mill equipment in Cloverdale, then close the mill three years later, asks Morris. Why did they invest another $6 million in the power boilers at Samoa for just one year's operation? Why did L-P upgrade the pulp mill, which is a by-products plant that runs on chips from their sawmills, while they were simultaneously closing so many sawmills that they no longer produce enough chips to feed the pulp mill, and are now "dangerously dependent on outside supplies" for raw materials?

The real reason, of course, is that by mismanaging the mills then shutting them down stocked with new equipment, L-P can take a tax write-off and Harry Merlo can disguise the true value of the mill infrastructure. If the takeover plan described in Morris' first memo ever went through, this would certainly put Harry in a position to enrich himself. But why would Harry want all this out-of-use mill equipment? The answer, with or without the Merlo takeover, is that it is needed for L-P's foreign ventures.

The best known of L-P's foreign operations is their Mexico mill, where they are currently shipping rough-sawn redwood to be planed by workers who make 85 cents an hour. The machinery in the Mexico mill was taken from the Potter Valley mill when it closed in 1989. I have seen a video of the Mexico mill in operation, and it is a huge, empty building with just one planer in it. That building is going to be filled with something, and it doesn't take an Einstein to figure out where the rest of the machinery is likely to come from.

But even more ominous than their Mexico mill is L-P's new Siberia operation. L-P has recently signed a contract to log the Siberian forest, where 57% of the old growth left in the world is located. But the Russians have stated that they are not interested in money. They want mill equipment in exchange for their logs, so that they can eventually become self-sufficient. And guess who has the mill equipment they need?

So, with this missing link, Harry Merlo's master

plan becomes clear. Because it never really did make sense for L-P to open this whole huge Mexico mill just for the few little shreds of redwood that are left up here. More likely, the Mexico mill will end up milling the logs from Siberia, which will be purchased with the remnants of the mill equipment from the north coast. Bob Morris mentions neither Mexico nor Siberia in his leaked memos, but it is undoubtable that he is aware of these connections. For now that Morris is no longer L-P's Western Division resource manager, he has gotten himself a new job working as a broker, middling the Siberia deal for L-P.

Such is the cynical world of the corporate executive. But what does this have to do with Albion? Well, Judge Luther, if you remember, this whole thing started when L-P got you to overrule the California Department of Forestry's stop order on the Enchanted Meadow cut. L-P told you that they would be forced to close their Ukiah mill if they didn't get this 300 acres down, and you believed them.

What we're saying is that L-P lied to you. The Ukiah mill (and the Potter Valley, Covelo, Cloverdale, and all the other mills) are not closing because we are trying to save a few trees before L-P completes its cut-and-run. The mills are closing and the forest is being blitzed because of a deliberate and conscious business decision that Harry Merlo made in 1988. He decided to sacrifice the redwood region by liquidating both the woods and the mills in order to capitalize his foreign ventures in Mexico and Siberia.

L-P claims that our little protests are causing them irreparable economic harm. Of course this is ridiculous. We are incapable of causing this multinational corporation any significant economic harm, even if they were to give us the entire Albion water-shed, which, by the way, is not a bad idea.

The real reason L-P wants to stop us so much is that we are exposing Harry Merlo for the cold-hearted Corporate Criminal that he really is. And that, Judge Luther, as you pointed out in court, is our First Amendment right. Which brings me to my final point. The only question left unanswered in the L-P Memos is why Harry Merlo never completed his private takeover plan for L-P. And I'm not really sure why, but I do have a theory. Morris states in that first memo that the takeover plan is dependent on their ability "to convince financial people that the bulk of the value is in the timber." I think we thwarted that plan when we held Redwood Summer and managed to tell the world that the redwood ecosystem is almost gone.

So that's why we're demonstrating in Albion, and that's why we're going to keep demonstrating. We are committing minor crimes of trespass to pre-vent Harry Merlo's much greater crimes. Crimes against our community, which is being stripped of its resource base. Crimes against the timber work-ers whose livelihood is being sacrificed to Harry's global schemes. Crimes against the forest, which can never recover from the loss of the last of the redwood trees. And crimes against the Earth, whose life support system is collapsing under the weight of Harry Merlo-style corporate greed.

L-P Logging Stopped in Albion!

AVA, June 24, 1992

Just when we were getting ready to pull out all the stops and really go for it in Albion, the courts have stepped in and stopped L-P for us. To our unending surprise, three separate judges have just issued court orders stopping logging on eight L-P timber harvest plans, seven of them in the Albion watershed. And for the time being at least, L-P has actually been forced to stop logging in Albion!

Most of the credit for this of course must go to the activists and lawyers who have been putting their bodies and brains on the line to save these trees. It's a lot easier for a judge to see the wisdom of granting a court restraining order when he knows that if he doesn't, a "people's restraining order" will be imposed by the Albion Nation. But some of the credit must also go to L-P itself, whose arrogance seems to have finally backfired.

This spate of court rulings came about when L-P, bolstered by Judge Luther's rulings against us and Albion, decided to throw its weight around the legal system. Declaring that it was tired of waiting for the courts, L-P decided they were just going to go in and start cutting without court approval on four plans comprising 500 acres on the south fork of the Albion River. L-P had been ordered to revise these plans after it was challenged by the Albion River Watershed Protection Association (ARWPA), and L-P claimed the court was taking too long to approve the revised plans.

ARWPA lawyer Rod Jones pointed out that the new plans were 738 pages long, in no particular order, filled with technical information that was fragmented and hard to follow, and still did not include important facts like where and when water temperature tests were taken. L-P's lawyer Frank Bacik responded that it was Rod Jones' fault the plans were so long because he filed the lawsuit, and anyway, "There are no rules to say the record should be indexed or follow pagination." (Pagination is a lawyer word for page numbers.) This apparently did not sit well with Judge Cox, who, although he is no friend of the forest in general, placed a temporary restraining order on L-P, saying iut would have to wait at least until July 17 for a ruling.

At the same time as it was threatening to cut the south fork of the Albion, L-P also said they were going full speed ahead on an outrageous plan to helicopter-log a few remnants of old growth on steep slopes in Greenfield Ranch near Ukiah. Rod Jones was the lawyer on this one too, and Luther was the judge. The thought of L-P assaulting Mendo County by air and land, pulling out the last of the old growth with helicopters no less, was too much for even Luther's cold heart. So he granted a temporary restraining order for three days, which gave Rod enough time to get an appeal in to the court in San Francisco, where they ordered L-P not to log until the case is heard. L-P sniveled that its helicopter logger was leaving in three weeks, so they won't get to play at all this year if they can't do it now.

The next two plans to go to court were THPs

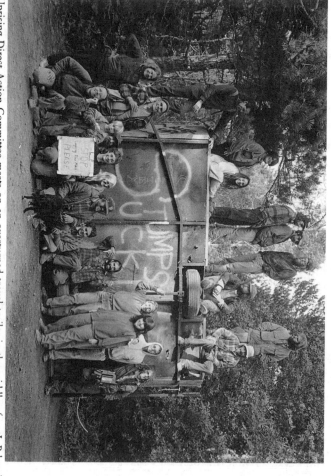

Albion Uprising Direct Action Committee meets on an overturned travel trailer in the middle of an L-P logging road. (photo by Gary Moraga)

L-P Logging Stopped in Albion!

100 and 145, the infamous Enchanted Meadow that Albion Nation has been so valiantly defending for the past eight weeks. Lawyer JoAnne Moore appealed Judge Luther's decision to allow the logging, and the appeal went to San Francisco judge Clinton White, who immediately did what Luther should have done long ago and ordered L-P to stop cutting until the case was heard. But L-P doesn't give up that easily. It claimed that the judge's order was unclear, and according to L-P's interpretation, it didn't really mean stop logging. So L-P attorney John Behnke wrote a letter to Judge White whining about the devastating effect that stopping logging would have on the poor contract loggers. Of course if L-P really cared about its contract loggers it could easily afford to pay them for the downtime, and provide health insurance too, but never mind all that.

Anyway, L-P actually put in writing to the judge its intention to go ahead and log without approval if the judge didn't hurry up and clarify his order. "Louisiana-Pacific," wrote lawyer Behnke, "does not want to appear to be disrespectful of this court's orders in any respect and therefore has wanted to refrain from operations until a clarification can be obtained." But, he added, "It is our intention to inform Louisiana-Pacific that this court's order in its current form does not preclude timber operations and we understand Louisiana-Pacific will give serious consideration to commencing operations within the next few days in the absence of an additional order from this court." Unfortunately for L-P, though, city judges are not as easily intimidated by Big Timber as our home-grown judges are. So Judge White clarified his order for L-P. No logging, no road building, no hauling. Is that clear enough? This order will last at least until July 8, when it may be extended until all appeals are heard.

The final court decision in this landmark week was THP 114, again in the Albion, right near Enchanted Meadow. This time it was Luther's court again, and believe it or not even he ruled against L-P. L-P claimed that ARWPA did not have standing to challenge its logging plans because the letters that had been entered into the record objecting to the plans early on were form letters. Of course L-P's timber harvest plans are mostly computer generated form letters too, but who said the law was fair? Anyway, Luther acknowledged that one of the letters, from Betty Ball, was not a form letter, so we do have standing to sue. And miracle of miracles, he even extended the court's restraining order so L-P could not cut before the case was heard.

And there you have it. Eight L-P logging plans in Mendocino County stopped by court order in one week. Unfortunately, although we now have standing, a disturbing number of the trees near Enchanted Meadow no longer do. And no favorable court ruling can bring back a 600-yea- old tree. For those trees that are still standing, we can thank the Albion Nation Uprising. Now that the chainsaws have stopped, the demonstrations have mostly stopped too, but people are still on alert. And these people are neighbors, L-P. If you try to start up again, they'll definitely hear you, and we'll definitely be back.

An Encounter with Bobby Simpson

AVA, August 12, 1992

Q—*Why did L-P hire 33-year-old Bob Simpson to head its Western Division?*

A—They don't want to have any corporate executives older than their oldest tree.

Bob Simpson, the new boy-wonder vice president of the kinder, gentler L-P, came to Albion Nation last Sunday to talk to the demonstrators. Simpson was hired to replace Joe Wheeler, who lost his job when (in response to our Albion demos) he accidentally released L-P's secret inventory figures showing that 90% of their trees are under 45 years old. Joe Wheeler has long been Harry Merlo's chief henchman in this area, and shock-waves rippled through the company as Merlo summarily fired Wheeler and replaced him with 33-year-old Bob Simpson, whose primary qualification for the job seems to be that his daddy is a top L-P executive and personal friend of Harry Merlo.

Bob Simpson flew into Little River Airport to meet us, along with L-P Resource Manager Chris Rowney. The last time we had met with L-P in Albion, Chris Rowney had been the highest executive at the meeting. That was back in April, at the beginning of the Albion Uprising, and when Rowney had refused to budge an inch on any point, including our entirely reasonable demand of "L-P Out of Mendo County," we had walked out of the meeting, saying we can't negotiate with terrorists. Now it was Rowney's job to chauffeur young Bobby around and introduce him to us radicals. Rowney did not look pleased.

Bob Simpson, on the other hand, was all smiles as he stepped out of Chris Rowney's company pick-up truck, looking like he had just stepped out of the country club. Wearing a Ralph Lauren-style button-down shirt, white with pastel pinstripes, with light khaki dockers and clean white sneakers, he lacked only a tennis racket to complete the outfit. To our stifled giggles, Albion Nation activist Bill Heil told us not to be so critical of Bob Simpson's clothing. The man had dressed down for us as far as was possible within the limits of his wardrobe. And Bill, wearing clean blue jeans, dusty black suspenders, and a brand new Ecotopia Bike Ride T-shirt, had dressed up as far as possible within the limits of his.

Bob Simpson's breeding even showed in his handshake—a dainty, fingers-only style for the ladies and a full-on manly handshake for the men. On our side we had a representative sampling of the Albion activists, including six adults, one of whom was six-months pregnant, one teenager, two children and two dogs from Friends of Enchanted Meadow, Earth First!, and Albion Nation. Simpson had agreed to meet us anywhere we wanted, so we piled into the back of the L-P pickup truck and headed down to the log deck near Enchanted Meadow. As we rounded a curve in the logging road, we caught sight of our banner, still hanging in the trees above the Meadow, and let out a spontaneous howl. "Earth First!/Albion Nation," it read, "L-P We Have You Surrounded."

The forest on that side of the river doesn't actual-ly look so bad, having been logged selectively in a timber harvest plan submitted by L-P's predecessor company seven years ago, right around the time L-P bought it up. Bill Heil, sitting in the back of the pickup, saw Chris Rowney in the cab of the truck pointing to the hillside, and, without even hearing a word, Bill knew that Chris was taking credit for the cut. "It's not an L-P cut!" Bill began yelling. "That's not an L-P cut!" Visibly agitated, Chris Rowney stepped on the brakes and turned to his new boss. "Should I stop the truck now and settle this?" he asked. But Bobby's cooler head prevailed, and we drove on to the log deck.

Once we got there we sat down on the stacked-up redwood logs in the middle of the carnage of what had until recently been a healthy second-growth forest. The first time they logged this place, back at the turn of the century, they had taken out some of the hugest redwoods I've ever seen pictures of, 12–15 feet in diameter. Now there was nothing left but a sparse covering of pecker poles—scraggly, undersized baby trees—with a few decent second-growth redwoods scattered around. These would have been taken in a few years, in stage two of L-P's two-stage clearcut logging method known as shelterwood removal.

Apparently oblivious to all this, Bob Simpson stood in front of us and began his spiel. He told us that he was a man who didn't like anger, and we were all going to have a peaceful discussion. He said he had instructed Chris Rowney to be there to answer questions, but Chris was to speak only when spoken to. Chris stood over to the side with smoke coming out of his ears.

Bobby assured us unconvincingly that, despite his age and inexperience, he was indeed in charge of L-P now. He admitted that L-P had "made mistakes" in the past, even overcut its land, and he said he had told that to his dad, right out. But now he was here to turn things around, and if he couldn't, well, he'd just quit. "I don't need this job," he said, gesturing with manicured hands. "I was making quite a comfortable living as a commodities trader."

As his first project, Bobby had flown over the Western Division and seen the ten closed mills that L-P had abandoned when it was done liquidating the trees. Those worthless old mills are an eyesore, and to show what a good corporate citizen L-P really is, he had committed to dismantle and restore its mill sites. Only L-P would call the demolition of its mills a restoration project, I thought. "And when you've dismantled those worthless old mills," I asked, "what are you going to do with the $6 million worth of state-of-the-art mill equipment at Cloverdale?"

Bobby said he would sell the mill equipment. "Want to buy it?" He said that no, that machinery was not going to end up in the Mexico mill, and we all had the wrong idea about the Mexico mill. It was just a little planing operation. It was never meant to mill Siberian logs with Western Division mill equipment. In fact, he confessed, it may have been a mistake. If it's just a planing mill, I asked, why was it built so big, and what was all that empty space going to be filled with? "Oh, Harry just likes to think big!" was his ridiculous reply.

Unconvinced that Harry Merlo would just accidentally build a redwood planing mill in Mexico, I pressed the point. Wasn't this part of a financial scheme to liquidate the Western Division in order to capitalized L-P's foreign operations? "You don't think we're that smart, do you?" responded Bobby. But what of the famed L-P memos, written by fired Resource Manager Bob Morris, in which he lays out a corporate takeover scheme for Harry Merlo to acquire the mills and equipment while leaving the stockholders with the depleted forestlands? "Bob Morris is a piece of shit, and he isn't worth the Earth he stands on!" snapped the man who doesn't like anger. "Can we quote you on that?" asked Zia. "Yes," answered Bobby. So I am.

Bob Simpson told us that he intended to bring L-P's cutting rates in line with tree growth, but there would be some sacrifices. He said he would soon be announcing the layoff of the second shift at both the Ukiah and Samoa mills. "And the Willits mill—well, it's just going to have to go!" he said with a shrug, blithely putting another 46 people out of work in my home town. So now we're down to the last two L-P mills in Mendo County, but Bobby Simpson was unmoved by our concern for the economic impacts on our community, finding it "inconsistent" with our environmental views.

We said that L-P has made a fortune stripping our county of its resource base, and it owes us reparations. With its recent 400% profit increase (or, as Naomi had the audacity to suggest, by cutting its multi-million dollar executive salaries) L-P could easily afford to employ all its laid-off loggers and millworkers doing much-needed restoration work on 300,000 devastated acres. "What? And have all those unqualified people out in the woods?" Bobby responded incredulously. "The loggers are unqualified to work in the woods?" I answered, equally incredulous. And Bill Heil said there must have been a lot of unqualified people out in the woods already, or they wouldn't look the way they do.

Bobby said his new program was called "enviro-nomics," but I said I prefer to call it "corporocracy"—an out-of-town corporation is ruling our area. "There's nothing wrong with corporations," Bobby shot back. "We can't all be blue-collar workers. Who would there be to work for?" And we really weren't trying to be impolite, but we couldn't help bursting out laughing. This guy was turning out to be the Dan Quayle of L-P. Hey, Bobby, I think you're on to something here!

Bob Simpson was most ignorant, though, when we tried to discuss forestry. He proudly announced that he planned to go to 60-year rotations of redwood trees, and seemed surprised when we informed him that redwoods don't even reach reproductive age until around 120 years. He didn't know if he was sitting in a clearcut or not. He didn't know what shelterwood removal was.... Anything of any substance about L-P's forestry practices, Bobby would turn to Chris Rowney and ask him. Even when Nick made reference to Joe Wheeler's famous charts showing the 90% depletion figures, Bob Simpson said, "Chris, have I seen those charts?"

Meanwhile, Chris Rowney was having a hard time containing himself. Pacing like a pit bull on a leash, chewing tobacco and spitting, picking up sticks and whittling them furiously, as if symbolically cutting Bobby down to size. In all the time I've dealt with L-P around here, I've never felt an ounce of sympathy for Chris Rowney. But watching him having to subordinate himself to this privileged son, this arrogant dough-boy, even my hardened heart went out. I mean, Chris Rowney may be a corporate sleaze, but at least he's real. So I told Bob Simpson that I didn't think "I don't know" was a good answer, and if every time we ask him anything he has to ask Chris Rowney, then maybe he's not qualified for the job, and maybe Chris Rowney ought to have his job. At that, Chris Rowney almost smiled and Bob Simpson almost lost it. "I don't have to take this abuse!" he said huffily. But he quickly regained control and resumed his amiable conversational style.

After a while it was time to go, so we all piled back in Chris Rowney's pickup. All except Alicia Little Tree, that is. She decided it would be easier to walk home across L-P land rather than go all the way up to the gate with us and walk around. So she took off by herself, but we soon overtook her in the pickup truck. Chris Rowney stopped and asked her to get in. "Oh, that's okay," Alicia replied nonchalantly. "I always use this road to walk home." And she sauntered off like she owned the place, thereby getting Bob Simpson's tacit approval for the prescriptive right to passage on L-P land that we claim in our court pleadings against L-P's trespass charges.

Back up at the top of the hill, Bob Simpson engaged me in a conversation right before we went out the L-P gate. He said something about our tactics, and don't we spike trees? "Of course not," I responded. We're non-violent activists, and we've stood up non-violently to everything they've thrown at us, including me being nearly killed by a car-bomb. "If I had been around at the time," Bob Simpson said in an inappropriate attempt at humor, "I would have given you lessons in how long a fuse to use." I looked at him without smiling. "It wasn't a fuse. It was motion device," I said coldly. "You don't think L-P bombed you, do you?" Bob Simpson asked. "Well, you're certainly not off my list," I replied. "You had the most motive," and Simpson made no denials, but soon changed the subject.

"Next time, don't just go out and demonstrate," he said, referring to our blockade of an L-P clearcut on Table Mountain in Albion the day before. "Call me first." I assured him that as long as L-P kept clearcutting, we would keep demonstrating, and he told me to wait until next week and I would see that he meant what he said about changing things. And the next week he really did do something unprecedented. He stopped cutting on the Table Mountain clearcut, with no court order and no legislation, just in direct response to us.

Of course this is no more than a bone being thrown our way to placate us while Bobby finishes liquidating and shutting down the Western Division. But even a bone is more than the old L-P ever gave up, and it shows the power of direct action and community-based resistance. Bob Simpson also called Nick the next day and told him that, in response to our concerns about allowing redwoods reaching productive maturity, he is considering going to 100-year rotations instead of 60-year. Sure, I told Nick, why not 1,000-year rotations? L-P is just as likely to be here in 1,000 years as they are in 100 years.

And as for Bobby Simpson, we're figuring L-P is down to about six-month rotations for corporate executives.

P.S. As unlikely as it may sound, this is not a fictional story. The dialogue and events described here are true and accurate, and can be confirmed by the other people who were there.

Taking Back the Woods

Interview with Ernie Pardini,

AVA, July 29, 1992

(Once a month I host the Environment Show *on KZYX. This month I interviewed fifth-generation logger Ernie Pardini. These are some excerpts from the show.)*

Judi: *I want to start by you talking a little about who you are. What's your background, how long have you been in this county, how long you've been logging?*

Ernie: Let's see—how old am I? I was born and raised here. My great-grandparents came here from Italy. They actually moved to Navarro during a logging boom, and built a hotel there in the days of the boom. But my family's been in the logging business in some capacity or another ever since, and I've been logging since I was 17. I'm 37 now, so that puts 20 years behind me. I am currently a licensed timber operator.

Judi: *And just so the listeners will know who they're listening to, everybody knows that the timber operator at the Albion cut is Pardini, so what relationship to you is the Pardini in Albion?*

Ernie: Well, that's my uncle. He just happened to be the unlucky guy who got the bid.

Judi: *And are you currently employed?*

Ernie: I'm self-employed right now. I'm starting a fledgling, struggling business. It's logging in a sense— I do some commercial logging. Probably by now it's clear that I won't do a job that's not in line with having timber in the future to log on that same piece of property. But I'm not against logging. Logging has to be done and should be done, I feel, but in a conscionable manner. And that's my complaint with the corporations, that they're not doing that.

Judi: *In your article in the AVA a couple of weeks ago, you said you left the area for a while, and when you came back you saw things that opened your eyes. Could you describe that?*

Ernie: Yes, I could. The business that I'm in now requires that I'm out and about a lot. I see a lot of country, a lot of the woods. And when I got back from New York—I was there for four and a half years—I found myself in areas that I had logged 10 years previously, when I worked for Masonite, on Masonite lands at the time, which are now L-P lands for the most part. And I saw areas that were logged when I was actively involved with Masonite that had been re-logged—and when I say re-logged I mean re-logged, there was nothing left but stumps and tan oak scrub—with entire new road systems cut in on steep ground, across the roads that we used when we were in there, which wasn't necessary as far as I could see. There's no logical reason for that, but it was done. This one job that sticks out in my mind looked like a checkerboard effect—it was skid roads this way and skid roads that way. And no trees. I thought, well maybe that's an isolated case, and then as I saw more and more of the corporate lands I saw more and more that it wasn't an isolated case—that there is very, very little timber out there on corporation lands.

Judi: *And yet you had never said anything for all this time, as have very few people who work for the timber industry, especially people whose families have been established here for a long time. Why were you silent? What were your feelings when you saw this?*

Ernie: Probably much the same as most loggers feel right now. I had mixed emotions. I mean, logging was my life, it's a tradition. It had always been happening, and always before it looked like there was always going to be enough trees, and that it would be an ongoing thing with no concern on our part as far as having trees to log somewhere down the line.

Judi: *And why do you think this is happening?*

Ernie: Well, I never really had any misconceptions about why it was happening. I feel it's happening because the corporations—L-P specifically—came in here with the intention of strong-arming Masonite out of the area and making a quick profit, and bailing out. That's what I felt when they moved in here. Most of the loggers that I know are going to do as good a job environmentally as they can with what they have to work with. But if L-P says, okay, this is a clearcut, cut every tree that's 12 inches at breast height and under, you're going to go in there and cut every tree that's 12 inches at breast height and under. Either that or you're not going to get the job.

Judi: *Well, when you're doing that kind of job— or when people are doing that kind of job, because I know you just said that you won't do that—do you think most of the loggers are aware that they're cutting themselves out of work?*

Ernie: I think a lot are, but don't have any choice. Some maybe don't see it or don't want to see it, but are in a position that dictates this kind of thinking to them. If they've got a million dollars invested in heavy equipment, they don't want to believe that in two years this equipment's going to be sitting in the yard with nothing to do.

Judi: *And what you're saying about not having any choice—yeah, I know. I used to build yuppie houses out of that old-growth redwood you cut down. And that was the best job I could get to support two kids with. So I don't think that's so much a point of contention. At any rate, you had some interesting things to say about the relationship of the environmentalists to L-P. Could you go into that a little bit?*

Ernie: Yeah. I feel that the environmentalists—no offense intended—are playing right into L-P's hands.

Judi: *I think the loggers are.*

Ernie: I think both are. I think the corporate timber industry is manipulating the entire struggle. They're ready to bail out of here. They've already laid off hundreds of people, and they're going to lay off hundreds more.

Judi: *They've actually laid off about 1,200 employees since 1989.*

Ernie: Well, if it hadn't been for the environmental faction—they're going to run out of timber. They're going to cut logging back to the point where they can't operate their mills. When their mills can't operate any longer, they've got no logs left, they're going to have to leave. That makes them look like bad guys in the public eye. By having the environmental battle going, THPs are harder to get through, there's new rules coming out. It's those damn hippies, that's what they're telling the loggers. I know that's what they're receiving, and L-P is fueling that.

Judi: *And in L-P's case, not only are they destroying the timber, they're destroying people's livelihoods. That means people's ability to live in a rural lifestyle. And when they talk of things like retraining, basically what they're talking about is displacement, because there has to be something that people can do here.*

Ernie: But there is. There is and there always will be. You know what people don't remember? They don't remember that when the clearcutting was done at the beginning of the century and in the '20s, they did create a lag for about 20 years. Through the Depression, actually until post-World War II, when the baby boom hit and all, the building was started again. But in those lapses they logged tan bark. My grandfather was a tan bark contractor. He had a mule train hauling tan bark out of the mountains to make tannic acid. So they found something to fill in.

Judi: *But this time, you know, these woods are trashed. We're going to have to hold some of this stuff in trust to prevent it from being turned into subdivisions. To me the problem is not whether people can survive in down periods of the economy. It's whether we're going to be* allowed *to survive. Or whether they're going to turn this into vineyards and subdivisions, because this timber gap is 50-year. Ninety percent of L-P's trees are less than 40 years old.*

Ernie: What I don't think most of the loggers realize is, yeah, we can wait out this lapse in the timber industry. We'll have to scale down, obviously, we'll have to get much more diversified in terms of the kinds of products we're going to be out there after. I think they're not seeing that it's not just waiting for this land to reproduce, it's making sure this land doesn't fall into developers' hands so that you'll never go back there to log it. I think pressure should be put on the county to pass some sort of law stating that what is now timberland must stay timberland. You know, it's easier to get a timberland conversion permit than it is to get a timber harvest plan through. That means it's easier to go in there and knock everything down and turn it into vineyard than it is to cut every other tree.

Judi: *That's a good point. And it does seem like a lot more people are beginning to see what's going on. But you know, at the FAC meeting I saw a lot of people waving yellow ribbons and cheering for their own demise. And I have to say that I thought, how long are the loggers going to let themselves be used as chumps for the corporations? How do you think this could be avoided? How can we stop being manipulated like this?*

Ernie: Well, first with the timber workers—and this is understandable because they're up against the wall—but they're not organized. I've thought for years that there should be a timber workers union. It's hard because there's so many levels of employment. There's a guy out there working in the woods, there's a guy hauling logs to the mill, there's a lot involved. But without organization, well what good's it going to do me to quit when Joe Blow down the road is going to go ahead and take the job?

Judi: *Ernie, we have a caller.*

Caller: I'm standing here looking out at the Noyo

watershed and seeing a lot of clearcuts, and listening to Ernie talk about the workers not being able to organize, and thinking how the big strike of '47 was crushed by the company. And I wonder if Ernie's folks ever talked about that, and what kind of attitude towards the company makes people continue to cave in.

Ernie: I don't think that company ever tried that in Boonville! All kidding aside, L-P I'm sure would try to break a union. In those years, though, you're looking at immigrant crews, mostly. And I think it's a lot easier to scare someone who's afraid of having to go back to something worse.

Judi: *Do you know about the history of the Wobblies organizing the timber workers?*

Ernie: No, I'm not familiar with it.

Judi: *Well, there actually was a union in the nineteen teens that succeeded in uniting all of those different factions of the loggers with different nationalities, different languages, and they actually did succeed in organizing the loggers. And they were crushed with a level of violence that's hard to even comprehend.*

Ernie: That may be. But I don't think companies can really exert that kind of muscle these days, with the media the way it is.

Judi: *Somebody bombed me, Ernie.*

Ernie: I know, Judi. I'm going to speak for most of the loggers I know, and I'm going to tell you that— they're not good at organizing labor unions, but if one of us got bombed and they thought that L-P was responsible, there wouldn't be a place big enough to hang the L-P sign over there in Ukiah at their plant. If it was you, if I knew who did it, if I had solid proof that L-P bombed you, I'd be going after them. We have to stand together as a community in that respect. You can't let corporate business crush the rights that we've been given as Americans. If the loggers ever got backed against the wall to the point that they would try and organize, I don't think that would deter them in the least if individuals got picked out. It would give them more incentive, more purpose. It would create martyrs.

Judi: *And that's what it's done to us.*

Ernie: You know, when I first started thinking about organizing timber workers is when my boss subletted me and my piece of equipment to a contractor to do some highway work. It was in the wintertime when logging was not going on. I was getting $8.50 an hour to run my piece of equipment, and there was an 18-year-old girl that was standing there holding the flag all day, and she was getting paid $22.50. And I thought to myself right then, I'm a trained professional—this is not something that you can just learn in an hour's time, so why am I getting $8.50 and she's getting $22.50? Ah! She's in the union!

Judi: *We have another caller. Go ahead.*

Caller: This is Tony Pardini, Ernie's brother. I just got in from the woods, and I just want to say a couple of things real quick. Judi Bari, some of the things that you guys stand for I agree with, some of your tactics I disagree with.

Judi: *Which tactics do you disagree with? Because some of the tactics we're blamed for, we don't do. For example, we've publicly renounced tree-spiking, and we don't sab your equipment.*

Tony: Okay, thank you. I'll give you one example. Turning a house trailer over in the middle of the truck road.

Taking Back the Woods

Judi: *Okay. That one I admit somebody did it.*

Tony: Okay. Stopping men just like me from going to their jobs and earning a living to feed the babies. Earth First! stands for Earth first. I look at it as feed the babies first, because they're here on this Earth, and they're the ones that are going to be taking care of the Earth. Okay, now I got something to say to Ernie. Ernie, I think there's a lot of loggers that agree with a lot of things you say. But I don't think they have the guts to say it because of the repercussions. And I just want to say I'm proud of you, standing up and saying what you feel regardless of repercussions from other loggers, L-P, or whatever.

Ernie: You're not doing too bad yourself there, little brother.

Tony: Yeah, well, if you get too many repercussions, let me know. I'll give you a hand.

Ernie: Yeah, I figured I could count on that.

Tony: But Judi, you got some good points, and I don't want to see the trees disappear either.

Judi: *Great! And as far as feeding the babies, I've got kids too, and I agree with that too. But I feel that we're at a state where, if this keeps going there's none of us going to be able to feed our babies. And one quick response to the turned-over trailer and the many other things we've done in the past eight weeks out in Albion—because Ernie in his article says why aren't we organizing boycotts and stuff like that instead of stopping people from working? And the reason is because we feel like this is an emergency. I mean, L-P admits they've taken 90% of the trees. They're leaving anyway, and they're going to leave us with nothing. And once a 600-year-old tree is gone, it's gone. I'm really glad to see Ernie proposing alternatives because* *that's exactly what we would like there to happen, that people can still work in the woods without destroying the woods. But we're taking drastic actions now because this is an emergency.*

Tony: Yeah, well I've got friends that work for my uncle, and their feelings are the same as mine. Feed the babies first. And, if you're going to turn a trailer upside down, turn it—now I'm going to say something that's going to cause repercussions for me. I'll never get a job on L-P land again for saying this, but I don't really care. I'm going to say what I feel, just like Ernie. Turn a trailer over in front of Harry Merlo's office, because I don't think Harry Merlo is concerned about his babies. I think he's concerned about his pocketbook, and that caseload of money that he's going to leave this county with.

Judi: *Thank you. You know we did do that. We actually went into his hot tub once at his secret Shangri-La at 3400 Scaggs Springs Road out near Healdsburg.*

Tony: Yeah. Maybe I'll be there with you next time, because I'm not going to get a job on L-P land now anyway.

Judi: *Well, there aren't very many more jobs on L-P land for anybody, and that's really the point. And I think we need to be aware about the people trying to make their livings too. So thanks a lot for calling in.*

Tony: Thanks for listening to me. I'm proud of you, Ernie.

Judi: *Ernie, you didn't get a chance to answer, and I'd really like to hear your answer, what you think of the demonstrations in Albion, the issues and the tactics.*

Ernie: Well, you're talking to a logger, so when

you're stopping loggers from trying to make a living, I could never participate in something like that. I think that what you've done so far has been beneficial in the sense that it's gotten a lot of media attention. Now my suggestion is let's use this media attention to start fingering L-P themselves, and stop picking on the little logger guys.

Judi: *Well, our signs say L-P Out of Mendo County and our bumper-sticker says L-P = Logger Poverty. But I think this is a dilemma too, because I don't want to protest against the people who are just earning a living out there. But I don't think that's what we're really saying. What we're saying is long-term versus short-term. If we're stopping a job today and keeping one last watershed of healthy trees for when L-P inevitably leaves, then maybe people can see it in a longer term. We have another caller. Go ahead.*

Caller: Oh, hi. This is one of the protesters from out in Albion. I was there the morning when we dumped that travel trailer. You know it's really wishful thinking to think that we really stopped the loggers. At most we stopped them for two or three hours at a time. And it's really been an issue with me to try and decide whether I could in good conscience even stop somebody for a few hours. But I know those timber fallers make a couple of hundred dollars a day, and it seems to me that if we stop them for an hour, it wouldn't break them. But I would really like to figure out a way to organize the timber fallers, who seem to be the real key in this issue—if they would organize into a guild and only do what they in good conscience could cut, I think we'd be a long way towards solving this whole thing.

Judi: *Real men don't cut pecker poles...*

Caller: But on that Enchanted Meadow cut, most of the fallers, at least from my contact with them, all they could see was that one job. They couldn't see that what we were trying to do was stop a destruction that was going on over the whole watershed.

Ernie: Exactly. That's why there's a need for communication between both factions, and that's what we're working to do. I'm finding out things I was unaware of. I saw an aerial photo that Judi showed me the other day that blew me away, and I already know they're devastating their timberland.

Judi: *That aerial photo, taken by Nick Wilson, showed 20 square miles of redwood clearcuts between Willits and Fort Bragg. And I have another one that's right next to it geographically that shows 16 miles of clearcuts. So I only showed you half of what I had to show. But there's another thing I want to say about the protesters. It's based in the area, people who live here. And many of the protesters live off the land in one way or another, either as fishermen and women, homesteaders—one of the protesters owns a small mill. So there isn't really this conflict of whether we can use the woods or not. I think we agree on that, that these woods could support us if they weren't abused.*

Ernie: That's why there's got to be communication. It's not enough to say, we're not going to let you work today. You've got to tell them why. And I think when all is said and done, the two groups can come to terms.

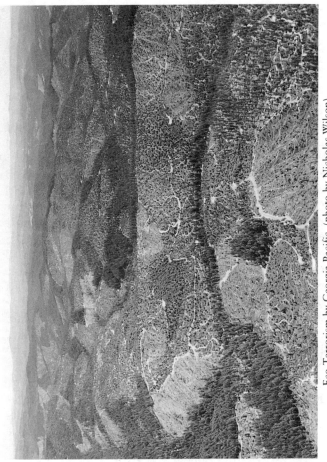

Eco-Terrorism by Georgia Pacific. (photo by Nicholas Wilson)

The Secret History of Tree-Spiking—Part 1

AVA February 17, 1993

In May 1987, millworker George Alexander was nearly decapitated when a spike shattered his saw-blade at the Cloverdale L-P mill. This grisly accident sent shock-waves through our community, and eventually led Northern California Earth First! to renounce tree-spiking. Southern Oregon EF! joined us, but that's all. The rest of Earth First! still endorses spiking, and many of them reacted to our no-spiking policy by denouncing us as traitors or dismissing us as wimps, without ever examining the reasons for our actions. Because of this, and because some of the new activists in our area have been talking about tree-spiking as if it may be a viable tactic, I think it's time to re-examine the issue. Recently, George Alexander and his wife, Laurie, agreed to talk about the 1987 tree-spiking. The following account of the incident is based on my conversations with them.

"I was the perfect victim," began George Alexander. "I was nobody." George, a lifetime Mendocino County resident and son of an old-time Willits logger, was 23 and just married, with his wife Laurie three-months pregnant at the time of the accident. George's job at the mill was called off-bearer. The off-bearer operates a huge band saw that makes the first rough-cut on the logs as they come into the mill, sectioning off slices of wood that will later be cut to standard lengths and planed for finished lumber.

Off-bearer is one of the most dangerous jobs in the mill. The saw that George Alexander worked on was sized for old-growth logs—52 feet around, with a 10-inch blade of high-tensile steel. "That saw was so powerful that when you turned it off you could make three more cuts through a 20-foot log before the saw stopped," George told me. One of the dangers of working as off-bearer is that, if the blade hits a hard knot or metal debris (from old fences, choker chains, nails, etc., embedded in the wood) the sawteeth can break off and can go flying. If it's bad enough, the sawblade can break. To protect against this, workers have to wear a heavy face mask and stay on the alert, checking each log as it goes through.

George knew the job was dangerous, but he was also confident of his skill. "I always figured that if that blade ever hit me, it would hit me on the run," he said. He knew every sound the saw made, and could tell by listening when something was going wrong. He also knew to look for the tell-tale black stains that usually show up on the smooth surface of the debarked logs if metal is present in the wood.

Although George Alexander was an L-P employee, he was no company man. L-P management had earned his disrespect long ago through the callous way it treats its employees. "We're not even people to them," he said. "All they care about is production." The perfect example of this L-P management attitude was Dick Edwards, the day-shift foreman. Edwards was always after everyone, but he seemed to go out of his way to harass George. In the months before the tree-spiking, Edwards would often stand on the cat-walk overlooking George's work station with L-P Western

Division head Joe Wheeler, just watching George work.

L-P has never been known to spend too much time maintaining equipment or worrying about worker safety. But in the weeks preceding the tree-spiking incident, conditions had gotten even worse than usual. Cracks had begun appearing in the band saw blade, and the blade was wobbling when it ran. But when George and other workers complained, foreman Dick Edwards shined them on, saying the new blades were not in yet, and they would have to make do. "That blade was getting so bad," said George, "that I almost didn't go to work that day."

Normally when a big tree is sawed, they start from the outside and square off the edges first. But the tree that George was sawing on May 8, 1987, was a 12-inch pecker pole, and because it was so small he took the first cut down the middle. Halfway through the 20-foot log, the saw hit a 60-penny nail. "That nail must have been recently placed and counter-sunk," George told me. He had checked the log when he started cutting it and had seen no sign of the metal. And, because the saw hit the nail square-on, there was also no warning sound. "Usually there's a high-pitched metal sound and you have time to get out of the way," explained George. "This time I didn't hear nothing but 'Boom!'"

The next thing he knew, George was lying on the floor covered with his own blood. "I knew I was dying. And all I could think about was Dick Edwards, and all the shit he gave me when I complained about the saw. I tried to get up but they pushed me back down. I tried to beckon to Edwards so he would come close enough for me to get my hands around his throat in a death grip. If I had to die, I wanted to take that bastard with me."

A 12-foot section of the huge sawblade had broken off and hit George in the throat and face, ripping through his face mask and cutting into his jugular vein. His jaw was broken in five places and a dozen teeth were knocked out. The blade was wrapped around him, and his co-workers had to blowtorch it off while they tried to keep him from bleeding to death. "The saw hit me flat," said George. "If it had hit me with the teeth I'd be dead. I'm only here because my friend Rick Phillips held my veins together in the hour before the ambulance came."

L-P didn't call the press right away, but when they did they had a field day. "Tree Spiking Terrorism," screamed the headline in the Press-Democrat, while the Eureka Times-Standard proclaimed, "Earth First! Blamed For Workers' Injuries." Mendocino County's Sheriff Shea put out a widely quoted press release that was almost gleeful in its condemnation. "This heinous and vicious criminal act is a felony offense, punishable by imprisonment in State Prison for up to three years," he wrote. "Still undetermined in the investigation is the motive of the suspect or suspects, to deter logging and milling operations or inflict great bodily injury and death upon lumber processing personnel." Even L-P President Harry Merlo got into the fray, blaming "terrorism in the name of environmental goals" for George's injury.

Meanwhile, George and Laurie Alexander had a different take on the incident. "I'm against tree-spiking," said George from his hospital bed, "but I don't like clear-cutting either." Laurie also tried to include L-P in the list of culprits. "I hate L-P," she told me. "I like trees." But the press wouldn't print a word that Laurie said, and George's comments about mill safety and clearcutting were mentioned in only one news article, by Eric Brazil of the *San Francisco Examiner.*

Earth First! was much less generous in its reaction, displaying practically no sympathy for this innocent man who had just been through such a terrifying ordeal caused by a spiked tree. And after advocating the tactic for years, even putting out a manual on how to do it, when the shit came down EF! tried to disassociate. "This is probably the first time we've made international news, and we weren't even involved in it," was EF! co-founder Mike Roselle's flippant statement to the press. "This raises the whole question of violence. Not just tree-spiking, the violence of cutting down ancient forests." Dave Foreman was even less concerned about George Alexander. "I think it's unfortunate that somebody got hurt, but you know I quite honestly am more concerned about old-growth forests, spotted owls and wolverines and salmon—and nobody is forcing people to cut those trees."

This moral arrogance didn't win Earth First! many supporters in our area. But did EF! spike that tree? The answer is probably no. Back in 1987 EF! was just getting started in Mendocino County, and the only issue at the time was old-growth. There was no consciousness yet about baby tree-logging, and the spiked tree was only 12-inches in diameter. There were also other signs that this may have been the work of a disturbed individual instead of an organized group. L-P traced the spiked tree to a cut on Cameron Ridge Road near Elk, where neighbors had been complaining about L-P liquidating the forest and threatening their water supply. One of the local residents was a strange man who drifted in and out of the area and mostly kept to himself. He was described by neighbors as a survivalist. Before the tree-spiking incident, loggers reported finding mutilated animals around the sight—a beheaded deer hanging from a tree, a skinned dog draped over a bulldozer—hardly Earth First! tactics, to say the least. But if this was the work of a lone crazy person, that still begs the question of where he even got the idea of spiking trees. The answer is probably Dave Foreman's book, *Eco-Defense*.

There is also reason to believe that the tree was not spiked at Cameron Road at all, but rather was hit while lying on a log deck after it was cut. The saw hit the spike about nine feet up the tree. If you figure a foot for the stump, that means it would have to have been spiked 10 feet off the ground. Bruce Anderson described the technique like this in the May 27, 1987 *Anderson Valley Advertiser*: "One average-sized person teams up with a midget. The midget gets up on the shoulders of his partner to hammer in the spikes. L-P can nail those pesky terrorists before they nail the trees by arresting any stray midgets they spot roaming around Mendocino County."

But it doesn't really matter whether an EF!er, a lone survivalist, or Harry Merlo himself spiked that tree. The point is that if you advocate a tactic, you had better be prepared to take responsibility for the results. And I don't want anything to do with causing the kind of injuries suffered by George Alexander. While George was convalescing from those injuries, he was contacted by someone from the yellow-ribbon gang of pro-timber stooges. George doesn't remember her name, just that it was "some woman from Humboldt County." She asked him to go on tour with her denouncing Earth First! for the tree-spiking. And George refused.

No matter what you think of L-P's forest practices, this much should be clear. George Alexander is not the enemy. He has no say over his bosses' policies, either in or out of the mill. I have heard EF!ers say that that doesn't matter, he shouldn't be working at an L-P mill. Well I shouldn't be driving a car either, but that doesn't make it okay to put a bomb in it.

After George refused to go on tour denouncing us, he was forced to return to work at L-P before his injuries were even healed. His and Laurie's baby was about to be born, he needed the money, and there are not many jobs in the Hopland where he and his family live. George got workers compensation for the time he was off work, but L-P didn't offer him a cent for the trauma and hardship he suffered. They made a big public show of putting up a $20,000 reward for information leading to the conviction of the spiker. But George Alexander had to file a private lawsuit against L-P to get anything at all. And while the company was crying crocodile tears over his injuries in public, in private they were fighting him tooth and nail over his damage claim. He ended up with just $9,000 and an involuntary transfer to night shift. "They used my name all over the country," George told me. "Then they laid me off when the mill closed down."

"L-P is just sorry I didn't die," said George Alexander. "Yeah, I know," I replied. "They're sorry I didn't die too."

The Secret History of Tree-Spiking—Part 2

AVA, March 8, 1993

Tree-spiking is a failed tactic by any standard. It has been practiced by Earth First! for 10 years now, and I think it's fair to say that the results are in. Here's Dave Foreman's description of tree-spiking from *Eco-Defense*:

> Tree-spiking is an extremely effective method of deterring timber sales, which seems to be becoming more and more popular. If enough trees are spiked in roadless areas, eventually the corporate thugs in the timber company boardrooms, along with their corrupt lackeys who wear the uniform of the Forest Service, will realize that timber sales in wild areas are going to be prohibitively expensive.

Believing this to be so seems to be an article of faith for some EF!ers. But a look at the actual history of Earth First! tree-spiking will show that it hasn't really worked out that way.

The most intensive spiking campaigns occurred in Oregon and Washington, although there have also been tree-spikings in California, Colorado, Montana, Idaho, New Mexico, Arizona, British Columbia, Southern Illinois, Kentucky, Maine and New Jersey, to name a few. And I'm not going to say that none of them saved any trees, because in a few cases they did, especially early on, or in areas without a timber-based economy. But the successes have been few and far between. Even unabashed EF! apologist Chris Manes, writing in his well-researched book *Green Rage*, could only come up with two timber sales that were canceled because they were spiked, one in the George Washington National Forest in Virginia, and one in the Wenatchee Forest's Icicle River drainage in Washington state. I don't know about the trees in Virginia, but the Icicle River sale has since been cut. EF! activists from Shawnee in Southern Illinois also report that when the hard-fought Fairview sale was finally clearcut, the only trees that were left were a few oaks that had been spiked.

But there have been scores and scores of tree-spikings, and in the vast majority of cases, the Forest Service or timber company just sent people in with metal detectors and, often with great public fanfare, removed the spikes and cut the trees. Sometimes spikes were missed, and sometimes they hit the blades in sawmills. But the timber industry has made it quite clear that this is a price they are willing to pay.

The first known tree-spiking in EF! history occurred in the Siskiyou Mountains of Oregon in 1983, on the Woodrat timber sale on BLM land. Notice was given of the spiking, and some of the trees were marked with yellow ribbons to make them easy to find and verify. The BLM reacted by having the loggers cut the trees and leave them on the ground for firewood cutters to saw at their own risk.

In 1984, a group calling itself the Hardesty Avengers mailed a letter to the Oregon Register-Guard announcing that a 132-acre sale on Hardesty Mountain in the Willamette National Forest had been spiked. The area was scheduled for helicopter logging by Columbia Helicopter. The Forest Service responded with a plan it called "Operation Nail," sending 20 Forest Service employees into the woods to remove the nails before they went ahead and cut the trees.

In 1985 in Southern Oregon, EF! was engaged in a high-profile direct action campaign to save Cathedral Forest in the Middle Santiam Wilderness. Demonstrators blockaded roads, staged the first tree-sits ever, and even occupied an area scheduled for blasting with dynamite, some of them actually sitting on the charges. In the midst of these actions, a few EF!ers took it on themselves to spike some of the trees at Pyramid Creek. And to read about it in Chris Manes' book, I can see where people get the false impression that tree-spiking is a drastic but effective last resort. "Despite continued opposition in the form of civil disobedience," writes Manes, "the road crept inexorably toward the sale. As a last ditch effort, (Mike) Roselle sneaked into the stand one night and spiked it. He sent a letter to the tim-ber company announcing the spiking, and signed it 'the Bonnie Abbzug Feminist Garden Party, a refer-ence to the voluptuous ecoteur in *The Monkey-wrench Gang*. The authorities caught neither the allusion nor the tree-spiker."

What Chris Manes doesn't tell us is that the spiking didn't work. It caused a spate of negative publicity, and it caused Mary Beth Nearing, one of EF!'s most inspirational organizers, to publicly dis-tance herself and the Cathedral Forest Action Group from the spiking and Earth First!. But it didn't save the trees. In fact, Mike Roselle himself, speaking in

Rik Scarce's book, *Eco Warriors*, admits that the spiking "barely slowed them down." The Forest Service sent rangers in to pull the nails, and the trees were cut.

Other areas in Oregon that were spiked and cut include the Hobson and the Deer Creek sales in the North Kalmiopsis, the Top and Skook sales in Hell's Canyon National Forest, Bull Run in the Mt. Hood area near Portland, and a Boise-Cascade sale in the Wallowa-Whitman National Forest. At this last site some of the spikes were missed by the loggers and made it into the mill, breaking teeth off of six saw-blades. The saw teeth shot across the mill like bullets, injuring no one but terrifying and angering the millworkers.

In fact, the main effect that tree-spiking seemed to be having in Oregon was to piss people off. In June 1987, EF! was protesting the Lazy Bluff timber sale in the North Kalmiopsis roadless area. Tree-sitter Randy Prince was perched 80 feet up in an old-growth fir when a logger cutting in an adjacent area hit an 11-inch spike and damaged his chainsaw. The logger stormed over to Randy's tree, revved up a saw, and, screaming something about tree-spiking, began cutting down the tree with Randy in it. He cut out a notch 1/3 of the way through the tree before he was talked into stopping. Shaken, Randy denounced tree-spiking and publicly distanced himself from Earth First! And the Lazy Bluff timber sale was cut.

By this time it was becoming clear that something was going wrong with the tree-spiking strategy. It seemed that all this publicity was backfiring, putting the timber industry in a position of having to cut the trees or lose face. So when Holcomb Peak in the Siskiyou Mountains was extensively spiked in June 1987 the spikers tried to correct past mistakes and do it "right." No notification was sent to the press. Instead, the BLM, the logging contractor, and the millowner were quietly notified, in order to give them an opportunity to quietly back out and cancel the sale. No luck. Instead, they called the press and made the incident into a media circus, with BLM rangers posing for photos in the woods with tree spikes, and the timber industry rallying to raise a $13,000 reward for information leading to the arrest of the spikers. And the trees were cut.

The ultimate media manipulation in the tree-spike wars, however, came in 1988 when Senator Mark Hatfield and Congressman Bob Smith (known to jaded Oregonians as the Representatives from Timber) were on a tour of the Gregory Forest Products sawmill near Glendale, Oregon. In an amazing display of synchronicity, at the very minute when the congressional delegation was watching the operation of a band saw, that very band saw just happened to hit a spike and explode. The delegation had just been shown spikes found in logs from the Silver Fire in the North Kalmiopsis. None of the dignitaries was hurt by the flying sawblade, but they were predictably impressed. "Tree-spiking is a radical environmentalist's version of razor blades in halloween candy," was Congressman Bob Smith's comment.

Meanwhile, some of the Oregon EF! activists were getting tired of answering for this ineffective and marginalizing tactic. "Personally I don't think it works," EF!er Steve Marsden told the *Seattle Times* when asked about tree-spiking in June 1988. Fellow

EF!er Bobcat expressed the same frustration, complaining that it makes them have to talk about "tree-spiking pro or con instead of old growth pro or con." But pressure was great within Earth First! to refrain from criticizing a tactic that others still engaged in. And tree-spiking was certainly going on outside of Oregon.

Spiking in Washington state was just as extensive as Oregon, and its results no better. Starting with the temporarily successful Icicle River spiking in 1986, sale after sale was spiked and cut, including the Lake Creek and Naches areas of the Wenatchee National Forest, Green Mountain and Granite Falls in Mt. Baker-Snoqualmie, and Storm King Mountain and Karamip in the Colville National Forest. The only spiked sales that I could verify as "probably still standing" are the Spoon sale and Olston Quirkendale in Mt. Baker-Snoqualmie, and they were set aside in the spotted owl ruling, not due to the spiking. In 1989 the Sugar Bear sale was spiked in the Cedar River area near Seattle. Although the cut in the watershed was eventually halved due to a public campaign by EF! and others, the spiked area was cut.

Spiking was not saving many trees in Washington, but it was certainly raising the ire of the timber industry. Band saw blades were broken by tree spikes in four different Washington sawmills between 1987 and 1989, resulting in the standard cries of "terrorism." Finally in September 1989, the timber industry and corporate press mounted an all-out assault on Washington Earth First! A four-part series was printed in the Bellingham Herald listing acts of sabotage in the area, quotes from *Eco-Defense*, and the names, addresses, places of employment and photos of key Earth First!ers. No proof was given to show that these public EF!ers were actually responsible for any of the sabotage listed, but the atmosphere was so hostile that no proof was needed. The Earth First!ers had to leave town for their own safety.

The classic example of tree-spiking, regularly cited by EF!ers as proof that the tactic works, occurred on Meare's Island in British Columbia in 1985, where the Society to Protect Intact Kinetic Ecosystems (SPIKE) drove 26,000 helix nails into old growth cedar trees. What the tree-spike advocates don't tell you is that there was a whole campaign going on over Meare's Island, and the spiking was only part of it. The issue on Meare's Island is native land rights, as the Claquet people who lived there have never ceded the land or signed any treaties. When the Canadian government attempted to sell timber rights on the island to MacMillan Bloedell, a coalition of natives and whites fought back with a lawsuit and a five-month occupation. When MacMillan Bloedell tried to come in and cut before the court could grant a restraining order, hundreds of people massed on the beach to prevent their helicopters from landing. The court finally halted the logging until the final ruling. That ruling is expected soon, and the Canadian government has stated that if M-B wins in court they will take the timber, spikes or no spikes.

Closer to home, California has had far fewer spikings than our northern neighbors, with many of them occurring in 1987, the same year George Alexander was hurt by the spike at the Cloverdale L-P mill. Just one month after that accident in

TIMBER WARS

Mendocino County, Trout Creek was spiked in a last-ditch attempt to save it from being cut by its owner, Pacific Gas & Electric. Friends of Trout Creek had been negotiating for a compromise, but when the spikes were discovered PG&E angrily broke off negotiations. Things looked bad until EF!er Sequoia came up with a plan. She organized a protest in which people were asked to withhold $1 from their PG&E bill and mail in a green card to show public support for saving Trout Creek. PG&E received so many green cards that it backed down and agreed to save the whole grove with no compromise.

There were also a few tree-spikings in California's National Forests. A minor uproar occurred in June 1987 right after the Trout Creek spiking when it was discovered that a spiked sale in Mendocino National Forest had been cut anyway and sent on to the mill, despite injuries to George Alexander one month earlier. A 202-acre sale in Tahoe National Forest was spiked and cut, as was a 240-acre sale at Running Springs in the San Bernardino National Forest, sold to L-P at Inyokern. One of the strangest tree-spiking incidents in California was again on L-P land, this time near Guerneville in Sonoma County. The newspapers received a notice that the Sonoma County Coalition to Stop L-P had spiked trees at the Silver Estate. No spikes were found, but nonetheless L-P said it had a suspect. He was described as "a black man with a bone through his nose who rides a bicycle and carries bows and arrows," obviously a better example of L-P's racism than its investigative capacities.

As tree-spiking continued across the US, the government increasingly tried to crack down on it.

Although no spiker has ever been caught, laws were passed to make spiking a felony in California, Washington, Oregon, Idaho and Montana. In 1989 the federal government passed its own laws, and that brought the FBI into the picture. When the Post Office timber sale in Clearwater Forest, Idaho, was spiked, the FBI responded by rounding up University of Montana professor Ron Erikson and several of his Earth First! students. They were forced to give hair samples and fingerprints, write "Stumps Suck" 25 times, and submit to a federal grand jury investigation. No evidence was found to link them to the spiking, and no charges were brought. But this intimidation served to separate Missoula EF! from its support in academia. And the trees were cut.

With this kind of history, you have to wonder why some EF!ers cling so tenaciously to the myth that tree-spiking works. One of the explanations commonly given is that, regardless of whether it saves individual trees, spiking is an economic constraint on the industry. "The idea could have come straight from the Chicago Business School," says Chris Manes in *Green Rage.* "If the cost of removing spikes is high enough, the cut will not be made, or at least the decreased profit margin will discourage logging in [controversial] areas." With this logic, Chris Manes would have flunked Econ 101. There are several flaws in this theory. The strategy of tree-spiking was designed for federal lands, where most remaining old growth in the US is located. In these cases it is the Forest Service, not the timber company, which bears the cost, both of removing the spikes and of charging lower rates for the timber to make up for the risk of broken saws. The Forest Service is not required to make a profit, since it is financed by tax money, and one of the scandals of the looting of our national forests is that the Forest Service subsidizes big timber by paying for log road construction and selling timber below cost. Between 1982 and 1987, the Forest Service received $800 million a year in federal timber sales, but spent $1.2 billion a year making the timber ready for sale. That's a loss of $400 million a year. There aren't enough tree spikes in the world to make a dent in this agency.

And even in the case of tree-spiking on private lands, this economic theory assumes that the price of lumber is fixed, so that any increase in production costs will result in a decrease in profits. But old-growth timber is so valuable, and there is so little of it left, that the timber industry could charge anything it wanted and still sell every stick. Any increase in production costs due to tree-spiking would simply be passed on to the consumers.

Nor are the timber companies put off by the threat of injury to employees, as we have already seen in real life. Dave Foreman tells us in *EcoDefense* that tree-spiking is "unlikely to cause anyone physical injury even should a blade shatter upon striking a spike, which is an unlikely event." But Foreman also admitted to the Christian Science Monitor in 1987 that he had never seen the inside of a sawmill. And it is clear that he doesn't understand the depths of depravity of the timber companies. The routine maiming and killing of timber workers is coldly calculated into the cost of the lumber, and a few more injuries are not going to stop them. L-P made this clear after George Alexander was hurt.... "L-P will not let tree-spiking be a deterrent," said spokeswoman Glennis Simmons. And she meant it. L-P kept running the logs from that same spiked sale through the mill, even though workers encountered two more spikes and broke another saw blade. Other timber companies were just as emphatic. After the Buse Company in Everett, Washington broke four saw blades on tree spikes in 1987, manager Ron Smith commented: "I assume they think if they do things like this the timber industry will get discouraged and will just quit cutting trees. But I don't thing that's going to happen."

And it hasn't happened. Yet just because Dave Foreman told us 10 years ago that it would, most of EF! continues to ignore reality, no matter how much experience we have. The forests that EF! had been instrumental in saving in this area (Trout Creek, Cahto Wilderness, Headwaters Forest, Albion and Owl Creek) have all been saved through blockades and public organizing campaigns, often combined with lawsuits. And it's time we faced the truth about tree-spiking. It is unquestionably dangerous to workers. It needlessly endangers EF! activists on the front lines. And it doesn't save trees.

Ironically, most of the early advocates of tree-spiking—including Dave Foreman—have left EF! for safer harbors after suppressing debate by treating any questioning of their tactics as heresy. And, although most of them have refused to make any public statements about it, the EF! groups that most strongly advocated tree-spiking in the early days have quietly abandoned the tactic. Yet the myth lives on.

Last month in Maine, a letter was sent to the local press stating that the trees at Mt. Blue had been spiked by EF! I don't know if the letter was real or fake, but a group of EF!ers blockading Mt. Blue were subsequently arrested, dragged though hot coals from their campfire, and roughed up in jail. And I wondered if a new generation of activists is going to repeat the mistakes of the last 10 years. Those of use who are out on the front lines putting our bodies in front of the bulldozers and chainsaws can't afford to be isolated and discredited by something as ineffective and incendiary as tree-spiking. If we are serious about putting the Earth first, we need to choose tactics because they work, not because they are macho or romantic. That's what no compromise really means.

Monkeywrenching

EF! Journal,
Feb-March 1994

Retreating into the hills after their impressive takeover of four towns in southern Mexico, the Zapatista army of National Liberation dropped two power lines and called on their supporters to engage in other acts of sabotage.

Unlike Earth First!, the Zapatista Army does not publish a "Zapatista Journal". complete with tips on how take down power lines, and listing the names, addresses, and phone numbers of the activists in a "Zapatista Directory." Unlike Earth First!, they understand the difference between above ground and below ground activities, and they understand that the survival of the movement requires separating the two.

Earth First! has treated monkeywrenching like a boy scout panty raid. Our failure to recognize the seriousness of this tactic has helped to endanger public Earth First!ers, isolate and discredit our movement, and drive away some of our best activists. Yet there are still people in Earth First! who think that if you won't publicly advocate monkeywrenching you are not a "real" Earth First!er. That the choice is between monkeywrenching and becoming, as Sea Shepherd captain Paul Watson called us, "a society of banner hangers."

I think these attitudes stem from a failure to analyze and understand our tactics. Earth First! stands for biocentrism, no compromise, and direct action. Direct action does not just mean theatrical demonstrations. It means action at the point of production, designed to stop or slow production. This is in contrast to indirect action, such as elections and lobbying. In a society where money is power and elections are just a facade to maintain corporate control, direct action at the point of production is one of the most effective places we can work. That's one of the reasons Earth First! has had power and influence beyond our numbers.

Civil disobedience and sabotage are both examples of direct action at the point of production. Both temporarily stop production. Both are principled and courageous. Both have been effective. And neither can work in the long run without public support.

People who put their bodies in front of the bulldozer are depending on prevailing moral standards and the threat of public outrage to protect them from attack. Unfortunately, prevailing public opinion in this country, at least in the timber region, is that if sabotage is involved, they have a license to kill. Until that changes, mixing civil disobedience and monkeywrenching is suicidal.

Similarly, people who put sand in gas tanks are depending on their anonymity to protect them from arrest or attack. They sure don't need the public spotlight that comes with a civil disobedience campaign. They also don't need the access provided for FBI infiltrators when they associate with a public group like Earth First!

None of this is theoretical. We have 12 years of experience to back it up. How many more of us to be bombed, jailed, run out of town, or scared away before we figure this shit out?

England Earth First! has been taking some necessary steps to separate above ground and clandestine activities. Earth First!, the public group, has a nonviolence code and does civil disobedience blockades. Monkeywrenching is done by Earth Liberation Front (ELF). Although Earth First!ers may sympathize with the activities of elf, they do not engage in them.

If we are serious about our movement in the U.S., we will do the same. Despite the romantic notions of some over-imaginative Ed Abbey fans, Earth First! is in reality an above ground group. We have above ground publications, public events, and a yearly national Rendezvous with open attendance.

Civil disobedience and sabotage are both powerful tactics in our movement. For the survival of both, it's time to leave the night work to the elves in the woods.

The Earth First!
Car Bombing

Earth First Journal,
February 1994

Part I
The Set-Up

I knew it was a bomb the second it exploded. I felt it rip through me with a force more powerful and terrible than anything I could imagine. It blew right through my car seat, shattering my pelvis, crushing my lower backbone, and leaving me instantly paralyzed. I couldn't feel my legs, but desperate pain filled my body. I didn't know such pain existed. I could feel the life force draining from me, and I knew I was dying. I tried to think of my children's faces to find a reason to stay alive, but the pain was too great, and I couldn't picture them. I wanted to die. I begged the paramedics to put me out.

I woke up in the hospital 12 hours later, groggy and confused from shock and morphine. My leg was in traction, tubes trailed from my body, and I was absolutely immobile. As my eyes gradually focused, I made out two figures standing over me. They were cops. Slowly I began to understand that they were trying to question me. "You are under arrest for possession of explosives," one of them said. And even in this devastated condition, my survival instincts kicked in. "I won't talk to you without a lawyer," I mumbled, and drifted back into unconsciousness.

Now, three and a half years later, even the FBI has given up saying that Darryl Cherney and I bombed ourselves. They slandered us all over the national press, declaring us guilty of transporting the bomb that was used to try to kill us. But in the end, they were unable to produce any evidence against us, and the district attorney refused to press charges. Still, no serious investigation of the bombing was ever conducted, and the bomber remains at large.

In the wake of this outrageous treatment, Darryl and I filed a lawsuit against the FBI and Oakland Police, charging them with false arrest and other civil rights violations. Last month, in a strongly worded 3-0 decision, the U.S. Court of Appeals turned down the FBI's third and last attempt to get the case thrown out of court. We are now headed for trial, and through the court procedures we have gotten access to police photos, reports, and depositions, and gained the release of 5,000 pages of FBI files on the case. As we peel back the layers of lies and deception surrounding this case, we can begin to reconstruct what really happened. I have had plenty of time now to ponder the magnitude and horror of this attack. And I think it' important for all Earth First! activists to know the story.

COINTELPRO

The events surrounding the 1990 bombing can only be explained in the context of COINTELPRO, J. Edgar Hoover's Counterintelligence Program to, in his words, "disrupt, misdirect, isolate and neutralize" radical groups in the U.S. The techniques of COINTELPRO include infiltration, surveillance, agent provocateurs, disinformation campaigns, fake documents, and framing or assassinating political leaders.

The FBI operation against Earth First! in Arizona was a classic example of COINTELPRO tactics (see Mark Davis's articles in the last two *EF! Journals*). Agent provocateurs infiltrated the group and misdirected them into doing an action they would not have done on their own, then busted them for it. The FBI also attempted to frame Dave Foreman, and certainly succeeded at neutralizing him as a spokesman and inspirational figure in Earth First!

The man in charge of my case at the FBI was Richard Held, director of the San Francisco FBI office. Held has a 25-year history as one of the principle operatives of COINTELPRO. He is known for producing fake documents, including death threats and insulting letters and cartoons, and sending them back and forth between different factions of the Black Panther Party in order to terrorize or enrage the leaders and destabalize the group. Held was personally involved in the framing of Black Panther Geronimo jiJaga (Pratt) and American Indian Movement leader Leonard Peltier, both of whom have been in jail for decades for crimes they did not commit. I cannot describe the cold terror of waking up in the hospital, crippled for life, and finding out that Richard Held was accusing me of blowing myself up with my own bomb.

COINTELPRO was publicly exposed in 1971 when Black Panther sympathizers, tired of seeing activists murdered and movements destroyed, broke into the FBI office in Media, Pennsylvania, and liberated the files. In 1975, the Senate Judiciary committee conducted a congressional Investigation and find the FBI's COINTELPRO activities to be illegal, involving massive violations of constitutional rights.

The FBI claims to have discontinued COINTELPRO after this exposure. Yet in the bombing case I find not only the resurgence of COINTELPRO, but also the privatization of COINTELPRO. Not just the FBI, but now the private corporations as well, are using the same counter-intelligence tactics that were declared illegal in the 1970's to try to discredit and destroy Earth First! in the 1990's.

The Uzi Photo

The effort to disrupt Ukiah Earth First! and paint me as a terrorist began in November of 1988, one and a half years before the bombing. At that time, a man named Irv Sutley came to Ukiah to attend an abortion clinic defense that I had organized with Ukiah EF! and other local groups. We were truly outrageous at that demo, singing our newly written song, "Will the Fetus Be Aborted" to the Operation Rescue thugs.

I knew Irv, although not well, from my earlier work in the Central America movement in Sonoma County. Irv was traveling with a good friend of mine, and after the demonstration we all went back to Darryl's house. We talked about our recent successful blockade of Cahto Wilderness, in which I had been arrested for vehicular trespass. We smoked dope and fantasized about imaginary actions, including creating an oil spill in our pro-oil congressman Doug Bosco's back yard swimming pool.

After a while, Irv opened the trunk of his car and showed us that he was carrying a modified Uzi submachine gun, which he told us was legal. We took turns posing for photos with the gun, laughing and trying to look tough. Irv placed the gun in my hands, showed me how to hold it, and arranged it so my Earth First! shirt was clearly visible.

About a month later, unknown to me at the time, the Ukiah Police received a copy of the photo of me holding the Uzi, along with a letter from an anonymous informant. The letter combined half-truths and outright lies to make me look like a terrorist. It read:

> I joined Earth First to be able to report illegal activities of that organization. Now I want to establish a contact to provide information to authorities. The leader and main force of earth First in Ukiah is Judi Bari. She is facing a trespassing charge in connection with the Earth First sabotage of a logging road in the Cahto Peak area. She did jail time in Sonoma County for blocking the federal building to support the Communist government in Nicaragua. Bari and the Ukiah Earth First are planning vandalism directed at congressman Doug Bosco to protest offshore oil drilling. Earth First recently began automatic weapons training...

The letter went on to offer to set me up for a marijuana bust. The police were instructed to take out a coded ad in the local newspaper if they were interested. We checked the archives of the local paper years later when we were investigating all this, and sure enough, we found that the police had indeed taken out the ad. Around that time, Irv Sutley called me up and asked me to sell him some marijuana. But, while I may have been stupid enough to pose for joke photos with an Uzi, I was not stupid enough to sell marijuana. I refused to get him the dope, and I was not busted.

The Uzi photo did not go to waste, though. Shortly after the bombing, the Ukiah Police released it to the press, and it was printed in all the large mainstream newspapers as "proof" that I was a terrorist.

Timber Industry Violence

During the years leading up to the bombing, Earth First! in Northern California had grown steadily in both size and prestige. We were everywhere, blocking log trucks, sitting in trees, protesting at the mills, or taking over the Board of Forestry dressed as animals. We saved Cahto Wilderness. We saved Trout Creek. By 1989, during EF! National Tree-Sit Week, we were able to pull off six strong actions in one week in the Redwood Region, with local watershed groups providing support, and EF!ers showing up to block logging in a new location each day.

Meanwhile, side by side with the Earth First! work, we were building alliances with progressive timber workers to oppose the corporations. We formed IWW Local #1, affiliated with the radical Wobblies union, and started signing up timber workers and representing them in workplace issues. We publicly denounced the timber corporations, not only for their treatment of the forest, but also for their treatment of their employees. We were getting

291

too popular, and the timber industry had to put a stop to it.

Increasingly, violence was being used as a means to repress us on the front lines. We were punched, shot at, and run off the road with log trucks, while the local police turned their heads and refused to intervene, arrest, or prosecute our attackers. The timber industry thought this was hilarious. When EF!er Greg King was knocked to the ground by a chainsaw-wielding logger at a demonstration in June of 1989, Maxxam executive Dave Galitz sent the following memo to CEO Charles Hurwitz: "Enclosed is an article on Cherney and King's latest stunt. As soon as we find the home of the fine fellow who decked Greg King, he has a dinner invitation at the Galitz residence."

The problem for big timber was to be able to continue the attacks on us without gaining public sympathy for Earth First! This was done, with the help of the highly cooperative press and local police, by creating the myth that both sides were violent. For example, in August 1989, my car was rammed from behind, at 45 mph by a log truck that we had blockaded less than 24 hours earlier. My car was totaled, sending three of us EF! activists and four of our children to the hospital with minor injuries. The police refused to investigate it as anything but a traffic accident, and the press refused to print the proven fact that the truck driver was the same one we had just blockaded.

Finally, months later, we were able to get this charge included in an article called "Logging Protesters claim Pattern of Violence," buried on page B-3 of the *Santa Rosa Press Democrat*. Two days later, front page metro headlines screamed, "Slashed Tire Leads to Attempted Murder Probe." A log truck had gone off the road when it blew a tire, and the owner claimed that the inside of the tire had been slashed. In contrast to the incident where I was rammed by the log truck, the sheriff decided to treat this case as an attempted murder, with EF! saboteurs as the implied suspects. The investigation of course went nowhere, but the headline certainly served its purpose.

Fake Documents and Disinformation

But by the spring of 1990, it was getting harder and harder to discredit us. We had put out a national appeal for people to come to Redwood Summer, calling for nonviolent demonstrations in response to timber's repeated violence. The Student Environmental Action Coalition (SEAC) had publicized our Redwood Summer appeal to students all over the country, and we had formed a coalition with Seeds of Peace and other peace activists to handle base camp logistics and nonviolence trainings. It was becoming clear that we had both the support and the infrastructure to actually pull off our grandiose plans, and big timber was getting nervous.

To make matters even worse for them, in early April we publicly renounced tree spiking as being dangerous to loggers and millworkers, who, we stated, are not to blame for the corporations' logging practices. "Their livelihood is being destroyed along with the forest," said our written proclamation. "The real conflict is not between us and the timber workers, it is between the timber corporations and the entire community."

Meanwhile, L-P closed yet another mill in Mendo County and laid off another 200 workers, the same day they announced record profits for the quarter. We responded by appearing at the county Board of Supervisors meeting for the first time in public with our timber worker coalition. Only a few loggers and mill-workers had the nerve to actually show up with the EF!ers, but our demands were so radical that we had an immediate impact. We demanded that the Board of Supervisors use their power of eminent domain to seize all of L-P's corporate holdings and operate them in the public interest, as the only way to save both the trees and the jobs.

Shortly after this meeting, things started to get crazy. Fake press releases containing the Earth First! logo but definitely not written by us, appeared in our community, distributed by the big timber companies. "We are in a 'war' with the north coast timber companies," read one of them. "We intend to spike trees, monkeywrench, and even resort to violence if necessary." Another, called "Some Thoughts on Strategy," rambled on incoherently about sabotage, randomness and invisibility. It was easy to prove this one was a fake, because they misspelled Darryl's name, and got my home town wrong.

These false documents were widely distributed to timber workers and to the local press, who treated them as genuine despite their inaccuracies and our repeated denials. Louisiana Pacific distributed the fakes to millworkers at a mandatory meeting held on the clock at their Somoa pulp mill. At that meeting, according to a grievance filed by Pulp and

The Earth First! Car Bombing

Paper Workers Union Local 49, plant manager Fred Martin encouraged employees to intimidate environmentalists by going to meetings and sitting down next to us "with rolled up sleeves, wearing work boots and hard hats."

Maxxam also distributed at least one of these false press releases to out-of-town newspapers after they had privately acknowledged that it was a fake. In an internal company memo dated April 18, 1990, executive Dave Galitz wrote, "Enclosed is a flyer with the Earth First! logo, however, as Darryl's name is misspelled, we are not sure who put it out." One week later, on April 25, columnist Robert Morse wrote in the *San Francisco Examiner* that he had just received this obviously false press release in the mail from Maxxam. "Things are getting pretty weird up there," wrote Morse. "Not only are trees being clearcut, but dirty tricksters are turning them into fake press releases."

But for all his city sophistication, Morse was right on the bandwagon with the others when I got bombed one month later. He wrote a column ridiculing our claim of nonviolence and supporting the judge's imposition of a $100,000 bail, without realizing that he was being influenced by the very disinformation campaign he had just exposed.

Another fake document making the rounds right before the bombing was a phony "Earth First! Terrorism Manual," distributed by the anti-environmental hate group, Sahara Club. In their April 1990 newsletter, they printed a diagram of how to make a bomb, claiming it was from an Earth First! manual. Of course this was false, but by saying it was from Earth First! the Sahara Club managed to simultaneously distribute information about how to make bombs, while inciting hatred against us and associating us with explosives in people's minds.

Through this disinformation campaign, the timber industry was doing their best to erode our credibility. But it's not as if we didn't help them along with some of our own mistakes. The worst of these was in March, 1990, when Darryl went on *60 Minutes* and told 10 million viewers, "If I had a fatal disease, I would definitely strap a body bomb to myself and blow up the Glen Canyon Dam, or the Maxxam building at night after everyone had gone home." Darryl, who has never even pulled a survey stake or lit a fire cracker, would never really do anything like that. He just wanted to get on TV. But that's why COINTELPRO works so well. They don't just make up what they say about you. They take your real weaknesses—in EF!'s case a tendency to brag about and exaggerate monkeywrenching—and turn it into something that will destroy you—in our case, an image of EF! as a domestic terrorist group.

Death Threats and Destabalization

Along with the disinformation campaign that preceded the bombing, there was also a destabalization campaign, designed to terrorize us and distract us from the organizing work that needed to be done. The most obvious form of this was the death threats we received starting in April of 1990. There were dozens of them, but the scariest by far was the infamous photo of me with a rifle scope and cross hairs drawn over my face. The photo was taken from a newspaper story about our Eminent Domain meeting with the Board of Supes, and I got the message loud and clear.

Unlike the violence on the front lines, I never believed the death threats were coming from unconnected individuals. For one thing, they all came around the same time, and I have never received written death threats before or since. Also, they were too good, often including artistic touches like hand drawn logger boots or a hangman's noose. But there is other evidence that at least one of these threats was written by a professional.

"Judi Bari, get out and go back where you came from," read the threat. "We know everything. You won't get a second warning." It was typed on a manual typewriter, and when we compared it to the informant letter that had been sent to the Ukiah Police along with the photo of me with Irv Sutley's Uzi one and a half years earlier, we discovered that they matched. The style of the typewriter, the irregularities of the individual letters, and the format in which the addresses were typed all looked the same, even when we enlarged the type on a document analysis machine.

The fact that one of the death threats matched a letter written by a police informant who had been conducting surveillance on me for a year and a half is not proof in itself that the FBI was involved in the death threat campaign. But matching letters are certainly a reason to investigate, and the FBI's refusal to do so makes me even more suspicious of them. We publicly handed the two matching letters to the FBI and declared that Irv Sutley was our prime suspect for the author, since he owned the Uzi, had easy access to the photo, and had personal knowledge of all the info in the letter. The FBI assured us they would investigate, but in my entire 5,000 pages of FBI files, neither the matching documents nor Irv Sutley's name appears even once.

Not all of the threats were received in writing. Wise Use Movement activist Candy Boak, leader of the Maxxam front group Mother's Watch, was a specialist at another type of harassment. I remember her calling me on my home phone as soon as I got back from a Redwood Summer organizing meeting. She told me she had been watching us, and accurately described the people at the meeting and the cars we were driving. Then she said, "Me and my husband John are coming over to visit you this weekend. We know where you live, over there in Redwood Valley."

I tried to ignore the death threats, but it was getting hard to concentrate. I was scared for my children. I considered going underground. I took the written death threats to the county sheriff, but Lt. Satterwhite just told me, "We don't have the manpower to investigate. If you turn up dead, then we'll investigate." I went to the County Board of Supervisors and complained about this treatment by the sheriff's office. But Supervisor Marilyn Butcher responded, "You brought it on yourself, Judi."

Besides the death threats, there were other forms of destabalization. At one of our Redwood Summer planning meetings, for example, a man who was brand new to the group and unknown to any of us jumped up and got in my face when I suggested that we organize collective child care. "Hey, it's not my fault your old man ditched you and left you with the kids!", he shouted. I had to be physically restrained to keep from decking him. Later I realized I was being baited into a fight which would have discredited our call for nonviolence. People just don't say things like that in real life.

Weirdness was everywhere. On Earth Day 1990, an expert team of EF! tree climbers had been planning to climb the Golden Gate Bridge and hang a huge banner in protest of the corporate greenwash. The night before, to the climbers' surprise, three power lines were cut down in Santa Cruz. We all thought it was great at the time, and I, naively thinking I was safe because I was not involved, even told the press that the people who did it were heroes. But the communiqué taking credit for downing the power lines was signed Earth Night Action Group. Darryl had recently produced his famous Earth Night poster, and I realize now that whoever chose the name Earth Night Action Group for the Santa Cruz power lines action was either equally naive, or maybe a provocateur. Because, no matter what you think of the action itself, the use of that name implicated Darryl, a highly public EF! organizer, in a serious act of sabotage that he had nothing to do with.

When the EF!ers were arrested on the Golden Gate Bridge trying to hang the Earth Day banner, Darryl, who was committing no crime making press calls from a nearby phone, got caught up in the sweep. And strangely, even though the arrests took place on the Marin county side of the San Francisco bridge, the Oakland Police Intelligence Unit was on the scene, as well as the FBI. They impounded and searched Darryl's car without a warrant, and confiscated his belongings. Included in the items taken from Darryl was the pasted up master copy of the Earth Night poster. Yet no public statements were made about this find, and the police simply let Darryl go without questioning him about it.

This lack of comment on Darryl's link to the Earth Night poster was especially odd because the Golden Gate Bridge climb and the Santa Cruz power lines were blended together in the press coverage, in the FBI's internal files, and in the public's mind. Headlines like "Eco-Terrorists Cut Power" and "Earth First! Militants Storm Golden Gate Bridge" equated the two, and photos of the downed power lines accompanied stories about the banner hanging.

The worst of these "eco-terrorist scare" stories appeared in the *San Francisco Examiner* a few days after the bridge climb. It began with this fantasy. "The scenario: Terrorists, whether religious fanatics or political zealots, attack the Bay Area. They plant explosives on the transmission towers of key electric lines. They bomb telephone switching stations. They poison the water..." The article went on to talk about the Golden Gate Bridge climb, the Santa Cruz power lines, Earth First!, and Redwood Summer.

So while the real Earth First! in northern California was renouncing tree spiking, building coalitions with workers and peace activists, and responding to timber industry violence by calling for mass nonviolence, the public was being taught to associate us with bombs and terrorism. By the time the bomb went off in my car they were well primed to accept the FBI's incredible lie: Not only are EF!ers violent terrorists who carry bombs around in our cars, but we are stupid violent terrorists who hide live anti-personnel bombs under our own car seats.

Part II
Frame-Up and Cover-Up

Normally, a car bombing in Oakland would fall under the jurisdiction of the Department of Alcohol, Tobacco and Firearms, not the FBI. So it was uncanny how fast the FBI showed up when the bomb went off in my car. The first agent arrived literally within minutes, and soon 12-15 agents from the FBI Terrorist Squad were on the scene.

The FBI told the Oakland Police that they were going to "assist" in this case, and they quickly briefed Oakland on me, Darryl, and Earth First! "They said that these were the types of people who would be involved in carrying a bomb," said Oakland Police Sgt. Sitterud in his sworn deposition. "They told us that these people, in fact, qualified as terrorists." Ten minutes after he arrived on the scene, based on information he got from the FBI, Sgt. Sitterud made an entry in his police log describing Darryl and me as "apparent radical activists with recent arrest for illegal demonstration on Golden Gate Bridge," and "Earth First! leaders suspected of Santa Cruz power pole sabotage, linked with federal case of attempted destruction of nuclear power plant lines in Arizona."

Meanwhile, Special Agent Frank Doyle, 20-year veteran bomb expert with the (aptly named) FBI Terrorist Squad, had taken over examining my car. The damage was obvious. A hole was blown in the driver's seat—you could see right through to the street below—and the car frame was buckled directly under it. When they unbolted the front seat and removed it from the car, there was a 2'x4' blast hole

Darryl and I were arrested based on the FBI's claim that the bomb was located on the rear seat floorboard, and therefore we were knowingly carrying it. Yet this photo shows a clear epicenter directly under the driver's seat. (photo: Oakland Police)

302

Taken immediately after the bomb exploded, this photo shows the front seat blown right through and the back seat intact. (photo: Oakland Police)

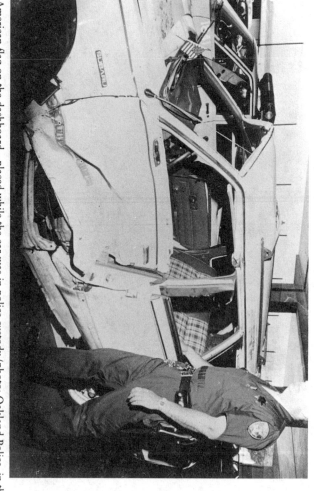

Notice the American flag on the dashboard—placed while the car was in police custody.(photo: Oakland Police, in the police lot.)

in the floor with the metal curled back from an obvious epicenter under the driver's seat (see police photos). Any honest observer would have concluded that a bomb had been hidden under my seat, and this was a case of attempted murder.

But Special Agent Doyle had other ideas. In defiance of all the evidence, he claimed that the bomb was located in clear view on the back seat floorboard, therefore Darryl and I knew we were carrying it, and that it was our bomb. That was all the Oakland Police needed to hear. The Oakland Police Department has a long history, dating back at least to the Black Panthers, of fronting for the FBI in COINTELPRO operations. So, with a wink and a nod, they ignored the evidence in front of their noses and went along with the FBI's lie. Three hours after the bombing, I was placed under arrest while still in surgery, charged with transporting the bomb that nearly took my life. Darryl was arrested 12 hours later.

The evening of the bombing, the FBI held a briefing meeting for the Oakland Police. They said that Earth First! was a domestic terrorist group who started a year ago downing power lines in Arizona, and were now on their way to California to do it again. They said Darryl and I were the prime suspects in the downing of the Santa Cruz power lines, and that I was also suspected in a recent pipe bombing in the Louisiana Pacific sawmill in Cloverdale, near where I lived. They also said that an undercover informant who was "close to the leadership of Earth First!" had told them that "the heavies from up north" were on their way to Santa Cruz for some kind of "action." And of course,

Photo 1 of 2 in a series. In this photo, the **FBI** has constructed a mockup of the bomb and placed it in an intact Subaru in the position where they claim it was in the arrest warrant—clearly visible on the back seat floorboard. (photo: Oakland Police.)

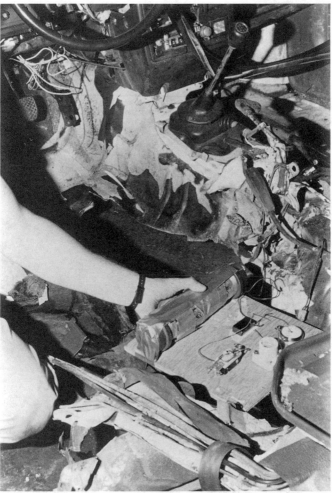

Photo 2 of 2. In this photo, FBI bomb expert David R. Williams is holding the mockup bomb in the damaged car, in the same position as the previous photo, showing that the epicenter of the blast hole does not correspond to a bomb positioned on the back seat floorboard. This photo also reveals the FBI and police in the act of knowing that they lied about the bomb's placement. (photo: Oakland Police.)

Photo 1 of 2 in a series. In this photo, the FBI has constructed a mockup of the bomb and placed it in a position hidden under the driver's seat. (photo: Oakland Police.)

Photo 2 of 2. In this photo, FBI bomb expert David R. Williams is holding the mockup bomb in the damaged car, in the same position as the previous photo, showing that the epicenter of the blast hole corresponds to the bomb positioned under the driver's seat. This photo shows the FBI and police in the act of knowing that they lied about the bomb being positioned on the back seat floorboard. (photo: Oakland Police.)

Darryl and I were indeed on our way to Santa Cruz. But the "action" was a concert, not a bombing.

After the briefing, Oakland Police Sgt. Chenault wrote an affidavit for the search warrant on Darryl's and my houses. Chenault has testified that the FBI agents literally dictated while he typed. The affidavit says, "(I) viewed the white Subaru along with Agents from the FBI. (I) was advised by these agents that the bomb device was on the floorboard behind the driver's seat when it was detonated." "(I) believe that Bari and Cherney are members of a violent terrorist group involved in the manufacture and placing of explosive devices. (I) believe that Bari and Cherney were transporting an explosive device in their vehicle when it exploded."

Press Smear

The media had a field day with this news, as the FBI and Oakland Police provided them with the images they needed to make it look like they had busted up a ring of terrorists. They raided Seeds of Peace House without a warrant, turned the place upside down in a fruitless search, and led the occupants away in handcuffs, only to release them a few hours later, after the reporters and cameras had gone home. TV news that night included not only the raid, but an interview with a neighbor who said there were strange goings on in the house, with lights on at all hours. When Seeds of Peace responded that they were a nonviolent collective who cooks food for mass nonviolent actions, the neighbor replied, "I don't know what they're cooking over there. It doesn't smell like food. Maybe PCP."

Another image shown over and over on the TV

news was the search of Darryl's van. Of course the police found nothing, but they sure put on a good show. They picked out a "suspicious" box of tapes of Darryl's incendiary music, cordoned off the block, and blew it up in front of the TV cameras, supposedly to see if it contained a bomb. "No additional explosives were found," reported the TV, as if explosives had been found in the first place.

The standard bail for the charge against us— transporting explosives—was only $12,000. Not only was this too easy to raise, but it was clearly not enough for the dangerous criminals they made us out to be. So, circumventing the normal procedures, the Oakland Police went straight to the judge, without even a lawyer there to represent us. Darryl and I were both declared a flight risk and a danger to the public, even though I was unconscious in the hospital with my leg in traction and my pelvis broken in 10 places. Our bail was raised to $100,000 each, spawning a new round of headlines and giving credence to the charge of terrorism.

The news quickly went national, with newspapers across the country screaming about Earth First!ers carrying bombs. It was the only time we ever made the front page of the *New York Times*. The press ate up the police lies with a big spoon, instantly convicting us in their stories. "Two members of the radical environmental group Earth First! were injured Thursday by their own pipe bomb," began the lead article in the *San Jose Mercury News*. "Earth First! leaders hurt in a pipe bomb explosion have no one but themselves to blame for their injuries," smirked the blow-dried talking heads on the TV news.

311

This really hurt Earth First!'s image on a national scale. Even today, particularly in places where there is no active EF! movement, bombs and tree spikes are the only things many people know about us.

The Lord's Avenger

Despite the image they were able to project in the press, the FBI must have known they would have a hard time pinning anything on us. The searches of our houses turned up no explosives, no weapons, and no incriminating items. And, as the FBI knew perfectly well, the damage to my car proved that the bomb had been hidden from our sight, discrediting their claim that we were knowingly carrying it.

Also, the Earth First!ers were just not acting like terrorists. Rather than hiding out, 200 of them gathered in the lobby of the FBI building, singing, chanting, hugging and crying, and refusing to leave until Darryl was released from jail. Karen Pickett, Pam Davis, Kelpie Wilson and others came across as strong and credible spokespeople, citing our commitment to nonviolence, holding up the death threats for the cameras, and calling for a nonviolent response to the act of terror that had been done to us. These views were getting some press attention, and if we managed to convince the public of our innocence, the FBI would need a good back-up story. Because if we didn't bomb ourselves, there were only two obvious suspects—timber and FBI.

One week after the bombing, a strange anonymous letter arrived at the *Press Democrat*, addressed to top timber reporter Mike Geniella. "I built with these hands the bomb that I placed in the car of Judi Bari," it began. "Doubt me not, for I will tell you the design and materials such as only I will know." In flowery, biblical language, the letter went on to describe my participation in the Ukiah abortion clinic defense several years earlier ("I saw Satan's flames shoot forth from her mouth, her eyes and ears..."), and cite my pro-abortion stance, as well as my "paganism" and defense of the forest, as reasons to kill me. The letter writer then described in exact detail not only the bomb in my car, but also the bomb at the Cloverdale sawmill, that the FBI had already tried to pin on me, taking credit for both. The letter was signed "The Lord's Avenger."

The Lord's Avenger letter was chilling, and at the time, it even fooled me. But in retrospect, its authenticity is not so clear. For one thing, the letter gave false information about the bombing, that led us off the trail. The Lord's Avenger claimed he put the bomb in my car while I was in a meeting in Willits, up in the timber region, two days before the bomb went off. But the bomb in my car had a 12-hour timer, so it couldn't have been placed anywhere but Oakland, where I stayed the night before it exploded. And, while it is true that the Lord's Avenger's detailed bomb descriptions were mostly accurate, I now realize that there were two sources who knew this information—the bomber himself, and the FBI.

The Lord's Avenger letter had several effects. It provided a plausible lone assassin not connected to timber or the FBI. It threw a veil of confusion over the motives for the bombing. And it removed the investigation from Oakland, where the bomb was actually placed, to Mendocino County, where there are many crazy people to use as suspects. And, masterfully, the FBI managed to simultaneously promote the letter as a key piece of evidence, while continuing their claim that Darryl and I bombed ourselves. Since we were the bombers, they reasoned, the Lord's Avenger must be our accomplice. So, with great fanfare, they raided my house a second time, this time looking for "typewriter exemplars" to match the Lord's Avenger letter, and never mentioning that nothing they found even vaguely matched.

No Evidence, No Charges

Not only did the FBI and Oakland Police say we were suspects in the bombing, they said we were the only suspects. Therefore they did not even attempt to investigate the death threats, fake press releases, or any other evidence of timber industry violence. Their entire investigation for the first eight weeks consisted of sending the bomb in my car, the Cloverdale bomb, and the Lord's Avenger letter to the FBI crime lab for analysis. They also sent in 111 items seized from our houses, including tools, solder, nails, glue, etc., to try and match them to the bomb.

But when the lab analysis came back, the FBI had a problem. The solder, tape, glue, etc. from the Cloverdale bomb and the bomb in my car matched exactly, and the two bombs matched the Lord's Avenger's description. But the solder, tape, glue, etc., seized from our houses did not match the bombs. Further, the lab determined that the bomb was an anti-personnel bomb, wrapped with nails for

The Earth First! Car Bombing

shrapnel effect. And they determined that, in addition to the 12-hour timer (which was used as a delay mechanism), the bomb also included a motion device, consisting of a ball-bearing that had to roll to connect two contact points. In other words, the bomb was a booby trap device, triggered by the motion of my car, and quite unlikely to have been knowingly carried under anyone's car seat.

The lab analysis of the hole in the floor of my car also showed that the epicenter of the blast was under the driver's seat, not behind it. And, to top it all off, they found that a blue towel had been placed over the bomb, making it even more unlikely that we would have seen it. The blue towel did not match the other blue towels seized from my house.

The FBI was hard put to keep the case going against us. But they managed to find a straw to cling to for a few more weeks. Of all the 111 items seized, two nails allegedly had the same tool markings as some of the nails in the bomb. By this it could be determined that they were made on the same machine. The supplier, Pacific Steel, told the FBI that the nails come in 50-LB. boxes from Saudi Arabia, and are distributed at over 200 outlets on the north coast. So, logically, it would be concluded that the nails were too common to compare.

But logic never stops the FBI. They just make up new lies. This time, instead of saying that the nails came from the same machine and therefore matched millions of other nails, Oakland Police Sgt. Sitterud claimed in an affadavit that the FBI bomb expert told him that the nails matched *in a batch of 200-1,000*. The FBI bomb expert now claims that he never said that, and apparently they didn't even try to make this argument in court. But they used it in the press for several weeks to counter emerging proof of our innocence, and they used it as part of the justification for the second raid on my house, in which they pulled finishing nails from the window trim in search of the elusive incriminating nails.

The Oakland Police, who were technically responsible for the arrest, went to court three times in the eight weeks following the bombing to try and get the district attorney to bring charges against Darryl and me. But each time they could produce no evidence against us, and asked for a delay. Finally, after the third try, the DA declined to press charges. Still, we were not exonerated. The FBI and Oakland Police, although chastened by their inability to charge us with the crime, continued to say that we were the only suspects. Dumb enough to carry a live anti-personnel bomb under my car seat, but, apparently, too clever to catch.

Part III
Investigating Earth First!

By midsummer of 1990, it felt like the FBI had already committed every imaginable atrocity against us in the bombing case. They lied and falsified the evidence. They arrested Darryl and me while we were still in shock from being bombed, and refused to even consider any other suspects. They smeared us as terrorists in the national press. But they were not done yet. The FBI still had one more trick up their sleeve for Earth First!

After the district attorney refused to bring charges against us for lack of evidence, public pressure began to mount on the FBI. A coalition of 50 mainstream environmental, labor, and women's groups, along with Congressman Ron Dellums, had demanded a congressional investigation of the FBI's handling of the case. And letters were coming in from all over the world, telling the FBI to stop blaming the victims and start looking for the bomber.

It was in this context that the FBI began their total farce of a bombing investigation. I did not know this part of the story back in 1990, but only discovered it recently when I got my FBI files on the case. In response to public pressure, the FBI did indeed widen their pool of suspects beyond Darryl and me. But they widened it only to include all other EF!ers and redwood region environmentalists. They refused to follow-up on legitimate leads, and never seriously considered any non-environmentalist as a suspect. Instead, they used this case as an excuse for a sweeping campaign of surveillance of activists. My files contain names and information on nearly 800 environmental activists and our associates, both locally and nationally.

Newspaper Monitoring

The FBI began their "investigation" by sending a letter to the local newspapers in the redwood region. "As part of the [bombing] investigation, the FBI is attempting to identify the author of the Lord's Avenger letter," it read. "In that regard, we are asking for your cooperation in making available for review letters you have received regarding the redwood timber and abortion issues."

Only the *Press Democrat*, the largest and most urban corporate newspaper in our area, said no, cit-

TIMBER WARS

ing the chilling effect it would have on free speech if
people knew that their letters were being turned
over to the FBI. But in the rural areas, ten small-
town newspaper editors, flattered by the attention,
let the FBI go through their files and pick out originals of published and unpublished letters. Once out
in the field, the FBI seemed to forget all about the
abortion letters, a strange oversight given the Lord's
Avenger's views on abortion. Nearly every letter they
confiscated was from an environmentalist, and none
had any apparent connection to the bombing case.

Most of these letters were simply collected and
added to the FBI's case file, with no follow up. But
one letter writer became a full-on suspect. His letter, sent to the *Humboldt Life and Times*, was a
poem that began, "Has anyone ever known their
spirits?", and was signed "First Impressions,
Pokhara Valley."

There was no imaginable connection between
this letter and the bombing, neither in handwriting,
typing, style or content. Yet it was fingerprinted,
handwriting analyzed, and sent to the FBI's
Behavioral Science Lab to determine if the person
who wrote it had the personality type that could
also have written the Lord's Avenger letter.

Besides snooping through the letters-to-the-edi-
tors files, the FBI also engaged in other scandalous
behavior involving freedom of the press. In one
memo to headquarters, San Francisco FBI Director
Richard Held complained about an article written by
Press Democrat reporter Mike Geniella. In that article, Mike Geniella documented the FBI's targeting of
Earth First! in Arizona, Montana, and California. To
my knowledge, this is the only article ever printed in

318

the mainstream press anywhere that linked these various FBI operations against Earth First! groups. Richard Held states in his memo that he intends to complain to the *Press Democrat*'s editors about Mike Geniella's reporting, and suggests that FBI chief William Sessions complain to the *Press Democrat*'s parent newspaper, the *New York Times*. A few weeks later, Geniella was disciplined by the *Press Democrat*, and removed from his position as timber reporter, despite his award-winning coverage of the issue.

Information Gathering

The FBI also interviewed the local police in the timber region. They asked them questions like who do they "consider to be prominent environmental activists" in their town. Without ever questioning why, police gave out names and addresses of various "respectable" environmentalists, as well as Earth First!ers. Humboldt sheriffs were asked for a list of "individuals capable of engaging in violent activity." The list consisted entirely of nonviolent Earth First! activists, none of whom engaged in any violent activity before, during, or since that time. Names of timber supporters, who had committed many well-documented assaults on environmentalists in our region, were not solicited by the FBI or included on any police lists.

Humboldt and Mendocino Sheriff's "Intelligence Officers" also came up with some wild stories about supposed internal jealousies and intrigues within Earth First! One had Mickey Dulas and me pulling a coup on Darryl Cherney to squeeze him out of the picture. Another had Mickey crying "from being upset with Judi Bari, as Judi Bari was dictating how things should be run from her wheelchair." In reality, we were all working together, standing up to lethal force with principle, courage, and nonviolence in a terrifying situation.

A Mendo sheriff report claimed that monkey-wrenching was being done by the Nomadic Action Team, led by Mike Roselle. The fact that there was no monkeywrenching going on at all didn't seem to bother him. Another fictitious "intelligence" report of an event that never happened quotes Humboldt sheriffs as saying that "members of the Earth First in the tri-state area, believed to mean Washington, Oregon and California and possibly Arizona are planning to travel to the north coast and attempt to take over, as they feel the local leadership is not doing enough. These outside Earth First! members, many of whom are former followers of Dave Foreman, are planning a build-up of activities... and there is something unknown that is being planned."

In addition to interviewing local cops, the FBI also interviewed management personnel from the timber companies, and anti-EF! organizers from the Wise Use Movement. They were asked to turn over any and all information about environmentalists, as well as any leaflets or printed material from the environmental movement. "Come to the Air Quality Hearing," says one of these leaflets turned in. "Hemp Awareness Day, Music, Teach-In and Festival," says another.

John Campbell, president of Pacific Lumber (Maxxam) was the most active snitch of the bunch. He turned over *Country Activist* newspapers, a timber industry-produced booklet of "Earth First

The Earth First! Car Bombing

Quotes," and a copy of the *Live Wild or Die* newspaper. He also turned in a list of 53 names and addresses that he claimed were Earth First! trespassers, even though the company admitted that "not all were formally charged, and I don't know the disposition."

Wise Use Movement anti-environmental organizers also submitted names and information on enviromentalists. Candy Boak of Mother's Watch, who is well known in our region as one of the worst of the pro-timber hate mongers, told the FBI that of all EF!ers she knows, Larry Evans and Bill DeVall are the ones she fears the most. Larry is a nonviolent activist with an academic background in and exceptional knowledge of forest biology. Bill DeVall is a Humboldt State University professor and co-author of *Deep Ecology*. The very same week that Candy talked to the FBI, she organized a "Dirty Tricks Workshop" with the anti-environmental hate group Sahara Club, to teach local timber goons new ways to terrorize us. This, of course, is not mentioned in the interview.

Paula Langager of the pro-timber group WeCare also had some interesting things to say to the FBI. She told them there is a "core group" of Wise Use activists who "like to play little jokes on Earth First! members and have issued false press releases." (These press releases, printed on EF! stationery and calling for violence, were discussed in Part I of this article as part of the lead-up to the bombing.) Paula gave the FBI copies of the fakes, and named a local timber stooge, Dave Cruzan, as the author. But the FBI never followed up on this info, never interviewed Dave Cruzan, and continued to treat the fake press releases as if they were real, as if they were evidence of our "terrorism."

Another surprise witness was John DeWitt, director of the Save the Redwoods League. DeWitt did not have any inside info at all, but he was sure eager to help the FBI convict Earth First! He turned over a letter he had received from EF!er Greg King in 1987, pleading with Save the Redwoods to stop selling out the forest. He also turned over a list of EF! activists and associates, stating how much each of us had donated to Save The Redwoods League. To our credit, none of us had given him a cent except Darryl, who only gave $5. And finally, a year later, John DeWitt turned over to the FBI a well-known Wise Use poster that said "Wood And Paper Products No Longer Available, Wipe Your Ass With A Spotted Owl." DeWitt told the FBI that this flyer had been sent to his office by Earth First!

Death Threats

The FBI refused to investigate the death threats I had received, even when we gave them leads to follow. Although my lawyer turned over the originals of eight written death threats, the FBI listed them only as "possible evidence," and did not even send them to the lab for fingerprinting, typing, or handwriting analysis. In contrast, death threats received by Maxxam CEO Charles Hurwitz were included in the bombing file and listed as official "evidence" in the bombing case, even though the FBI could find no link between us, the bombing, and these threats. Hurwitz's threats were immediately sent to the FBI lab for handwriting, fingerprinting, and behavioral analysis. Obsequious letters were sent to Maxxam,

322

expressing the FBI's concern for Charles Hurwitz's safety, and an agent was sent out to teach Maxxam's secretaries how to handle letter bombs, even though none had been received or even alluded to.

The most obvious omission in the FBI's non-investigation of the death threats was the matching death threat and police informant letter (discussed in Part 1 of this article). Through the work of investigative reporter Steve Talbott, we had discovered that one of the death threats I received before the bombing was apparently typed on the same typewriter and addressed in a matching style as an informant letter sent to the Ukiah Police along with the famous Uzi photo of me a year and a half earlier. We took copies of the matching letters to the Willits Police, in my home town, and used their document analysis machine to establish the apparent match. But you cannot prove a forensic match without the original documents, and we had already turned those over to the FBI.

The Willits Police gave their copies of the matching letters to the FBI and told them that Irv Sutley was the suspected author (see Part 1). The FBI assured the Willits Police that they would send the letters to the lab and investigate. Steve Talbott also handed these two matching letters to the FBI on TV, and was also assured they would investigate. But in my 5,000 pages of files, the FBI never acknowledges receiving these letters from either the Willits Police or Steve Talbott. And neither the police informant letter nor Irv Sutley's name appear even once in the case file.

One final death threat that I received right in

the middle of the FBI's month-long investigation in our region was the strangest one of all. In late July, the FBI wrote a memo saying that they had "determined that Judi Bari has a cabin outside Willits" that has no electricity. In fact, this is my home, where I live with my two children, and I was just getting ready to move in after getting out of the hospital. The FBI described my cabin as my "hideout" and "safe house," and instructed Mendocino Sheriff Steve Satterwhite to "attempt to locate Judi Bari's hideout." Satterwhite indeed investigated, according to FBI files, and in mid-August an anonymous tip was recorded in my file giving exact directions to my house. One week later I received a death threat saying that the "hippys" in my area had "built a hideout for radical terrorist Judi Bari." The threat, which was found on my landlord's mailbox, gave exact directions to my "hideout", using the same language as the anonymous tip in my FBI file, and offered a "case of Coors to the stud who burns her out." The original copy of this threat was turned over to the Mendocino Sheriffs, and the Willits Police have told me it was discussed at a meeting between local law enforcement and the FBI. Yet neither the threat letter nor any mention of it appears in my entire FBI file.

Phone Sweep

This totally bogus local investigation went on for about a month, and the names of about 150 local environmentalists were collected. Still the FBI found nothing to link any of us to the bombing or any other crime. But rather than give up their ridiculous presumption that the bombing was the work of an environmentalist rather than a pro-timber assassin, they hatched a new plan to expand their investigation nationally. In November of 1991, Richard Held issued a memo to headquarters saying that he still considered Darryl and me to be the prime suspects in the bombing. And, he wrote, "investigation indicates a number of people who associate with one another to include, in some cases, being arrested with each other." Therefore, he states, "the investigation remaining will involve the computerization of the toll records" of these core EF!ers phone calls.

With that, Richard Held and the FBI embarked on the most outrageous wild goose chase of the entire phony "bombing investigation." They came up with a list of 634 out-of-state phone calls we had made during April-May 1990, and proceeded to investigate every one of them. The files that the FBI gave me never tell who these core activists are whose phone calls are being compiled. But we can tell from the phone numbers they investigate that many of the people arrested in the Golden Gate Bridge climb in April 1990 were among this group.

The phone numbers were listed by area code and sent out to every FBI office in the country. And for the next year, the reports trickled back in, listing, at Held's request, names, addresses, places of employment, physical descriptions, criminal records and political associations of the 634 people whose only "crime" was receiving a phone call from an EF!er.

Our parents, grandparents, uncles and cousins were investigated. When a phone number was found to be unlisted, making the info on it unobtainable without a search warrant, the FBI made a "pretext call" to the number to see if they could get anything. One woman in Wisconsin, Louisa Hemachek, who received a call from an EF!er, was cited for having a phone she called "the green line." For no other reason than this, the FBI talked to the local sheriff, who told them that Louisa was considered a "hippie", and was an environmental activist. Another phone number on the FBI list for receiving a call from an EF! belonged to the Center for Constitutional Rights (CCR), a nationally known public interest law firm. The FBI reported that their "indices reveal" that the CCR is associated with the Revolutionary Communist Party and the American Indian Movement, because they helped people from those groups file Freedom of Information Act requests for their FBI files.

All in all, the phone sweep was an absolutely unjustified intrusion, violating people's rights to privacy and freedom of association, recalling the red scares of the 1950's. It is also similar to the CISPES spying scandal of the early 1980's, in which the FBI conducted surveillance on thousands of people who did nothing more than attend a meeting or demonstration about Central America. But in the Earth First! case, you didn't even need to go to a meeting. You were vilified just for knowing us.

Case Closed

When the FBI field offices around the country finished sending in their reports on our phone calls in October 1992, Richard Held had still not found anything to incriminate us. So he quietly closed the case, saying that he had run out of leads to follow. He didn't even notify the district attorney or

Oakland Police that the case was closed until March 1993. And even though we had a lawsuit against him for his handling of the case by then, he never notified us at all that he had closed it.

In May 1993, we released the Oakland Police's damning photos of my bombed car, showing that the FBI had lied about the bomb being in the back seat. The day after we announced our press conference, which was held in front of the FBI office in San Francisco, Richard Held resigned from the FBI. He was 53 years old, and at the height of his career, with 25 years experience in counterintelligence operations. But he left the FBI to take a job as head of the fraud department for VISA company.

Of course, Held claims that there is no relationship between this case and his sudden early departure. But the timing of us waving incriminating photos on his doorstep while he sits upstairs in his office cleaning out his desk to leave is hard to ignore. I'm sure there are other reasons, and we can't take full credit. But the man ruined my life, and I certainly hope I ruined his career.

I don't know how far our lawsuit and congressional investigation will eventually take us with this case. No matter how right we are, the same U.S. Dept. of Justice that is in charge of the federal court system is also in charge of the FBI, and our case could get thrown out at any time under the court's draconian rules. Still, I have to pursue this course, because I don't know what else to do to keep the case alive and try to find justice.

I hope I can someday find out who bombed me. I hope we can expose the FBI's systematic attempt to disrupt, discredit, and destroy Earth First!, starting with the infiltration and set-up of the Arizona 5, and including the bombing and framing of Darryl and me, as well as many other operations across the country. EF! has taken some heavy hits, and we have definitely suffered from them. But, incredibly, we have survived, and we're still together as a movement, still out on the front lines battling for the life of the planet.

We can't minimize the forces we're up against. But I hope we can learn from these experiences, so we won't be so vulnerable next time.

Index

Index

Index

Index

Index

Index

Index

Index

Index

Index

Index

Index

Index

Index

photo: Eugene Louie

About the Author

Judi Bari was born in Baltimore, MD in 1949. She attended the University of Maryland, where she majored in anti-Vietnam War rioting. As a blue collar worker she became active in the union movement and helped to lead two strikes. As a carpenter in northern California, she became a member of Earth First! Disabled for life by a bombing, Judi now resides in Willits, CA with her two children, Lisa, age 13, and Jessica, age 9.